English for Academic Resear

C000088549

Series editor
Adrian Wallwork
Pisa
Italy

This series aims to help non-native, English-speaking researchers communicate in English. The books in this series are designed like manuals or user guides to help readers find relevant information quickly, and assimilate it rapidly and effectively. The author has divided each book into short subsections of short paragraphs with many bullet points.

More information about this series at http://www.springer.com/series/13913

Adrian Wallwork

English for Presentations
at International Conferences

Second Edition

 Springer

Adrian Wallwork
English for Academics
Pisa
Italy

English for Academic Research
ISBN 978-3-319-26328-1   ISBN 978-3-319-26330-4   (eBook)
DOI 10.1007/978-3-319-26330-4

Library of Congress Control Number: 2016933456

Springer Cham Heidelberg New York Dordrecht London

Springer International Publishing AG Switzerland is part of Springer Science+Business Media
(www.springer.com)

Preface

Who is this book for?

This book is part of the *English for Research* series of guides for academics of all disciplines who work in an international field. This volume focuses on preparing and giving presentations. Problems with language (both written and oral) are dealt with extensively, whereas the technical/graphical elements of creating slides are given less space.

The book is designed to help both those who have never done presentations before and researchers whose English is already good (or who are native speakers) but who want to improve their presentation skills.

Chapter 19 is specifically designed to help native speakers present to an audience of non-natives.

The majority of the guidelines given are appropriate for any language, i.e. not just English.

EAP trainers can use this book in conjunction with: *English for Academic Research: A Guide for Teachers.*

What does this book cover?

English for Presentations at International Conferences will help you to

- learn how to assess other people's presentations, including those on TED

- overcome problems with nerves and embarrassment

- prepare and practice a well-organized, interesting presentation

- highlight the essential points you want the audience to remember

- avoid problems in English by using short easy-to-say sentences

- attract and retain audience attention

- decide what to say at each stage of the presentation

- improve your pronunciation

- learn useful phrases

- deal with questions from the audience

- gain confidence and give a memorable presentation

- network and find new research opportunities

How is the book organized?

Chapters 1-5 cover the initial preparation: learning from others (analysing TED presentations) deciding what to say, creating slides in support of what you want to say, etc.

Chapters 6-11 break down the presentation into its separate parts from the first words to the Q&A session.

Chapters 12-15 focus on practising and improving your presentation and your delivery (including pronunciation), and handling your nerves.

The final chapters, 16-19, deal with other aspects of international conferences -networking and posters - plus a chapter dedicated to native English speakers.

Chapter 20 contains a list of useful phrases.

How are the chapters organized?

Each chapter has the following three-part format:

1) FACTOIDS / WHAT THE EXPERTS SAY

In most cases, this section is a brief introduction to the topic of the chapter. Occasionally, the factoids are simply interesting in themselves and have no particularly relevance to the chapter in question. However, they can be used by EAP teachers as warm-ups for their lessons. All the statistics and quotations are genuine, though in some cases I have been unable to verify the original source.

2) WHAT'S THE BUZZ?

This is designed to get you thinking about the topic, through a variety of useful but entertaining exercises. These exercises can be done either by the reader alone, or in class with an EAP (English for Academic Purposes) teacher / trainer. The final part of each *What's the buzz?* section is a brief outline of the contents of the chapter.

3) The rest of each chapter is divided up into short subsections in answer to specific questions.

How should I read this book?

This book is designed to be like a manual or a user guide—you don't need to read it starting from page 1. Like a manual it has lots of short subsections and is divided into short paragraphs with many bullet points. This is to help you find what you want quickly and also to assimilate the information as rapidly and as effectively as possible.

You can use the Table of Contents as a checklist of things to remember.

Differences from the first edition

There are two main differences from the first edition. Firstly, each chapter now begins with Factoids and a *What's the buzz?* section. Secondly, there are four new chapters (Chaps. 16–19) on networking, preparing and presenting posters, and advice for native English speakers on how to present to a non-native audience.

I am a trainer in EAP and EFL. Should I read this book?

If you are a teacher of English for Academic Purposes or English as a Foreign Language you will learn about all the typical problems that non-native researchers have in the world of academia. You will be able to give your students advice on writing quality research papers and getting referees and editors to accept their papers. In addition, you will generate a lot of stimulating and fun discussions by using the factoids and quotations, along with the *What's the buzz?* exercises.

There is a teacher's guide to accompany this *English for Academic Research* series, with notes on how to exploit all the books: *English for Academic Research: A Guide for Teachers*.

Are the examples in this book taken from real presentations?

Most of the examples are taken from real presentations. Others are manipulated versions of the originals. A few are complete inventions, but nevertheless generally contain real data. All the statistics in the factoids are, to the best of my knowledge, true. Most, but not all, statistics in the example presentations are true.

The author

Since 1984 Adrian Wallwork has been editing and revising scientific papers, as well as teaching English as a foreign language. In 2000 he began specializing in training PhD students from all over the world in how to write and present their research in English. He is the author of over 30 textbooks for Springer Science+Business Media, Cambridge University Press, Oxford University Press, the BBC, and many other publishers

Other books in this series

This book is a part of series of books to help non-native English-speaking researchers to communicate in English. The other titles are:

English for Academic Research: A Guide for Teachers

English for Writing Research Papers

English for Academic Correspondence

English for Interacting on Campus

English for Academic Research: Grammar, Usage and Style

English for Academic Research: Grammar Exercises

English for Academic Research: Vocabulary Exercises

English for Academic Research: Writing Exercises

Pisa, Italy   Adrian Wallwork

Contents

Chapter 1

The Importance of Presentations

Factoids

CONFERENCE - The Latin word *ferre* (*conferre* - bring together) derives from an ancient Sanskrit word meaning to 'sustain and nourish'. So a *conference* literally means a bringing together of people for nourishing new ideas.

CONGRESS - In the Middle Ages in England a *congress* was an encounter during battle, but the original Latin word simply meant 'walking together'.

DEBATE - In ancient times to *debate* meant to *beat* or stir a mixture very vigorously so that it became less viscous. The term then came to mean to examine something in depth.

FORUM - The principle public squares in ancient Rome, where in addition to commercial activities, magistrates would judge legal cases. Today it means an organized event or meeting that encourages round-table discussions.

KEYNOTE VS PLENARY - A *keynote* is a presentation by a high profile expert, aimed at generating enthusiasm amongst the audience for the theme of the conference. Keynote is a musical term meaning the first note of the scale of any key. A *plenary* (from the Latin *plenus* meaning full) is a presentation / speech that is expected to be attended in full (i.e. by all participants).

MEETING - An informal conference. In fact *meeting* has a Germanic, rather than a Latin/Greek origin, and as with all Germanic / Anglo Saxon words it has a warmer feel denoting something more friendly (*a talk* vs *a presentation*, *chat* vs *conversation*, *speech* vs *discourse*, *welcome* vs *reception*). The original word *meet* meant to come across, find or come face to face with someone who was walking towards you.

POSTER SESSION - An alternative to an oral presentation, where research is displayed pictorially (Latin: *ponere* = to place].

PRESENTATION - To *present* originally meant to put something or someone under a person's eyes (Latin: *praesum* = I am in front).

SYMPOSIUM - A prestigious conference, with a low acceptance rate for abstracts for presentations. In ancient Greece a symposium was a drinking party (*sumpotēs* means a 'fellow drinker'). After a dinner, other guests were invited to gather round the table and discuss philosophy, politics and literary questions.

© Springer International Publishing Switzerland 2016
A. Wallwork, *English for Presentations at International Conferences*,
English for Academic Research, DOI 10.1007/978-3-319-26330-4_1

1.1   What's the buzz?

A good presentation of a paper can be a delightful experience, an elegant performance, a memorable show for its audience. During the course of my scientific career I have seen thousands of presentations. Most go immediately into oblivion, but some stay in the memory for a lifetime. There's no doubt about it: good speaking skills are more important than dazzling PowerPoint slides

Osmo Pekonen, Finnish author and mathematician

Read the quotation above and think about the answers to these questions.

1. Why is it important for you to give presentations at international conferences?
2. Is merely attending a conference (i.e. without actually presenting) useful for your career?
3. Which is more important: your slides or how you explain them?
4. What kinds of presentations do you like to see?
5. What typical faults do you notice in other people's presentations? Do you personally have the same faults?
6. Is being a good presenter an innate talent or can you learn to give better presentations?

****

This book is designed to help you give presentations in front of international audiences, and to prove that it doesn't have to be a terrifying experience!

Three key points are worth making straight away.

1) Don't be obsessed by your spoken English. If you make mistakes in your English when you talk, the majority of your audience will probably not care or even notice. However, they may notice written mistakes. Don't be creative with your English. Only write what you know is correct. Generally speaking, the shorter the sentence, the less likely you are to make a mistake.

However, the less text you have, the more evident any grammar or spelling mistakes are. These final slides from three different presentations (all real) did not make a good last impression on the audience!

End

Thank!

Any question?

The presenters should have written "The end," "Thanks," and "Any questions?"

2) Consider having two versions of your presentation.

THE VERSION YOU SHOW TO YOUR LIVE AUDIENCE: this contains the main results with minimal detail and minimal text. This book focuses only on this version.

THE FULL VERSION: this contains more text, more details and possibly more slides. You can tell the audience at the beginning of the presentation where they can download the full version (you can include this in your title slide and / or conclusions). This means that the audience can upload your presentation onto their phone and use it as an aid to their comprehension while listening to you.

3) Consider uploading your presentation (either the 'live' one of the full one) onto your smartphone and hold it in your hand during the presentation. This solution is already acceptable in the business world and is now increasingly being found at scientific congresses. The advantages are clear: you can glance at your phone to remember where you are and what you want to say. This will considerably reduce your anxiety (see Chapter 11, 13.6 and 15.2).

This chapter analyses the benefits for you of presenting at a conference. It also identifies some of the basic differences between a good and bad presentation.

Posters are covered in Chapter 18.

1.2   Giving presentations gives you visibility and advances your career

By giving a presentation at a conference, you can gain visibility and inform others of the results you have achieved. This may enable you to increase your chances of getting feedback on your work, establishing new contacts, collaborating with other research groups, and maybe of even getting more funds so that you can carry out better research.

A presentation is an opportunity to talk about factors that you probably wouldn't mention in your paper, e.g., ideas and conjectures, negative results, unfinished work— all of these might stimulate useful questions and feedback from the audience.

You will also be able to exploit the review process that takes place before the conference, and of course you can list the presentations you have given in your CV, in applications for grants, and in grant progress reports.

1.3 Simply attending, without presenting, is not enough

All the networking benefits are considerably improved if you have given a presentation. You will find that people will come up to you after the presentation and ask for more details or even suggest collaborations—this means that the effort to make face-to-face contact is principally made by them not you. In any case, if you have gained visibility through a presentation, then you will find it much easier to introduce yourself to other people and begin a conversation.

1.4 Good presentations: typical features

Audiences from all parts of the world appreciate presentations that:

- are professional and are delivered by someone who is credible and confident

- look like they were prepared specifically for us and make it immediately clear why we should be interested

- have clear slides, with minimal detail and helpful and/or entertaining images

- tell us interesting, curious, and counterintuitive things

- don't make us work too hard to follow what is being said—two or three main points, lots of examples, and not too much theory

- are delivered in a friendly, enthusiastic, and relatively informal way

- entertain us and interact with us

1.5   Bad presentations: typical features

No audience will be pleased to attend a presentation where the speaker:

- has clearly not practiced the presentation

- has no clear introduction, a confused structure, and no conclusions

- appears to be talking to himself/herself rather than engaging with the audience

- reads the slides

- has a series of similar slides full of text and diagrams

- relies on animations

- fails to address the audience's interest and only sees things from his/her point of view

- is too technical, too detailed

- speaks too fast, speaks with a monotone, speaks for too long

- shows little interest in his/her topic

1.6   The key to a professional presentation

A "professional" presentation is one where you put the audience first. You think about how the audience would most like to receive the information you are giving.

The key to an effective presentation is that you have a few main points that you want the audience to remember and that you highlight these points during the presentation in an interesting, and if possible, enthusiastic way.

The important thing is to be relaxed. To become more relaxed, the key is to prepare well and concentrate on the content, not on your English. Your presentation is not an English examination—your English does not have to be perfect. Be realistic and don't aim for 100% accuracy, otherwise you will be more worried about your English than about communicating the value of your research.

Chapter 2

TED and Learning from Others

Factoids

TED stands for *Technology, Entertainment, Design* and was founded in 1984 as a one-off event.

TED organize conferences under the slogan "Ideas Worth Spreading".

TED originally focused on technology and design, but now the conferences include scientific, cultural, and academic topics - some very serious, some very funny.

Presenters have a maximum of 18 minutes to deliver their ideas in innovative and engaging ways, including using a story-format.

Three of the shortest TEDs, all under 3.30, are entitled: *Try something new for 30 days; 8 secrets of success*; and *How to start a movement.*

Over 2000 talks are freely available on the website and have been watched over one billion times worldwide.

TED has become a regular word in the dictionary: *I watched two TEDs today. Did you watch that TED on …?*

TED is watched by millions of non-native speakers who can use subtitles (in English, or their own language), or see the full transcript (again in English or their own language). TED's Open Translation Project aims to reach out to the 4.5 billion people who do not speak English. TED also has its own series of short books.

© Springer International Publishing Switzerland 2016
A. Wallwork, *English for Presentations at International Conferences*,
English for Academic Research, DOI 10.1007/978-3-319-26330-4_2

2.1 What's the buzz?

Think about the answers to these questions.

1. TED's mission as stated on their website is: *TED is a global community, welcoming people from every discipline and culture who seek a deeper understanding of the world. We believe passionately in the power of ideas to change attitudes, lives and, ultimately, the world. On TED.com, we're building a clearinghouse of free knowledge from the world's most inspired thinkers — and a community of curious souls to engage with ideas and each other.* How important and how achievable do you think this mission is?

2. Have you seen any TED presentations? Which ones do you like the most?

3. Are TED presentations different from the kinds of presentations you have seen at your university or at conferences in your country? Do you think it would be appropriate to use a TED-style presentation at your next conference? Why (not)?

4. Which features of TED do you use? Have you ever tried the 'surprise me' feature or used the playlists?

5. Do you watch in English? With or without subtitles?

6. Have you ever based your own presentations on the style and/or structure of a TED presentation?

7. How can you use TED to improve your speaking style and pronunciation?

8. Is it possible to learn from others? Do we tend to be blind to our own mistakes?

****

This chapter discusses the benefits of TED by analysing some typical TED presentations. It also provides checklists to enable you to assess the slides and presentation styles of various presenters (not just TED presenters, but your colleagues too, and of course yourself).

You can access TED from your computer or by downloading the TED app onto your smartphone.

Most of what is said in this chapter will make much more sense if you actually watch the TED presentations in subsections 2.3-2.6.

In addition to TED, there are several sites on the Web dedicated to presentations. There are some where you can share slides, for example:

slideshare.net

myplick.com

authorstream.com/slideshows/

These sites are useful for seeing how other people in similar fields to yours create their slides. Examining these presentations should help you to understand that packing a presentation full of detail is not usually a good approach.

2.2   Choosing a TED presentation and learning the benefits

You can choose the topic of the presentations you want to watch by using TED's search engine, and you can also choose whether to have English subtitles on or not. The subtitles report every single word, and are particularly useful for seeing (not just hearing) how many words a presenter uses in a sentence. This highlights that the shorter the sentence is, the easier it is for the presenter to say, and the easier it is for the audience to understand.

You can see or download a full transcript (called 'interactive transcript') of the presentation in English, plus translations in several other languages. This means that you can note down any useful phrases that the speaker uses that you think you could use too.

By reading the transcript and listening to the presentation at the same time, you can also improve your pronunciation and intonation by trying to imitate the presenter.

A good TED presentation to start with is Jay Walker's *English Mania* (19.5). Jay's talk highlights how preparation, and speaking clearly and slowly in very short sentences, are key to a good presentation. This presentation is less than five minutes long and is easy to follow even without subtitles!

2.3   TED example with use of slides: *Let's bridge the digital divide!*

You may be concerned that many of the presentations you watch on TED are given by very dynamic presenters. Economist Aleph Molinari in his presentation *Let's bridge the digital divide!* is not dynamic, he doesn't run around the stage entertaining us. But he does know how to inform us and how to bring important data to our attention, which is all you need to give a good presentation at an international conference. For another example of a good but not particularly dynamic presenter see Jay Walker (19.5).

In his presentation, Aleph Molinari tells us that five billion people don't have access to the Internet and then explains what we should do about it. This presentation may seem rather dated when you watch it, so concentrate not on the statistics themselves but on how Molinari presents these statistics.

EXAMPLES AND STATISTICS

Aleph immediately starts with concrete examples of victims of the digital divide. He then moves on to some statistics. He shows a slide with the number of people in the world: 6,930,055,154.

Why not 7bn? Because the length and exactness of the number emphasizes firstly the incredible number of people who live on our planet and at the same time that they are individuals. The long number also looks dramatic on the screen. But when he actually mentions the number verbally he says "nearly seven billion people" - there would be no point in reading the exact number. He then gives the number of people who are digitally included, which on the slide appears as 2,095,006,005. What he says is "Out of these, approximately two billion are digitally included, this is approximately 30% of the entire world population, which means that the remaining 70% of the world, close to five billion people, do not have access to a computer or the Internet .. five billion people, that's four times the population of India".

Aleph's technique is thus to:

1. show a statistic in a simple clear way (i.e. not along with several other distracting statistics)
2. talk about the statistic in three ways (first as a whole number, then as a percentage, then by comparison with India). Aleph thus offers his audience different ways of absorbing the information, his aim being to help them to really understand the true significance of the numbers involved
3. interpret the statistic by saying what the implications are

TEXT, BACKGROUNDS AND FONTS

Aleph's slides have a black background with a yellow font. They are incredibly clear. The majority of his slides that contain text only have one or two words. The slide with the most text, which is his first slide and contains a definition of the digital divide, contains 19 words. At least half his slides are just photographs, which support his speech. Essentially, the information contained on each of his slides can be absorbed in less than two seconds. This means that all the audience can listen to him with 100% of their concentration, rather than some of the audience reading the slides and some listening to him.

ALEPH'S PRESENTING STYLE

I may be wrong, but I imagine that Aleph is quite introverted. This reveals itself in the fact that he spends too much time (in my opinion) looking at the screen rather than the audience. Although he does try to emphasize his key words, his voice is rather monotonous. The combination of these two factors could lead to the audience losing interest.

However, Aleph compensates for this lack of dynamism by

- having a clear logical structure

- having excellent slides - clear, easy to follow

- being professional

This makes him very credible in the audience's eyes. They will certainly be motivated to follow him and listen to what he has to say. And this also means that although his conclusion in itself lacks impact (his voice does not sound very impassioned), as a whole his presentation will have a positive impact because he appears to the audience as being totally committed to his project and also very sincere.

2.4   TED example with minimal slides, delivered from a lectern: *The forgotten history of autism*

The TED website introduces this presentation as follows:

> Decades ago, few pediatricians had heard of autism. In 1975, 1 in 5,000 kids was estimated to have it. Today, 1 in 68 is on the autism spectrum. What caused this steep rise? Steve Silberman points to "a perfect storm of autism awareness" — a pair of psychologists with an accepting view, an unexpected pop culture moment and a new clinical test. But to really understand, we have to go back further to an Austrian doctor by the name of Hans Asperger, who published a pioneering paper in 1944. Because it was buried in time, autism has been shrouded in misunderstanding ever since.

This presentation contains only four slides - one graph and three photos.

FULLY WRITTEN SPEECH

Steve is speaking from a lectern upon which he has his full speech. He looks down frequently (but very rapidly) to remind himself what to say next. If someone on TED can rely on looking at their written speech, then so can you. A better option however, may be just to have notes (see 19.5, and also see 13.6 and 15.2 on how to use your smartphone).

STRUCTURE

There is a clear logical structure - i) introduction to the issue of autism, ii) how and where misconceptions arose, iii) how these misconceptions were overcome, and iv) finally the positive aspects of autism and the key contribution of having a diversity of brainpowers in our society.

EYE CONTACT

Notice how Steve looks at one section of the audience for a few seconds, and then turns his head to look at another section. Maintaining eye contact is essential to maintaining audience attention.

GRAPH

Steve only uses one graph. Note how the information on the graph is extremely simple to absorb very quickly.

BODY LANGUAGE

When you are standing at a lectern there is less opportunity to use your body. However Steve makes great use of his hands to emphasize points (see at 4.0, 5.45, 7.23, 12.32 minutes)

VOICE

When reading from a prepared script, there is a danger of adopting a monotone. Note how Steve modulates his voice to give emphasis and raise the audience's interest in specific points.

2.5 What might Steve have done differently if he had been giving a more formal version of his talk at an international conference made up of a multilingual audience?

I think he would simply have used more slides for the following:

STATISTICS: He mentions a number of statistics. Given that numbers can be quite difficult to process by speakers of another language, and given that some English numbers can create confusion (e.g. *thirteen* vs *thirty*), having the numbers on a slide is useful.

MORE PHOTOS: He mentions the famous movie *Rain Man* starring Dustin Hoffman. It might have been useful to see a photo of the movie poster. There is a chance that the audience knows the name of the film in a translated version and may pronounce Dustin Hoffman in a very different way. This means that they may miss the point.

QUOTATIONS: He quotes from many people and it might have been helpful for the audience (as well as creating variety) to have seen these quotes on a slide - after all his quotes were well chosen as they were all very concise.

When you are giving a presentation from the lectern you have fewer opportunities to engage your audience and attract their attention. Having a few slides will grab the audience's attention if they are becoming distracted due to the mental effort required to follow someone who is speaking a language that is not their own.

2.6   TED example delivered from a lectern: *This is what it's like to teach in North Korea*

Suki Kim's talk begins as follows:

> In 2011, during the final six months of Kim Jong-Il's life, I lived undercover in North Korea.
>
> I was born and raised in South Korea, their enemy. I live in America, their other enemy.
>
> Since 2002, I had visited North Korea a few times. And I had come to realize that to write about it with any meaning, or to understand the place beyond the regime's propaganda, the only option was total immersion. So I posed as a teacher and a missionary at an all-male university in Pyongyang.
>
> The Pyongyang University of Science and Technology was founded by Evangelical Christians who cooperate with the regime to educate the sons of the North Korean elite, without proselytizing, which is a capital crime there. The students were 270 young men, expected to be the future leaders of the most isolated and brutal dictatorship in existence. When I arrived, they became my students.
>
> 2011 was a special year, marking the 100th anniversary of the birth of North Korea's original Great Leader, Kim Il-Sung. To celebrate the occasion, the regime shut down all universities, and sent students off to the fields to build the DPRK's much-heralded ideal as the world's most powerful and prosperous nation. My students were the only ones spared from that fate.

I have chosen this talk because apart from being a very moving and interesting presentation, it is a wonderful example of how to speak clear English. Suki Kim is not a native speaker, although she does speak almost perfect English in this talk.

You can learn a lot from Suki about how to speak slowly (around 100 words per minute) and enunciate each word very clearly. She is able to do this, because like Steve Silberman (see 2.4), she is reading from a prepared speech.

Her script contains a series of relatively short sentences. The average sentence length is 17 words. She has one long sentence (34 words - the first sentence in the fourth paragraph), but this sentence has places for natural pauses (*who ..., which ...*). She also has two 7-letter sentences, where she is able to be more dramatic.

She wrote her script in a way that would enable her to read it aloud without difficulty. She also wrote it in short paragraphs. This means that at the end of each paragraph she would remember to have a longer pause than the time she paused at the end of each sentence.

Whether you are a scientist or humanist, you can certainly see the advantages of having a written script - for more on this see Chapter 3.

I strongly recommend that in any case, you watch this extremely powerful and inspiring talk.

2.7   What can you learn from these three TED presentations?

1) *Dynamism is not key to a good presentation*

None of the three presenters were particularly dynamic, none of them were funny or tried to tell any kind of humorous anecdote (which in any case can be dangerous).

This was in fact one of the reasons why I chose these three presenters. Being dynamic and entertaining is great, but certainly not essential. So, although you may not be a 'born presenter' this should not stop you from giving a good presentation.

2) *Consider reducing the number of slides*

Most TED presenters use a minimal number of slides, and some use none at all.

If you are a 'scientist' you may be likely to use more slides in your own presentations, but by watching TED you will understand why and when it is possible to reduce the number of slides.

If you are a 'humanist' you may not be required to use slides. However this puts a lot of pressure on both you and the audience (they have to concentrate just on your voice and what you are saying and maybe easily distracted). TED has many examples of where the presenter just speaks and you can learn a lot from their techniques.

3) *Preparation helps to ensure the level of credibility and memorability of your presentation*

What the three presentations outlined in the three previous subsections all have in common, is that it is clear that the presenters were well prepared. The audience feel that they are being led forward in a logical progression and that the presenter has spent a considerable amount of time practising his/her presentation. This gives each presenter credibility in the eyes of the audience, and also helps to make their presentation memorable.

In fact, it is probably these two factors - credibility and memorability - that you should aim for. And you can achieve them through:

- uncomplicated language

- loud, clear, reasonably slow voice

- simple slides

- a clear logical structure

2.8   Should you opt for TED-style presentations?

Should you aim to give a TED-style presentation at your next conference? Probably not. The aim of TED presentations is to get an interesting message across to the audience, rather than necessarily presenting some key results of research that someone has done. If you are a scientist your presentations are likely to be more technical and require more slides. If you are a humanist, you may not have such an interesting story to tell as some of the TED presenters.

Another difference from TED is that at a presentation at an international conference, the aim of your presentation should not be merely to inform (or entertain). You should also be trying to 'sell' yourself, to get yourself noticed by other research teams who might be able to collaborate with you in your projects, or even invite you for an internship in their lab.

2.9   TED viewers rarely comment on non-native speakers' use of English

TED.com allows viewers to 'discuss' what they have watched. What is interesting is that nearly all the comments are on the content of the presentation rather than the delivery. This is true also for talks given by non-native presenters.

A classic example of this is Philippe Starck the well-known French product designer's talk entitled *Design and destiny*. Starck's talk is worth watching in order to prove to yourself that even if you don't have a good English accent it doesn't necessarily matter. His technique for dealing with his poor English is to immediately draw attention to it in a self-deprecating way by saying: *You will understand nothing with my type of English.*

His pronunciation is terrible. At least 20% of his first 100 words contain pronunciation mistakes (e.g. *'ere* instead of *here*, *zat* instead of *that*, the *u* in *usually* pronounced like the *u* in *under* rather than the *u* in *universe*) and he consistently puts the stress on the wrong part of a multi-syllable word (e.g. *comfortable, impostor*). He makes a series of grammar mistakes: forgetting the plural *s*, using the wrong part of the verb etc.

But because the audience are interested in what he is saying rather than how he is saying it, his poor English skills are not a problem. In fact if you read the comments on his presentation, not one reference is made to his poor English. Instead many viewers simply write: *Superb! Fantastic! Really the most brilliant talk I've heard on TED.*

However, note that Starck does speak slowly. If he had spoken very fast, his poor accent would probably have interfered with the audience's ability to understand him.

So, it is worth highlighting again: providing that the presenter does a reasonable job, audiences are more interested in content than in the presenter's use of English.

2.10 Note down what you remember about the presentations you watch

When you have watched five or six presentations on TED (or whatever site), write down what you remember about the content and about the presenter and his/her style. You will be surprised how little you remember about the information that was given. Repeat the same memory exercise a week later and you probably won't even remember how many presentations you watched. Instead, you will remember the impression that the presenter made on you and their style of presenting for much longer.

What this means is that there is no point filling your presentation with descriptions of complex procedures or masses of data, because the audience will simply not remember. What they will remember from that experience is their frustration in not being able to absorb the information that you gave them. Make sure you always give your audience a positive experience.

2.11 Assess other people's presentations

You can learn a lot from the presentations you watch, and not just from those on TED. Use the assessment sheet on the next page to decide which presentation styles you liked and why. Then you can perhaps think of ways to incorporate these aspects into your own presentations.

Also, analyse the audience's reaction. Is the audience attentive? Are you yourself attentive? Notice when and why the presenter starts to lose your attention. If you stop watching, at what point did you stop watching and why?

2.12 Using TED talks

I personally would like to thank the organization for providing one of the best ways of learning English on the Internet. This was clearly not their original intention, but is a fantastic byproduct of a fantastic service. See page 277 to learn about permissions to use TED presentations.

Assessment Sheet

	THE PRESENTER TENDS TO DO THIS	RATHER THAN THIS
CORE FOCUS	clarifies the main point of the presentation immediately - it is clear to audience why they should listen	the main point only emerges towards the end - audience not clear where the presentation is going
PACE / SPEED	varies the pace i.e. speaks slowly for key points, faster for more obvious information; pauses occasionally	maintains the same speed throughout; no pauses
BODY LANGUAGE	eyes on audience, moves hands, stands away from the screen, moves from one side of the screen to the other	eyes on screen, PC, ceiling, floor; static, blocks screen
STRUCTURE	each new point is organically connected to the previous point	there are no clear transitions or connections
FORMALITY	sounds natural, enthusiastic, sincere	sounds rather robotic and non spontaneous
STYLE	narrative: you want to hear what happened next lots of personal pronouns and active forms of verbs	technical, passive forms
LANGUAGE	dynamic, adjectives, very few linkers (*also, in addition, moreover, in particular*, etc)	very formal, no emotive adjectives, many linkers
RELATION WITH AUDIENCE	involves / entertains the audience - thus maintaining their attention	seems to be talking to him/ herself not to the audience
TEXT IN SLIDES	little or no text	a lot of text
GRAPHICS	simple graphics or complex graphics built up gradually	complex graphics
ABSTRACT VS CONCRETE	gives examples	focuses on abstract theory
STATISTICS	gives counterintuitive / interesting facts	makes little or no use of facts / statistics
AT THE END	you are left feeling inspired / positive	you are indifferent

Chapter 3

Why You Should Write Out Your Speech

Factoids: Women in Science

NOBEL PRIZES: Between 1901 and 1960 a woman received a Nobel Prize on average once every 4.2 years; 1961-2000 once every 2.4 years; and since 2000 every 0.75 years.

CHINA: When Yingying Lu, Ph.D., was made a professor at the College of Chemical & Biological Engineering at Zhejiang University, she was only 27 years old and possibly the youngest professor (male or female) in the world. Between 43% and 52% of teachers at higher education institutes in China are female.

IRAN VS UK: The total populations of Iran and the UK are approximately 65 million and 78 million respectively, yet there are more than twice as many female university students in Iran than in the UK (2.1 million vs 0.9 million).

JAPAN: Has one of the lowest share of female PhD students in the world (30%). Japan also has a very low share amongst researchers (18%) and professors (18%).

KOREA: More than 75% of Korean girls go to university. Yi So-yeon was the first Korean woman to go into space and is probably Korea's most famous female scientist.

LATVIA: Holds the world record for the highest share of women amongst scientific staff and the highest share of women with a PhD (Latvia 60%, USA 53%, Germany 45%)

SPAIN: Approximately one in three researchers are women, less than 20% of women hold a high position. 18% of Spanish women aged 55-64 hold a university degree or PhD, this rises to 47.5% for those aged between 25 and 34.

USA: There are more females graduates with a bachelor's degree in health professions (85% women, 15% men), public administration, education, psychology and languages than there are in math and statistics, architecture, physical sciences, computer science, engineering (83% men, 17% women).

© Springer International Publishing Switzerland 2016
A. Wallwork, *English for Presentations at International Conferences*,
English for Academic Research, DOI 10.1007/978-3-319-26330-4_3

3.1 What's the buzz?

This chapter is dedicated to women in science.

This came about by accident. In my mad quest for interesting factoids for this book and the others in the series I came across hundreds of famous scientists. Basically 99% were from the US, UK, Germany, France or Italy, and less than 1% were female.

This discovery was not surprising, but coincided with the fact that at the same time as writing this book, I was teaching several female researchers from Iran and the Baltic States. They told me that the percentage of women in science in their countries was very high, and in fact I remembered reading that Iran has the highest percentage population of students in the world.

This all triggered an interest in

- how search engines tend to provide very Anglo-American oriented information (something that I find extremely worrying given the potential for massive distortion of reality leading to a monocultural viewpoint)

- how it might be interesting to set my PhD students (both male and female) the task of doing searches in their native languages of the role of women in science in their countries

The results of this very small and very random project (just 10 PhD students, researchers and professors of 10 different nationalities) are presented in the factoids and have also been used to provide examples in the main part of this chapter.

1) Look at the six points below regarding some research whose aim is to investigate women's position in science and how it is perceived by today's young scientists. Imagine that you are the researcher. You have decided to select some of the points in order to include them in the first minute of an oral presentation. This presentation will be given at an international conference on social studies, which will be attended by both women and men. Choose which points you think would be the most suitable for inclusion, and decide exactly what you would say in the first minute or two of your presentation (you can also use any other info that you have access to).

   1. Academies of Science: Of the 454 members of the Russian Academy of Sciences only nine are women. Marie Curie was not accepted into the French Academy because she was a woman (Yvonne Choquet-Bruhat, mathematician and physicist, was the first to be admitted).

2. Famous female scientists in 19th and 20th centuries: Caroline Herschel, Mary Somerville, Lise Meitner, Irène Curie-Joliot, Barbara McClintock, Dorothy Hodgkin, Marie Curie.

3. Survey of 500 PhD students (male and female): only 10% were able to recognize more than one name in those listed in Point 2 above.

4. Editorial boards and peer review: the majority of editors of scientific journals are male, and this majority is entrusted with selecting reviewers, the majority of whom are again male.

5. Women in national parliaments. Top 5: Rwanda 63.8%, Bolivia 53.1%, Cuba 49.9%, Seychelles 43.8%, Sweden 43.6% (Yemen 0%).

6. "When the whole world is silent, even one voice becomes powerful" Malala Yousafazai (2014 Nobel Prize Winner)

2) When you have written your script, decide at which points you would insert slides and what these slides would contain.

3) If you opt not to do exercises 1 and 2, write the introduction to a presentation on your own research by answering the following questions.

- What is the current situation?

- Why is this a problem?

- What should be done?

- Benefits of doing it.

- Drawbacks of doing it

- What happens if it isn't done?

****

In this chapter you will learn how to write your speech. You may think that writing out your speech is a waste of time. However there are huge advantages (if you are not convinced see 2.4–2.6). You can:

- email your speech to an English-speaking colleague to revise or you can even submit it to a professional service. Then you can be sure that at least the grammar and vocabulary will be correct. This will give you confidence and make you feel less nervous

- show your speech to a colleague (without forcing him/her to watch you performing)—this is a quick way to see if your presentation is clear and interesting.

- insert your speech into the space for notes under your slides on PowerPoint and other presentation software. You can then glance at your monitor to remember what to say.

- upload your speech onto your smartphone and hold the smartphone in your hand while doing the presentation (see 13.6 and 15.2).

3.2 Write down your speech

This chapter is designed to make you aware the benefits of using a script and will help you decide exactly what to write and how.

Most presentations in scientific fields are not read from a script with the presenter standing at the lectern.

However, in the humanities they often are (see 2.4 - 2.6 to learn about using a script).

If you are presenting more purely scientific research, the reasons for writing the script are absolutely NOT for you to then learn every word. Memorizing a script is not a good idea. You will not sound natural when you speak and you might panic if you forget your "lines."

However, writing a script is useful for other reasons—to help you to decide

- what the best structure is and thus the best order for your slides

- if certain slides can be cut

- if the audience really needs to know what you plan to say

Obviously you do not need to write down every word you will say; though you may be surprised to learn that a typical ten-minute presentation only requires 1200–1800 words.

For the more technical parts of the presentation, when you explain your methodology and results, it may be enough to write notes. This is because these technical aspects will probably be the easiest for you to talk about, as you will be very familiar with them and will probably have all the correct English terminology that you need.

The beginnings and endings of presentations tend to be less technical and are the places where presenters tend to improvise the most. At least 20% of the words and phrases that inexperienced presenters use tend to be redundant, i.e., they give no information that is useful for the audience. That's 20% less time for explaining and emphasizing the key points.

So write down exactly what you want to say in your introduction and conclusions.

3.3 Don't lift text directly from your paper

An easy way to write the speech for your presentation would be to cut and paste from your paper.

However the style of a paper and the style of a presentation are very different. Papers tend to be more formal, with longer sentences and considerably more detail.

Compare these two versions:

ORIGINAL PAPER	PRESENTATION
The period of the Union of Soviet Socialist Republics (1922-1991) provided ample opportunities for women to enter higher education in all fields and sectors, including natural or physical sciences (e.g. chemistry, biology, physics, or astronomy). In 1985 the number of female undergraduate students stood at 40%, with 10% undertaking a doctorate.	The Soviet period was not all bad news. Women were able to get into higher education in all fields, including hard sciences, in a way that was unimaginable in Western Europe. In 1985, six years before the break up of the USSR, the number of female students was 40%.
The post-Soviet period is witnessing a so-called feminization of science, in which there has been an emigration of highly trained or qualified scientists. Notable individuals who decided to leave Russia include Pavel Durov (the founder of VKontakte Russia's version of Facebook), and the economist Sergei Guriyev. In contrast, female Russian scientists have remained in Russia and the number of female researchers in such underrepresented areas of sciences as physics, maths, and life sciences has shown a marked tendency to increase.	What is changing in the post-Soviet period is the feminization of science. There has been a brain drain with male researchers going abroad. And it's not just the academics who leave. Chessmaster Garry Kasparov left in 2013. He was followed the next year by the founder of Russia's version of Facebook. But the women tend to stick with the motherland. Consequently, the number of female researchers in previously underrepresented areas of sciences such as physics, maths, and the life sciences is growing.

The two texts are the same length, but the style and content are quite different. The presentation version

- is much more listener-friendly (compare the first sentence in each version)

- generally uses shorter sentences and is thus easier for the presenter to say

- uses less formal language (e.g. *brain drain* vs *emigration of highly trained or qualified scientists*; *is growing* vs *has shown a marked tendency to increase*)

- has fewer hard facts (e.g. the exact dates of the Soviet Republic, the name of the founder of Russia's equivalent to Facebook)

- has more interesting facts, or the facts are presented in more audience-related way (Kasparov, a well-known Russian for all audiences is used as an example of the brain drain rather than Guriyev, who is from a more specialized field)

- uses a narrative style

3.4   Only have one idea per sentence

Each sentence should only contain one idea. This makes it easier for you to say and for the audience to understand.

Use the simplest English possible by using short phrases containing words that you find easy to say.

The original sentence in the example below has 75 words. In a text form it is not difficult to understand. However, having such long sentences in a presentation creates problems for:

- the presenter, as by the end of the sentence you will have no breath left!

- the audience, as it will be much more difficult for them to follow

ORIGINAL	REVISED
Although most academies of science around the world are now open to women, this has not always been the case, as exemplified by Marie Curie whose application to join the French Academy in 1911 was rejected despite her having won a Nobel Prize in 1903 but heavily influenced by the fact that not only was she a woman but was also of Polish origins and rumored to be Jewish (though in reality she was not).	Most academies of science around the world are now open to women. This has not always been the case. A classic example is Marie Curie whose application to join the French Academy in 1911 was rejected. This was despite her having won a Nobel Prize in 1903. In fact it was heavily influenced by the fact that not only was she a woman, but was also of Polish origins. She was also rumored to be Jewish, though actually her father was an atheist and her mother a devout Catholic.

Notice how in the revised version

- there are four short sentences rather than one long sentence. This gives you natural pauses when you're speaking

- emphasis and drama can be created by very short phrases interspersed with pauses

For details on how to break up long sentences see Chapter 4 in *English for Writing Research Papers*.

3.5 Be concise—only say things that add value

Thomas Jefferson, chief author of the Declaration of Independence once commented: *The most valuable of all talents is that of never using two words when one will do.*

The more words you use

- the more mistakes in English you will make!

- the less time you have to give the audience important technical info

Here are some examples of sentences from the beginning of a presentation that could be deleted because they delay giving important information to the audience.

> The work I am going to present to you today is …

> My presentation always begins with a question.

> I have prepared some slides.

> This presentation is taken from the first draft of my thesis.

> The title of my research is …

Here are some phrases that could be reduced considerably, as shown by the brackets:

> Testing [can be considered an activity that] is time consuming

> The main aim of our research [as already shown in the previous slides] is to find new methodologies for calculating stress levels. [In order to do this calculation,] we first designed …

Finally these phrases below could be reworded to make them more concise:

> Another thing we wanted to do was = We also wanted to

> In this picture I will show you a sample = Here is a sample

> Regarding the analysis of the samples, we analyzed them using = We analyzed the samples using … *or* Let's have a look at how we analyzed the samples.

For details on how to reduce redundancy see Chapter 5 in *English for Writing Research Papers*.

3.6 Simplify sentences that are difficult to say

Try reading this sentence aloud:

> S1 In 2016, Kay proved that most people speak at a speed of one hundred and twenty to two hundred words per minute, but that the mind can absorb information at six hundred words per minute.

How easy did you find it?

It is difficult to say because it contains a lot of numbers plus a repetition of sounds (twenty to two hundred).

Your aim should be to create sentences that you find easy to say. Writing a script will help you to identify sentences, such as the one in the original version below, that do not come out of your mouth easily or naturally. So, read your script aloud, underline any phrases that are difficult to say, and then try to rewrite them until you find a form that is easy for you.

S1 could be improved in two ways:

> S2   In 2016, Kay proved that most people speak at a speed of *nearly* two hundred words per minute. *However*, the mind can absorb information at six hundred words per minute.
>
> S3   In 2016, Kay proved that most people speak at a speed of around two hundred words per minute. However, the mind can absorb information at six hundred words per minute—that is four hundred words more than the speed of speech.

S2 gives an approximate number and splits the sentence into two parts. S3 states the same fact in a different way so that the audience will remember it better.

3.7   Do not use synonyms for technical/key words

Never use more than one term to refer to the same key concept. If you do, the audience may think that each word has its own specific meaning and wonder what it is. For example, if you use the term *gender studies* don't suddenly use *gender politics*, *feminist studies* or *women's studies* to mean the same concept. If there is a difference, for example, between *gender* studies and *feminist* studies then you should explain it, but if they have an identical meaning then just use one or the other.

3.8   Only use synonyms for nontechnical words

Having a written speech will also stop you from unnecessarily repeating the same word. Note below how in the original version the word "aim" appears three times in two sentences, and the second sentence does not appear to add any new information.

ORIGINAL	REVISED
The aim of this research project was to estimate the number of female editors of international journals with an aim to reveal possible shortcomings due to male predominance. In addition, this study aims to look into the effects of …	We wanted to / Our aim was to estimate the number of female editors of international journals. Secondly, we were interested in revealing possible shortcomings due to male predominance. Our final objective was to look into the effects of …

To resolve the problem of repeated non-key words, you can do as in the revised version or

- find a synonym—in the first occurrence *aim* could be replaced by *objective* or *target*

- delete it—in the second occurrence *with an aim* could be deleted with no loss of meaning

3.9   Use verbs rather than nouns

Using verbs rather than nouns (or verb + noun constructions) makes your sentences shorter, more dynamic, and easier to understand for the audience.

X is meaningful for <u>an understanding</u> of Y = X will help you <u>to understand</u> Y

When you take into <u>consideration</u> = When <u>you consider</u>

This gives you the <u>possibility</u> to do X = This means you <u>can</u> do X./This <u>enables</u> you to do X.

3.10   Avoid abstract nouns

Abstract nouns such as *situation, activities, operations, parameters, issues* are more difficult to visualize than concrete nouns and thus more difficult to remember. Often they can simply be deleted.

Our research [activity] focused on …

If you find that your speech is full of words that end in *-ability, -acy, -age, -ance, -ation, -ence, -ism, -ity, -ment, -ness, -ship*, you probably need to think about deleting some of them or finding concrete alternatives or examples.

3.11   Avoid generic quantities and unspecific adjectives

Replace generic quantities such as *some, a certain quantity, a good number of* with a precise number.

I am going to give you <u>a few</u> examples = <u>three</u> examples

We have found <u>some</u> interesting solutions to this problem = <u>four</u> interesting solutions

Audiences like numbers:

- they make us more attentive because we start counting and we have a sense that we will be guided

- they give the information a more absorbable structure and thus help us to remember it better

Clearly the number of examples has to be low, otherwise the audience will think you will be talking all day. Or you can say

> We believe that there are possibly 10 different ways to solving this problem. Today I am going to outline the top two.

3.12 Advantages of having a written script

Once you have written your script, you can then write the slides. The slides themselves will help you to remember what to say, so you can then practice talking about the slides without using your script.

A written script will also help you to

1. identify words that you may not be able to pronounce

2. check that the sentences are not too long or complex for you to say naturally and for the audience to understand easily

3. understand when an example would be useful for the audience

4. clarify where you need to make connections between slides

5. delete redundancy and unnecessary repetition

6. identify the moments in the presentation where audience interest might go down

7. check if there are any terms that the audience might not understand

8. think of how you could deliver your message in a more powerful or dynamic way

9. verify if you are spending too much time on one point and not enough on another

10. time how long the presentation will take

Important: You can upload your script onto your phone and use it as a memory aid during your presentation (see 13.6 and 15.2).

3.13   Mark up your script and then practice reading it aloud

When you have created a final version of your script, you can mark it up as shown below. You probably won't have time to do a full markup for your whole presentation. But it is important that you do it for your introduction, which is the time when the audience is tuning in to your voice and making their first impressions. You should also do it for your conclusions. Also, it is a good idea to mark all those words that (a) you intend to give EMPHASIS to (b) those words that you find difficult to pronounce.

> **First** of all / thank you **very** much / for **coming** here today. My name's **Esther Kritz** / and I am <u>cu</u>rrently doing **research** into **psycholinguistics** [sy/my] / at **Manchester** Uni<u>ve</u>rsity. / / I'd like to show you / what **I** think / are some INCREDIBLE re<u>sults</u> / that I got while …

KEY

slash (/)—indicates where you want to pause. You only need to do this for the first 30-60 seconds of your presentation. A typical problem of the first few seconds of your presentation is that you are nervous and this makes you speak very fast. If you speak too fast the audience may have difficulty understanding. If you insert pauses this should encourage you to slow down and also to breathe. By breathing more you become more relaxed.

double slash (//)—indicates a longer pause. If you pause between key phrases it will focus the audience's attention on what you are saying and also give them time to digest it. Long pauses can have a positive dramatic effect.

bold—words that you want to stress in each phrase. This does not mean giving them a lot of stress but just a little more than the words immediately before and after. This stops you from speaking in a monotone (i.e., with equal stress on each word) which is boring for the audience. Words that tend to be stressed are key nouns, numbers, adjectives, some adverbs (e.g., significantly, unexpectedly), and verbs. Words that are not generally stressed are pronouns (unless to distinguish between two entities, e.g., *I gave it to **her** not to you*), non-key nouns, prepositions, conjunctions, and most adverbs.

CAPITALS—these are words that you want to give particular emphasis to. You may want to say them louder or more slowly or in a particular tone of voice. You do this to draw the audience's attention to what you are saying. Words that tend to be given extra emphasis are numbers and adjectives.

<u>under</u>line—indicates the stress within a particular word

[ ]—insert in brackets the sounds of words or syllables. For example, if you write *psy = my>sy*, this will remind you that you don't pronounce the initial "p" and that "sy" rhymes with "my" (as in "my book"). Alternatively you can try to find words or sounds in your own language that sound similar.

3.14   Use your script to write notes to accompany your slides

Most presentation software allows you to write notes for each slide. On the basis of your script you can write down what you want to say for each slide in note form. You can then print your slides with the accompanying notes and have these next to you when you do the presentation at the conference. It is best to print several slides on one page, then you don't need to keep turning the pages. Having these notes with you will give you confidence, because you know that you can consult them if you forget what to say or forget where you are in your presentation.

Also, you can practice your presentation using these notes.

3.15   Use your speech to decide if and when to have slides and in what order

If your usual preparation for presentations is 1) create the slides 2) practise your presentation, then your slides will dictate what you say.

It makes much more sense to 1) decide what you want to say, 2) create slides in support of what you want to say.

The script below is based on the second exercise of the *What's the Buzz?* section. You can compare your version with this version. The slides are indicated in italics and square brackets.

[*No title slide*] Herschel, Somerville, Meitner, Curie-Joliot, McClintock, Hodgkin - what do these names mean to you?

Have a look at them again on this slide [*slide with names: Herschel etc*].

OK, let's try this slide [*slide with the following names: Darwin, Newton, Einstein*]. OK, so you recognize these guys, right? And you know why? Because they are men. But you don't recognize these ones [*shows slide with Herschel, Somerville etc and their photos*].

Now look at this slide [*names of scientific units e.g. Celsius, Ohm*]. Are you getting the picture? All men again. Did you know that no female scientist has ever had a scientific unit name after her?

The aim of my research was to investigate women's position in science and how it is perceived by today's young scientists [*title of the presentation, presenter's name, etc*]. We conducted surveys of 500 PhD students at our university over a three-year period. We gave them the names of the female scientists that I gave you just now. Only 10% were able to recognize two names or more [*a table of results*], their list actually included Marie Curie as well. And only two students knew that Marie Curie had not even been accepted into the French scientific academy. And not much has changed. There are 454 members of the Russian academy, but only nine are women [*a table showing numbers of women and men in various scientific academies around the world*].

When we asked our students who is the most famous female scientist in your country, most were unable even to name a female scientist, let alone a famous one. The students that managed to think of a female scientist all tended to nominate physicists, mathematicians and chemists [*photos, names and nationalities of these female scientists*]. And ironically these are exactly the subjects which women tend to study the least.

Something has got to change. I mean it's changed in politics. Over fifty per cent of the Bolivian government is made up of women [*graph highlighting the rising number of women in politics in Bolivia, India, Israel and the US*].

So what's stopping women gaining a greater share in science?

The above script highlights how you can

- begin without the typical title slide - instead you can delay it until after you have captured the audience's attention

- get the audience interested immediately by getting them curious - most of the audience will not be familiar with the surnames of these scientists and will not realize that what they all have in common is that they are women

- adopt an informal style but still be professional

- give some unusual / interesting and relevant background detail before telling the audience what your main aim is

- use short sentences to enable you to remember what to say and also to help the audience to follow you

Notice how the script could be marked up (see 3.13) to help the presenter with her pronunciation and intonation, and to help her remember when to pause (by putting each sentence, or at least key sentences, on a separate line).

Something has got to change.

I mean it's changed in **politics**.

Over fifty per cent of the Bolivian government is made up of women /wimin/.

So what's **STOPPING** women gaining a greater share in **science**?

3.16   Tense usage

Tenses are used in different ways in different parts of the presentation. The most frequently used are

present simple: *I work*

present continuous: *I am working*

present perfect: *I have worked*

present perfect continuous: *I have been working*

past simple: *I worked*

future simple: *I will work*

future continuous: *I will be working*

going to: *I am going to work*

You can always either use full forms (e.g., *I will, I am*) or contracted forms (e.g., *I'll, I'm*). There is no difference in meaning, but the full forms can be used for emphasis, and the contracted forms sound more informal.

You don't need to have a perfect understanding of English grammar in order to be able to use the tenses correctly. I suggest that you consider the examples given in this subsection as useful phrases which you know that you can say at particular moments during your presentation.

More precise rules on the usage and meaning of these tenses can be found in Chapters 8-12 of *English for Research: Grammar, Usage and Style*.

Outline / Agenda Three tenses are usually used in outlines. When you outline your first point, just use either going to or the future continuous. For the other points, you can also use the future simple.

Let me just outline what **I'll be discussing** today.

First, **I'm going to tell** you something about the background to this work.

Then **I'll take** a brief look at the related literature and the methods we used.

Finally, and most importantly, **I'll show** you our key results.

Referring to future points in the presentation Use either the future simple or the future continuous. In this context, there is really no difference in meaning.

As we **will see** in the next slide ...	As we **will be seeing** in the next slide ...
I'll **tell** you more about this later ...	I'll **be telling** you more about this later ...
I **will give** you details on that at the end ...	I **will be giving** you details on ...

Don't use the present continuous to refer to future parts of presentation. Only use it when informing the audience about what you are doing now or when hypothesizing about what they are probably thinking as they see the slide.

I **am showing** you this chart because ...

Why **am I telling** you this? Well ...

You **are** probably **wondering** why we did this, well ...

Explaining the background and motivations Use the present simple to talk about the general situation, established scientific fact, and to explain your opinions and hypotheses.

As **is** well known, smoking **causes** cancer. But what we **don't know** is why people still **continue** to smoke

Despite some progress, not much **is known** about ...

Current practice **involves** doing X but we **believe** that doing Y would be more effective

Use the simple past for events and situations that have ended.

We **decided** to address this area because:

We **started** working on this in May last year.

Our initial attempts **failed** so we **had** to adopt a new approach.

Use the present perfect to talk about open issues, the progress that has been made in your field so far and when; the precise time is not important.

Several authors **have published** their findings on Y.

Other researchers **have tried** to address this problem, but no one **has yet managed** to solve it.

Not much progress **has been made** in this field so far.

Our experience **has shown** that ...

INDICATING WHAT YOU DID IN (A) YOUR RESEARCH (B) WHILE PREPARING YOUR SLIDES You need to make a clear distinction between what you did in your research (simple past) and the choices you made when preparing your slides (present perfect).

We **selected** patients on the basis of their pathology

We **used** an XYZ simulator which we **acquired** from ABC.

We **concluded** that the difference between A and B must be due to C.

I **have included** this chart because ...

I **have removed** some of the results for the sake of clarity ...

I **have reduced** all the numbers to whole numbers ...

TALKING ABOUT THE PROGRESS OF YOUR PRESENTATION When you refer to what you have done up to this point in the presentation, use the present perfect. This is often used for making mini summaries before moving on to a new point.

So we **have seen** how X affects Y, now let's see how it affects Z.

I **have shown** you how this is done with Z, now I am going to show how it is done with Y.

But when you are talking about moments earlier in the presentation use the simple past.

As we **saw** in the first/last slide ...

As I **mentioned** before/earlier/at the beginning ...

EXPLAINING AND INTERPRETING RESULTS Use the simple past to say what you found during your research. But to explain what your findings mean, use the present tense plus modal verbs (*would, may, might*).

We **found** that in most patients these values were very high.

This **means**/This **may mean**/This **seems to suggest** that/This **would seem to prove** that patients with this pathology should ...

GIVING CONCLUSIONS Make sure you distinguish between what you did during your research (past simple) and what you have done during the presentation (present perfect).

Okay. So we **used** an innovative method to solve the classic problem of calculating the shortest route, and this **gave** some interesting results which we then **analyzed** using some ad hoc software.

During this presentation, I **have shown** you three ways to do ...

OUTLINING FUTURE RESEARCH Various forms of the future will be needed here. Use the present continuous for actions in progress, and with verbs such as *plan, think about, assess the possibility* and *consider* to talk about possible plans. With *plan* and *hope* you can also use the present simple.

We **are currently looking** for partners in this project.

We **plan/are planning** to extend this research into the following areas ...

We **hope/are hoping** to find a new way to solve PQR.

You can use a mix of the future continuous and the future simple to give the idea of an already scheduled plan:

In the next phase we **will be looking** at XYZ.

This **will involve** ABC.

Chapter 4

Writing the text of your slides

Factoids

1. Over a three-day conference the average attendee will see between 300 and 500 slides.

2. *Death by PowerPoint* is a state of boredom and fatigue induced by information overload due to bullet-driven presentations with a series of very similar slides.

3. Using overly complex language prevents the audience from interpreting what a presenter is saying, and renders the presentation less convincing.

4. Ideas are perceived as being more persuasive if they are in a font that easy to read.

5. Professors Trevor Hassall and John Joyce of Sheffield Hallam University (UK) state that: "The audience does not need to see, or hear about, all the data you have collected. The data needs editing so that you only present concise and relevant evidence to justify any point you make".

6. Over 50,000 presentations have been uploaded onto the web containing the typo "tanks for your attention" most of which have no reference at all to armored vehicles!

7. 'Nobel Peace Price' gets 200,000 returns on Google, and *zebra strips* gets only ten times fewer returns than *zebra stripes*.

8. Words that native speakers typically misspell on slides include: *accommodate, finally, forty, government, grammar, laboratory, maintenance, necessary, performance, transferred*

© Springer International Publishing Switzerland 2016
A. Wallwork, *English for Presentations at International Conferences*,
English for Academic Research, DOI 10.1007/978-3-319-26330-4_4

4.1   What's the buzz?

1) Think about how you feel when you come out of someone else's presentation. Which of the following (a or b) do you regularly say to yourself:

   1a) I now know everything I need to know about X.

   1b) Now that I have seen the presentation, I would like to know more about X.

   2a) Thank goodness I remember everything that the presenter told me about X.

   2b) I only remember a couple of points about X.

   3a) It took me a long time to form an impression of the presenter.

   3b) I quickly formed an impression.

   4a) The presentation was too short - I would have like to hear more.

   4b) The presentation was too long - I stopped listening after a while.

   5a) There was too much text - I couldn't concentrate on the speaker.

   5b) There was just the right mixture of text, graphics etc.

   6a) I was able to concentrate 80-100% on everything the presenter said.

   6b) I concentrated for about 50% of the presentation.

What can you deduce from your answers?

2) Answer the questions

   1. How can you reduce the amount of text you use in your slides? Think of three ways or more.

   2. What are the pros and cons of minimal text in slides? For you? For the audience?

   3. What should you include in your title slide?

****

This chapter discusses what to write on your slides.

Audiences will potentially see thousands of slides during a conference. An audience will be more attentive if they believe you have made a special effort for them to make your talk not just useful, but also interesting and entertaining: limiting the amount of text and number of bullets is a sign of such effort.

Your aim should be for the audience to quickly assimilate the information on your slides and then focus on you. The less text there is, the quicker the audience will focus on what you are saying. You will also be less tempted to "read" your slides.

Text on slides needs to be concise, so in order how to remove any possible redundancy, read sections 5.3 to 5.15 in Chapter 5 'Being Concise and Removing Redundancy' in *English for Writing Research Papers*.

4.2 PART 1: TITLES - WHOLE PRESENTATION AND INDIVIDUAL SLIDES

4.2.1 *Make sure your title is not too technical for your audience*

The title of your presentation is a like an advertisement for a product, so consider not using the title of your thesis or paper as the title of your presentation. An interesting title is more likely to attract people to your presentation, and titles of papers and theses are rarely designed to attract the attention of an audience.

Attendees sometimes watch presentations in fields that are not strictly their own, but perhaps where they feel they might be able to apply their findings or because they are looking for new areas of research. It may thus be useful to think of titles to your presentations that are likely to engage a wider audience, which is not all made up of experts in your precise field of research.

Here are some examples of alternative titles:

TECHNICAL	NONTECHNICAL
1) A Pervasive Solution for Risk Awareness in the context of Fall Prevention in the Elderly	Stop your grandmother from falling!
2) An evaluation of the benefit of the application of usability and ergonomics principles to consumer goods	I hate this product! How the hell does it work?
3) Construction and validation of a carrier to shuttle nucleic acid-based drugs from biocompatible polymers to living cells	Q: How can we get nucleic acid-based drugs from biocompatible polymers to living cells? A: Use a shuttle
4) Contact Force Distribution in the Interference Fit between a Helical Spring and a Cylindrical Shaft	Will this fastener kill me?
5) Preparation, characterization, and degradability of low environmental impact polymer composites containing natural fibers	How can we stop the world disappearing under polyethylene bags? Using low environmental impact polymer composites containing natural fibers
6) Anti-tumor activity of bacterial proteins: study of the p53-azzurine interaction	Azzurrine binds to p53. Towards a nontoxic alternative to chemotherapy?
7) Investigation into the perpetuation of the classic stereotypes associated with lawyers.	Lawyer stereotypes vs reality: spot the difference.

Notice how in each case, the nontechnical titles contain verbs. Verbs give the idea of dynamism, nouns don't. You may think that the last title—Will this fastener kill me?—is too obscure. However you would probably be curious to see what it was about.

In examples 5-7, the non-technical titles consist of two parts. In typical two part title:

• one part (generally the first) is less technical and much more informal. It is designed to attract a more generalist audience to your presentation. It is often in the form of a question.

• the other part is more technical and should attract those who are already in your field

Another alternative is to have both titles in the conference program, and just the fun/more informal title on your title slide.

4.2.2 Remove all redundancy from your title, but don't be too concise

When you have decided on your title, rewrite it removing redundant words (in square brackets in the examples below) and leaving in only key words.

The ligno-cellulose biomass fuel chain [: a review]

[A study on] producing bread [in Andalucia] with [the] acid moisture [technique]

[Development of] a Portable Device for Work Analysis to Reduce Human Errors in Industrial Plants

[Issues of] language rights and use in Canada

However, don't remove too much! What is the problem with this title?

An innovative first-year PhD student scientific English didactic methodology

When you start reading it, it seems to have one meaning. But when you finish, it seems to have another meaning. The problem is that this title is a string of adjectives + nouns + nouns that act as adjectives.

A much easier title to understand would be

An innovative methodology for teaching scientific English to first-year PhD students

Good titles put

- the adjective next to the noun it refers to (*innovative* refers to *methodology* not to *students*)

- have a verb (*teaching*)

- use prepositions (*for, to*)

Some more examples showing the use of verbs are given below:

NO VERBS	WITH VERBS
The *implementation* of sustainable strategies in multinational companies	*Implementing* sustainable strategies in multinational companies
TOF-SIMS: an innovative technique for *the study of* ancient ceramics	TOF-SIMS: an innovative technique for *studying* ancient ceramics
Fault *detection* of a Five-Phase Permanent-Magnet Motor - a four-part solution	Four ways *to detect* faults in a Five-Phase Permanent-Magnet Motor
Effect of crop rotation diversity and nitrogen fertilization on weed *management* in a maize-based cropping system	How does crop rotation diversity and nitrogen fertilization *affect* the way weeds *are managed* in a maize-based cropping system?

4.2.3 Check that your title is grammatical and is spelt correctly

The rules of grammar, particularly the use of articles (*a, an, the*) also apply in titles. Can you find the grammatical mistakes in the ungrammatical titles below?

UNGRAMMATICAL	GRAMMATICAL
Multimodality in the context of Brain-Computer Interface	Multimodality in the context of <u>a</u> Brain-Computer Interface/of Brain Computer Interfac<u>es</u>
Importance of role of planning and control systems in supporting interorganizational relationships in health care sector	<u>The</u> importance of <u>the</u> role of planning and control systems in supporting interorganizational relationships in <u>the</u> health care sector
Iran Foreign Policy	Iran<u>'s</u> Foreign Policy

Titles of presentations often contain spelling mistakes. This is particularly true if the title of the presentation is also the title of your thesis. You have seen that title so often that when you look at it on your slide you don't actually read it because it is so familiar to you. Can you find the spelling mistakes in these titles?

The Rethoric of Evil in German Literature

Governance choice in railways: applying empirical transaction costs economics to the the railways of Easter Europe and the former USSR

Hearth attack! Cardiac arrest in the middle aged

In the first example *rethóric* seems correct because it looks as if it reflects the pronunciation (correct: *rhetoric*). In the second and third examples it should be *Eastern* and *Heart* respectively—unfortunately no spell check system would have found the mistakes because *Easter* and *Hearth* are also correct spellings (but with entirely different meanings). Also, there is the repetition (*the the*) which you may not notice: although they are in sequence they appear on different lines.

4.2.4 Deciding what else to include in the title slide

There is no standard way to construct a title slide, but most presenters prioritize information by using different font sizes. The two most important elements, which should be given the most space, are

1. the title
2. your name

Other things that some presenters sometimes include are

3. the name and date of the conference (this helps in web searches)
4. co-authors
5. the name and/or logo of your institute/research unit
6. your supervisor
7. acknowledgments
8. sponsors
9. a photo
10. a background image

Some of the best presenters use their title slide to attract audience attention. They do this either by completely ignoring points 3–7 above, or by putting such details in a very small font. Points 3–7 generally contain no information that 99.9% of the audience need to know or that they can't find out from the conference program.

Point 3 has become a kind of standard way to show that the presentation is not simply a recycled version of a previous one—this goes to the extent of putting the conference name and date on every single slide. This seems totally unnecessary.

Points 4–7 tend to be included exclusively to satisfy colleagues, professors, supervisors, and those that have helped during your research. It probably makes more sense to thank these people personally away from the conference. If you are part of a research team, there is no need to list all the names of the people in your team. If you absolutely must give acknowledgments to such people, then it is probably a good idea to put their

44

names in a small font and in a non-prominent position in your slide. Similarly, if you have participated in many projects, you don't need to write the names of these projects. This kind of information is very pertinent to you, but it is usually of no interest to the audience. You could simply say, *"There are 14 people in our team and we have already participated in 10 projects."* That is all the audience needs to know.

You may have a contractual obligation to mention sponsors (Point 8).

Points 9 and 10 may help to make your title slide look more interesting. Typical photos and background images include elements of your research or photos (or maps) from your country of origin.

The more information you have on your title slide the more it will detract away from the most important things: your title and your name.

For more on writing titles see Chapter 12 in *English for Writing Research Papers*.

4.2.5 Think of alternative titles for your slides

When thinking of titles for your slides, bear in mind the quantity of slides that an audience will see over a typical two-day congress. Ask yourself how much audience attention you are likely to attract by a series of titles such as, Introduction - Methodology - Discussion - Conclusion and Future Work - Thank you for your attention - Any questions?

If your slot is near the end of the morning or afternoon (particularly on the last day of the conference), you need to think of alternative titles. Avoid words that give no real information and which the audience has probably seen a hundred times since the beginning of the conference such as, *activity, investigation, overview.*

Here are some possible alternative titles to the typical sections of a presentation:

Outline:	Why?	Why should you be excited?
Methodology:	How?	Don't try this at home
Results:	What did we find?	Not what we were expecting
Discussion:	So what?	Why should you care?
Future work:	What next?	Men at work
Thank you:	That's all folks	See you in *name of location of next conference*

See also 8.7 to learn how to use slide titles to explain a process or methodology.

4.3 PART 2: KEEPING TEXT ON SLIDES TO THE MINIMUM

4.3.1 *Keep it simple: one idea per slide*

Limit each slide to one main idea or result. Any bulleted text, data, or graphics on the slide should be in support of this main idea.

You can check how many ideas there are in your slide by trying to give it a title. If a title doesn't come quickly to mind, it may mean you have covered too many points and thus that you need to divide up these points into further slides.

The moment to give detail is when you are talking the audience through the slide (i.e. explaining the significance of the information contained in the slide).

There shouldn't be too much text/detail within the slide itself.

4.3.2 *Where possible, avoid complete sentences*

Which is it easier for an audience to do—read or listen? The answer is probably read—it requires much less effort.

If you fill your slides with text, you are encouraging your audience simply to read and not to listen to what you say.

This habit will then continue throughout your presentation. At this point you could simply email the audience your paper.

By simplifying and cutting you will have much cleaner slides. The audience will then spend more time listening to you, and less time reading your slides.

Assuming your audience all understand English quite well, if you write complete sentences in your slides

- your audience will read the text on the slide rather than focus on you

- when you comment on the slide it will be difficult for you to avoid repeating word for word what is on your slide. Alternatively, you will be forced to para-phrase, which may lead to unnecessarily long sentences

- your slide will be full of text and to accommodate this text the font may be too small for the audience to read clearly

Moreover, if you have a lot of text on your slides but you say something very different from the text, then the audience has to take in two different sets of information—one written, the other verbal—at the same time. The human brain is not equipped to simultaneously read some information and to listen to something different.

So the solution is to do one of the following:

- cut the slide completely and simply talk

- reduce the text to three or four short bullet points which the audience can absorb immediately. Then expand on one or more of these bullets

- give the audience a few seconds to absorb the text (for example, an important definition or a quotation from an expert), and then blank the screen and start talking

Otherwise there will be two presenters—you and your text—and you will both be competing for the audience's attention.

4.3.3 Only use complete sentences for a specific purpose

Some audiences, however, appreciate complete sentences. They enable attendees with a low level of English to

- follow your slides, even if they can't follow what you say

- better understand your pronunciation if they can also see the written forms of the key words that you are using

- take notes

- memorize what you have said if they have a better visual memory than auditory memory

Four possible solutions for dealing with an audience with mixed levels of English are

- have a more complete version (i.e. more text, notes under the slides) of your presentation which the audience can download and follow during your presentation (see 1.1)

- have slides with complete sentences but keep them as short as possible, removing all redundancy and removing articles (*the, a/an*). Ways to do this are explained in this chapter. When you show these slides, give the audience up to five to six seconds to read them. Then, make general comments <u>without</u> reading the text. This allows the audience to absorb the information on the slide and then they can concentrate on what you are saying

- have short bulleted sentences. In addition, prepare photocopies of the same slides but with full text. You can then distribute these to the audience <u>before</u> you begin and the people in the audience with poor English can then refer to them during the presentation

- give the audience a handout <u>after</u> you have finished, where you can write more complete sentences, and add extra details, e.g., extracts from your paper, your contact details

Even if the audience has a high level of English, complete sentences can occasionally be used to emphasize a particular point, explain a difficult point, or give a quotation.

Again, it is important to remember that you

- should <u>never</u> read your slides, there is absolutely no advantage for either you or the audience, particularly as people read at different speeds and most will not be synchronized with your speech

- don't have to explain everything on your slides—if you have a series of four bullets, you may only need to comment on the first bullet, leaving the audience to interpret the other three

- need to have a variety of slide types. You cannot do what I have suggested in the first solution above (show slide, wait five seconds) throughout the whole presentation, as this will be very tedious for the audience. So try to have some slides with more text, some with less text, and as some with no text at all

4.3.4 Avoid repetition within the same slide

If the title of your slide is *How to free up space on your disk* don't have a series of bullets introduced by *The following are ways to free up space on your disk:*

To save space, don't repeat the first words in a series of bullets—either incorporate them into the introductory phrase or simply say them when you make your commentary.

ORIGINAL	REVISED
The advantages of using this system are	Advantages for researchers:
➢ *it will enable researchers to* limit the time needed in the laboratory	➢ limits lab time
	➢ finds relevant data
➢ *it will help researchers to* find the data they need	➢ produces more accurate results
➢ *it will permit researchers to* produce more accurate results	The system enables researchers to
	➢ limit lab time
	➢ find relevant data
	➢ produce more accurate results

In the original example above, the first three words on each bullet (*enable, help,* and *permit*) mean the same in this context.

4.3.5 *Use only well-known acronyms, abbreviations, contractions, and symbols*

In the following examples the shorter versions are in brackets: as soon as possible (asap); to be confirmed (tbc); for example (e.g., or eg), that is to say (i.e., or ie); information (info); against (vs); research and development (R&D); and, also, in addition etc., (& or +); this leads to, consequently (> or =); 10,000 (10 K); 10,000,000 (10 M).

However, don't use abbreviations, acronyms, and symbols unless they are well known. If you explain a new acronym in Slide 2, by Slide 3 the audience will already have forgotten what it means. It is much easier for them to see the full words.

4.3.6 *Choose the shortest forms possible*

Use the shortest words and shortest phrases possible. Here are some examples:

regarding = on; however = but; furthermore = also; consequently = so; necessary = needed

We needed to make a comparison of x and y. = We needed to compare x and y.

There is a possibility that X will fail. = X may fail.

Evaluating the component = Evaluating components

The user decides his/her settings = Users decide their settings

The activity of testing is a laborious process = Testing is laborious

No need for the following: = No need for

Various methods can be used to solve this problem such as = Methods:

4.3.7 Cut brackets containing text

Brackets tend to contain examples, definitions, or statistics.

Natural fibers (wool, cotton etc.,)

ISO (International Organization for Standardization) approval

In the examples above, it is generally not necessary for the audience to see the information in brackets, you can simply say

We analyzed some natural fibers such as wool and cotton.

Our device has been approved by the International Organization for Standardization.

By deleting the parts in brackets, you will thus have extra information to add when you comment on your slide.

4.3.8 Keep quotations short

Imagine that you are doing a presentation on Human Rights and you wish to quote what was said by a judge. There is no need to quote the full text. If you do you will force the audience to read it all and probably also force the audience to hear you reading it all. Your choices are either to paraphrase it using your own words; or you can cut the parts (i.e., the parts in *italics* in the original version below) that are not fundamental to an understanding of it, and replace them with three dots (…). More drastically, you may decide not to use three dots but tell the audience that you have removed a few words for the sake of space (the full quote could be given in a handout)—this leads to the revised version below, which takes a lot less time for the audience to read and absorb.

ORIGINAL	REVISED
I also concede that the Convention organs have *in this way*, on occasion, reached the limits of *what can be regarded as* treaty interpretation in the legal sense. *At times* they have perhaps even crossed the boundary and entered territory which is no longer that of treaty interpretation but is actually legal policy making. But *this, as I understand it, is not for a court to do; on the contrary,* policy making is a task for the legislature or the Contracting States *themselves, as the case may be.*	The Convention organs have, on occasion, reached the limits of treaty interpretation in the legal sense. They have perhaps even crossed the boundary and entered territory which is no longer that of treaty interpretation but is actually legal policy making. But policy making is a task for the legislature or the Contracting State.

4.3.9 Avoid references

References to other authors' works, legislation (e.g., EU directives, dates of laws), and manufacturer's instructions are generally not necessary on slides. You may think they give authority to what you are saying, but in most cases they are just distracting and add unnecessary text to your slides. However, check on the conference website whether such references may in fact be required.

You might be worried that in the Q&A session someone might ask you for such details, for example if there is some contention about which author made a certain finding. If so, you can create a separate slide showing these details and only show the slide if someone asks the question.

4.3.10 Don't put text in your slides to say what you will do or have done during your presentation

In an outline there is no need to write "*I will discuss the following ...*" Likewise on the Conclusions slide do not write "*We have presented a strategy for...*" In such cases, you simply need to say those phrases.

Imagine you are participating in a project to get more people in your country and surrounding countries to use the Internet. You are at a conference on the Internet, and you are reporting on what you have done so far. Below is the text contained in your first slide:

INTERNET DIFFUSION PROJECT

➤ Several research and technological projects have been activated. I am going to describe the results of the Internet diffusion project.

➤ The main goal of the project is to analyze Internet diffusion among households, companies, nonprofit organizations through the use of domain names.

Ask yourself

• does the audience need to see this information?

• what am I going to say when I show this slide?

The problem is that if you do not practice your presentation, you will not be prepared for the fact that in reality there will be nothing that you can say when you show this slide, apart from repeating what is on it. There is nothing complicated on the slide, no tables, no strange words, no pictures, in fact nothing that the audience would not be able to understand if you simply stood in front of them and told them.

This is the kind of slide that should be cut completely. Instead, when you show your title slide you could say something like this:

> Hi, I am here today to tell you about a completely new project—the first in Eastern Europe in fact. The idea is to find out how much the Internet is being used among various categories of users: households, companies, nonprofit organizations [you can count on your fingers to highlight each category]. To do this we are looking at the numbers of Internet domain names by type. My idea is to tell you where we are at the moment. Then it would be great if I could set up contacts with those of you here who represent other Eastern European countries. You might be interested to know that we estimate that there are around 25 million domain names registered in our part of the world and this represents ....

4.4 PART 3: BULLETS

4.4.1 *Limit yourself to six (standard) bullets per slide, with a a maximum of two levels of bullets*

Always use the standard bullet (•) unless the items

- need to be numbered to show the order or chronology in which something is done

- are in a list of things that were scheduled to be done and have been done. In this case you can use a tick (√).

- are better presented using bullets that you have created yourself

When you are giving lists keep them short. Six bullets are generally more than enough. And you only need to talk about a couple of them (e.g., the top two).

An exception is when you are not going to talk about any of the bullets but your aim is simply to show that, for example, your instrument has a lot of features, or that your research group has been involved in a lot of projects. Such features or projects can thus all be preceded by a bullet, or can simply appear as an unbulleted list. In such cases you do not need to read/say anything on the slide.

The slide below has three levels of bullets, which generally leads to messy slides.

ORIGINAL	REVISED
DISCUSSION	OPTIMIZATION GOALS

➢ Different optimization goals:
    ° Save storage
    ° Save CPU utilization
       • Only if multiple applications
         are being run together
	➢ Save storage
	➢ Save CPU utilization with multiple applications

As you can see from the revised version, you can reduce the bullets to one level by

1. changing the title of the slide from *Discussion* to *Optimization Goals*
2. incorporating the third level into the second level (*Save CPU use for multiple applications*). Alternatively you could delete the third level and simply give this information verbally

4.4.2   Choose the best order for the bullets

The normal practice is to order the bullets in terms of which ones you will be commenting on. Given that there is generally no need to comment on all the bullets in a list, it is best to put the ones you intend to talk about at the top of the list.

Sometimes you may have a list of bullets and you intend to make one general overall comment about them, without commenting on any of them individually. In such cases it is best to put them in alphabetical order to highlight that they are not in order of importance. Alternatively, you can say, "*By the way these bullets are in no particular order.*"

4.4.3   Do not use a bullet for every line in your text

The default settings of PowerPoint and other applications encourage you to use a bullet before every line of text.

Note how the bullets in the original version below have been misused in this slide from a presentation on detecting faults in a magnet motor.

ORIGINAL	REVISED
MODELING FAULT CONDITIONS	MODELING FAULT CONDITIONS
➢ Two main faults are investigated:	Two main faults are investigated:
➢ Open phase. In this case the current sensor in each phase.	➢ Open phase. In this case the current sensor in each phase.
➢ Shorted turns. In this case a percentage of the turns of the winding is shortened.	➢ Shorted turns. In this case a percentage of the turns of the winding is shortened. Under these conditions the faulty …
➢ Under these conditions the faulty …	

The first line (*Two main faults* …) introduces a list of two items. So only the second and third lines need bullets. The fourth line is not a *fault*.

4.4.4 Be grammatical in bullets and where possible use verbs not nouns

Using the least amount of words is generally a good tactic. But what you write has to be grammatical and the words have to be in the right order.

Make sure the first word in each bullet is grammatically the same:

- an infinitive (e.g., *study/to study*)

- an -ing form (e.g., *studying*)

- a verb (e.g., *studies/will study*)

- a noun (e.g., *researcher*)

- an adjective or past participle (e.g., *good, better, improved*)

BAD EXAMPLE (BULLET 1 —NOUN; BULLET 2— VERB; BULLET 3— ADJECTIVE)	GOOD EXAMPLE (ALL VERBS)	GOOD EXAMPLE (ALL ADJECTIVES)
Advantages for researchers: ➤ Lab time limited ➤ Finds relevant data ➤ More accurate results	Advantages for researchers: ➤ Limits lab time ➤ Finds relevant data ➤ Produces more accurate results	Advantages for researchers: ➤ Limited lab time ➤ Relevant data ➤ More accurate results

The grammar in the slide in the first column below may initially look correct, but it isn't.

INCORRECT GRAMMAR (DIFFERENT GRAMMATICAL FORMS)	INCORRECT GRAMMAR (ALL NOUNS)	GOOD EXAMPLE (ALL VERBS)
A Java infrastructure for	A Java infrastructure for	A Java infrastructure for
➤ MPEG-7 features processing	➤ MPEG-7 features processing	➤ Processing MPEG-7 features
➤ XML database managing	➤ XML database management	➤ Managing XML database
➤ Algorithms ontology exploiting	➤ Algorithms ontology exploitation	➤ Exploiting algorithms ontology
➤ Functions integrating	➤ Functions integration	➤ Integrating functions

In the first column above, the final word in each bullet ends in -ing, but unfortunately they are not all the same grammatical form. *Processing* can be a verb or a noun, but the other three (*managing, exploiting, integrating*) can only be verbs and cannot be in this position in a phrase. In the second column, there is a series of noun+noun+noun constructions, which is difficult for the audience to understand quickly and is generally not grammatically correct. The best solution is to use verbs, as in the third column.

Where possible, use verbs both in the introductory sentence and in the bullets themselves. Using verbs, rather than nouns, reduces the number of words you need.

NOUNS	VERBS
Testing is the activity of	Testing involves
➤ The observation and recording of results	➤ Observing and recording results
➤ The evaluation of the component	➤ Evaluating the component

4.5 PART 4: CHECKING YOUR SLIDES

4.5.1 *Print your slides as a handout then edit /cut them*

When you've prepared your slides, print them. You can generally print up to nine slides on a page—this is called "print as handout." When you see all your slides together like this, it gives you a clearer picture of the amount of text you have used throughout your presentation.

Look at each slide and ask yourself if the text is crucial. If it is not crucial, cut it.

If it is crucial then ask yourself—can I express it in a more succinct way? Could I use a picture rather than text? Do I really need a slide to express this point or could I just say it verbally?

If you think that a particular slide, photo, story, or statistic is likely to help you achieve your objective of getting people interested in your work and in you, and of generally making your presentation more entertaining, interesting, and memorable, then don't cut it. A presentation with interesting parts, even if less essential than other parts, will be far more digestible than a presentation with only essential parts and nothing interesting.

But don't keep a slide just because you personally think it is fun.

4.5.2 *Check for typos*

When you become very familiar with your slides it becomes almost impossible for you to notice typos. It is also pssobile to udnresnatd cmpolteely mssiplet wrods and snteecnes. So this means you may not see the mistakes.

Presentation software does not always manage to highlight incorrect spellings. To check the spelling of your presentation you need to convert the text into your word processing program.

Some typical examples that spell checkers won't find are *attach* vs *attack*, *constrains* vs *constraints*, *contest* vs *context*, *filed* vs *field*, *form* vs *from*, *price* vs *prize*, *some* vs *same*, *stripe* vs *strip*, *then* vs *than*, *though* vs *tough*, *three* vs *tree*, *through* vs *trough*, *where* vs *were*

To learn about typical spelling mistakes and how to avoid them see Chapter 28 in *Grammar, Usage and Style*.

Chapter 5

Visual Elements and Fonts

Factoids

Research has shown that of all the information the mind stores, 75% is received visually, 13% through hearing, and 12% through smell, taste, and touch.

Visual aids improve learning by 200%, retention by 38%, and understanding complex subjects by 25% to 40%.

A key quality of good presenters is that they spend about 95% of their time looking at the audience.

According to a blog poll, 76% of those surveyed used a font size of less than 20 in their presentations. The size should depend on the conference room and is likely to be at least 24 for the body and 34 for header.

Experts recommend pie charts for percentages (max 5 slices), bar charts for comparisons and rankings (max 7 bars), graphs for changes over time (preferably just two lines), and tables for comparisons (max 3x3).

Research has proved that capital letters are hard to read, as is dark text on a dark background.

In a study of advertising copy, color was found to increase readership and retention by as much as 80%.

According to a color preference study by Pantone Color Institute and Cooper Marketing Group, the color most favored by people is blue. The least popular color is a yellow-green shade like the color of sulfur.

© Springer International Publishing Switzerland 2016
A. Wallwork, *English for Presentations at International Conferences*,
English for Academic Research, DOI 10.1007/978-3-319-26330-4_5

5.1   What's the buzz?

1) How do you think the researchers established the percentages in the first two Factoids on the previous page? How reliable and useful are such statistics?

2) Complete the sentences:

1. My favorite font to use in a presentation is _____ .
2. I hate this font: _____ .
3. The best background/foreground color combination is _____ .
4. The ideal number of bullets in one slide is: _____ .
5. I tend to use pie charts for _____ .
6. The problem with many presenters' graphs and figures is _____ .
7. Often tedious text can be replaced with _____ .

****

A key element in the success of your presentation is the way it looks. This book focuses on the language, structural, and oral delivery elements of giving presentations, so this chapter only deals briefly with visual aids.

The key to whether an image, photo, figure, chart etc is necessary to presentation is whether it will

– add value for the audience
– relate to what you are saying
– look good

You don't need a visual aid in each slide. Sometimes you could just have a blank screen. Other times visual aids are essential to help the audience to understand something quickly that would otherwise take you many words to explain.

This chapter is designed to help you make decisions with when to use a visual aid, and what type of aid is most appropriate for your purpose. Sections 5.2, 5.3 and 5.4 outline the various uses of graphs, figures and tables. Sections 5.5 - 5.13. give some suggestions on when, if and how visual aids should be used, and how color affects audience understanding. The chapter ends with a few points related to presentation software. Note that the primary aim of this book is to help you with your English, so all the different possibilities offered by presentation software are out of the scope of the book.

To learn how to make the explanation of your graphs, figures and tables interesting for your audience see 8.11 and 9.4.

5.2 Use visuals to help your audience understand, but keep the visuals simple

We tend to enjoy the creative graphical side of preparing a presentation but think less about the actual utility for the audience of what we have created. The aim of visuals is to help your audience to understand, but often they confuse the audience.

To avoid confusion, experts recommend

TYPE OF GRAPH OR CHART	USEFUL FOR	MAX. NO. ELEMENTS
Pie	percentages	3–5 slices
Bar charts (horizontal), columns (vertical)	comparisons, correlations, rankings	5–7 bars/columns
Graphs	showing changes over time. Scatter graphs give clear overview of how data are scattered	1–2 lines
Tables	comparing small amounts of information	3 columns and 3 rows
Cartoons	clarifying all kinds of graphs and charts	1–2

In addition, you should

• minimize the amount of information contained

• include labels and legends, and locate them as close as possible to the data points they refer to

• ensure that labels are horizontal, otherwise the audience will find them difficult or impossible to read

• explain what the axes represent and why you chose them

• present comparative information in columns not in rows

Given that tables and graphs are difficult to interpret quickly, decide if it would be possible to present the same information in a much clearer way.

A sequence of related tables over several slides means that the audience have to remember what was in the previous tables. The best solution is to have all the information on one slide. You can only do this by significantly reducing the amount of information and having a maximum of two adjacent figures.

You can also use visuals to

- get audience attention

- inject humor

- vary the pace of the presentation

To learn how to comment on graphs etc, see 9.4.

5.3 Choose the most appropriate figure to illustrate your point

Imagine you want to present the following information:

- the number of different words used in a presentation does not rise significantly with the length of the presentation

- this means that even in a long presentation the number of words whose pronunciation you may have to practice does not increase very much.

With regard to point (1), a 10-minute presentation will contain a total of 1200–1800 words, of which 300–450 will be different. The words are "different" in the sense that a presenter may use a total of 300 different words to express himself/herself, but many of these 300 words he/she will use more than once (for example, *an, the, this, then*), which then gives the total number of words (total words). In a 20-minute presentation the "total words" will be twice as many as in a 10-minute presentation, but the percentage of "different words" will only rise slightly from 300–450 to 320–470. Likewise in a 40-minute presentation.

With regard to point (2), only a small number (around 20) of the "different words" will be words that a presenter does not know how to pronounce, as the vast majority of words should already be familiar to the presenter. In addition, this number does not rise significantly with the length of the presentation—for example, in a 20-minute presentation it may only rise from 20 to 22.

Below is a graph that is designed to illustrate the information given on the previous page.

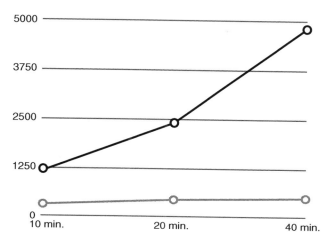

The presenter could say:

> This graph clearly shows that the total number of words, which is shown in the black line, in a presentation changes in direct relation to the number of minutes of the presentation. On the other hand, the number of different words, which is represented by the gray line, does not increase very much.

However, there are some problems with the graph and the explanation:

- there are no labels, either for the y-axis or for the two lines, so initially the audience will be confused and the presenter is forced to explain what the axes mean

- the most interesting information is contained in the gray line (which represents the total different words), but the way the y-axis has been scaled does not make it clear how many different words are used for each type of presentation

- the audience will be left thinking "what does this all mean?" or "why are you telling me this?"

In fact, there is nothing said about what the connection is with pronunciation (point 2 above), which is supposed to be the key fact that the presenter wants to give to the audience. If you choose the wrong type of illustration, you may find it more difficult to talk about your key points.

The bar chart below shows the same information as in the graph, but perhaps in a more dramatic and immediate way:

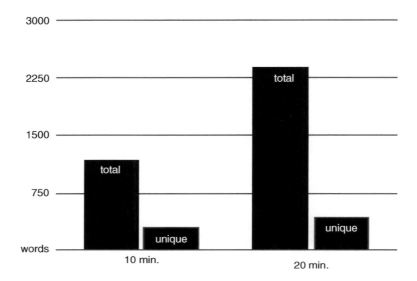

But again, there is no connection with pronunciation. In any case, it would be impossible to illustrate the number of words that could create pronunciation problems, because the number would be barely visible as a bar.

Below is a table that a presenter has cut and pasted from a paper

	total: all words	total: different words
10-minute presentation	1200–1800	300–450
20-minute presentation	2400–3600	320–470
40-minute presentation	4800–7200	340–490

There are a few problems with cutting and pasting from papers:

- readers of papers have, in theory, all the time they need to absorb detailed information; in a presentation the audience does not have this time frame

- by having so much information (i.e., the ranges of values and the coverage of three different lengths of presentation), the presenter may be tempted to describe everything, without telling the audience where they should focus. Clearly the more you describe, the longer you take, and potentially the more mistakes in English you will make

• the table in the paper may have been used for a slightly different purpose from what is needed for now—in fact this table tells us nothing about pronunciation Generally, the best solution is to

• have a really clear idea of what it is that you want the audience to learn about (in this case, the number of words they will have to learn to pronounce)

• choose the minimal amount of data that will clearly convey this idea

• choose the most appropriate format for conveying this idea (the graph and bar chart did not really work well for our purposes in this case)

• use the simplest possible form of this format

So a good solution could be the following table:

	all words	different words	words difficult to pronounce
10 minute	1200	300	10–20
20 minute	2400	320	12–22

This table is quick for the audience to read and absorb. The significance of the very slight rise in the total number of different words is very easy to see. Also, the data on a 40-minute presentation has been removed and just the lower value of the number of words is given.

And it also contains a new column "difficult words to pronounce." The information given in the second column is interesting, but the key information for someone who is preparing a presentation and who is worried about pronunciation is in the third column (which does have a range of values, but these are very easy to comprehend immediately).

The result is now that the presenter only gives the audience the information that they really need to know and excludes everything else.

This is what the presenter could say:

> I think that from this table it is clear that the number of different words we use in a presentation only increases slightly from a 10-minute presentation to a 20-minute presentation. The significance of this is in the third column. You don't have to learn the pronunciation of many words. In fact, most of those 300 or 320 different words you will probably already know how to pronounce. This is great news. You just have to learn between 10 and 20 words for a 10-minute presentation. And only a few words more for a presentation that is twice as long.

Note how the presenter

- does not describe the table

- tells the audience where to focus their attention (*the third column*)

- explains the importance of the data

- uses a lot of short sentences—they are easy for the presenter to say, and easy for the audience to understand

- shows enthusiasm (*great news*)

If you were the presenter and you were worried that someone in the audience might question your accuracy, then you could also say,

By the way, the number of words in a presentation obviously varies from presenter to presenter, so someone who speaks very fast may use up to 1800 words. And the number of different words will very much depend on the number of different technical words that a presenter needs. So instead of 300 it could be 450 different words. But in any case the number of different words doesn't rise considerably if you speak for 20 or 40 minutes rather than just 10 minutes.

5.4   Design pie charts so that the audience can immediately understand them

The two pie charts below represent the percentages of time spent on three aspects of preparing a presentation.

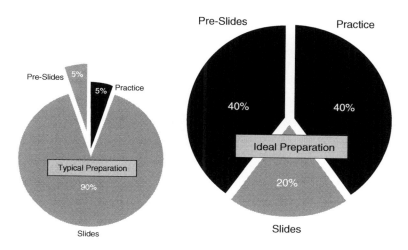

The secret to pie charts is not to have too many slices. Given that in the first chapter of this book I outlined 10 stages for preparing a presentation, there could have been 10 slices in the pie. But 10 slices would be hard for the audience to decipher on the slide and difficult for the presenter to explain. Plus it would be almost impossible to put clear labels on each slice. In any case, you can always tell your audience that you have considerably simplified the chart, and that if they are interested in seeing the full version they can see it in your paper, on your website, etc.

Notice how the two pie charts are not the same size. This tells the audience that the second chart is the one they should give the most attention to.

If you do reduce a pie chart to its most important elements, it will be easy for the audience to understand immediately. It will also require minimal comment by you, as highlighted by the revised version below:

ORIGINAL	REVISED
In the next slide we can see a comparison between the typical practice of presenters during their preparation of a presentation and the ideal practice. Pre-slide preparation in the normal practice is allocated 5% of the time in comparison with 40% in the ideal time. On the other hand, in the normal practice 90% of the presenter's time is dedicated to slide creation ... (63 words)	I think these pie charts are self-explanatory. People spend too much time on designing slides, rather than preparing what they want to say and then practicing it. (27 words)

Note how in the original version above, the presenter gives no extra useful information—it is merely a tedious description of the information contained on the chart. The revised version simply limits itself to interpreting the data.

An alternative to the above pie charts is not to have a slide at all. You could simply walk to the whiteboard and write 90 and 20% in large characters. You then say to the audience,

If you are like most presenters, you probably spend about 90% of your time preparing your slides. This leaves you only 10% to think about what you will actually say and to practice saying it. The result is often very poor presentations. Instead you should reduce the slide preparation time to 20% and use the other 80% of the time for deciding exactly what to say and then how to say it. (72 words)

Note how the presenter directly addresses the audience using *you* (rather than saying *"Typically presenters spend about 90% of their time preparing their slides"*). This alternative is useful if you already have lots of figures in your presentation and so it provides variety. Also, it immediately attracts the audience's attention if you walk over to the whiteboard. However, it does mean that you will have to spend more words explaining everything (72 words rather than 27).

So another alternative is to reproduce the pie chart on the whiteboard—which should not take more than about 10 seconds—and then give you explanation as in the revised version above.

The moral of the story is to always think about the most audience-oriented and quickest way to present information. In the case above, a pie chart (whether as a slide or on a whiteboard) is the quickest, easiest, and most effective way for you to convey information to the audience.

Sections 5.2-5.4 highlight that the easier a figure is to understand, the less time you will have to spend on explaining it. Likewise, the more complex it is, the more difficult it will be for you to explain—and the consequence will be that you will be less relaxed and therefore more likely to confuse the audience and make mistakes in your English.

Please note that all the information presented in these figures is only very approximate and is based purely on my personal observations.

5.5   Only include visuals that you intend to talk about

Only show graphs, charts, tables, and diagrams that you will actually talk about. If you don't need to talk about them, you could probably cut them.

Unless a visual is completely self explanatory, then ensure you explain its connection with your topic. If not the audience will become distracted or confused, and wonder what the significance is.

5.6   Use an image to replace unnecessary or tedious text

Using a picture rather than text has many advantages for both you and your audience.

•   once the audience has looked at the image, they will focus directly on you, the presenter

•   you don't have to "compete" with your slide, because your slide has no text and therefore "says" nothing

•   the audience does not have to read through information that they will never remember and in any case do not need to know. If such information on directives really is important, then it would be better to put it in a handout that could be given to the audience at the end of the presentation

•   you relate what you say directly to the audience. Everyone in the audience probably has a fridge and everyone knows (or can at least imagine) the problems of disposing of an old one. By involving the audience you can make your point much more strongly. And because they are engaged they will remember more

5.7 Only show a slide for as long as you are talking about it

When you show an image, chart etc, your audience will be immediately drawn to it. However they will equally quickly tire of it the moment you stop discussing it, or if you discuss it for too long.

When you stop discussing it, blank the screen (B button on PowerPoint) or move onto the next slide.

If you discuss it for too long, it probably means it is too complicated and you should have used a sequence of slides to explain it.

The moment a visual piece is presented, the audience's attention is drawn to it. Display a piece of visual material only when you are ready to talk about it and do not leave an image to "die" on the screen.

As with any slide - image or text - give the audience a couple of seconds to absorb it, and then talk about it.

5.8 Avoid visuals that force you (the presenter) to look at the screen

If you talk while looking at the screen you lose audience attention and also your voice is much more difficult to hear.

If your visuals are clear you shouldn't need to look at the screen or point. If you need to point, it means that you need to simplify what is on your slide. Simplification is obviously a benefit for the audience but also for you because it means that you will not get lost or confused in complicated explanations.

The problem with pointing with your hands/fingers, your cursor, or using a laser pointer is that it may be clear to you where you are pointing but it rarely is for the audience. It also means that you will have to turn your back on the audience for several seconds. This can be very distracting for the audience.

One solution is to show such slides to your colleagues and ask them for advice on how to cut out what is not truly essential. The result will be cleaner slides which only require you to point at them for a few seconds. You will consequently be able to maintain the audience's attention more effectively.

5.9 Make sure your slide can be read by the audience in the back row

Audiences will not be pleased if you say, "*I know that this is too small for you to read but ...*" This generally happens when you paste a figure from your paper directly into your presentation. This never works. Look at your figure and decide what is the key information that you want your audience to remember. Then start again with a completely new graphic whose sole aim is to show that key piece of info.

If a table or graph is too detailed, it can be distracting and confusing. One solution is to enlarge just one part of it, i.e., the key element you want your audience to understand. If showing the whole table is essential for your purposes, you can show it all in one slide. Then in the next slide show a reduced version but highlighting the interesting part through color, circles, or enlargement.

5.10 Use background color to facilitate audience understanding

Only use color to help audience understand your visuals, not simply to make them look nice. Be consistent with color; use the same color for the same purpose throughout the presentation.

Website designers know that the background of a website can have a significant effect on whether a surfer is likely to stay and look, and possibly buy. This implies that the background color of your slides may also affect how willing the audience will be to spend time looking at them. The experts suggest using dark text such as blue or black on a medium-light, but not bright background, or light colors on a medium-dark background. Dark colors on a dark background are very hard to read.

A lot of people have problems distinguishing red and green (and also, brown/green, blue/black, and blue/purple); so don't use those colors in combination. Avoid red as it has associations with negativity—it is the color often used by teachers to make corrections and in finance it indicates a loss.

If you project your slides you will see how different they look from on your laptop. The audience's ability to see your slides very much depends on the internal and external lighting of the room. If the sun is shining directly onto the screen it makes light colors (particularly yellow) almost impossible to see. Some beamers make red look like blue. Also, bright light considerably reduces the strength of color in photos.

5.11 Choose your font(s) wisely, and limit different types of formatting

There is no conclusive evidence that a san serif font works better than a serif font, or vice versa.

Some of the most overused fonts in presentations are Arial, Helvetica and Times New Roman; but their familiarity may also be a bonus.

Comic Sans is one of the most reviled fonts in existence, but is great if you are going to a conference where the audience is elementary schoolchildren.

Stick to one (at most two) fonts throughout your slides.

It may be tempting to use lots of formatting because it makes slide preparation seem more creative. However, your text will be easier to read if you limit underlining, italics, shading, and other forms of formatting to the minimum.

5.12 Remember the difference in usage between commas and points in numbers

The international convention is to use the US system of points for decimals (.) and commas (,) for whole numbers. For example, 3.025 is said *three point zero two five* and 3,125 is said *three thousand one hundred and twenty-five*. Ensure you make this change when you convert graphs and tables from a figure or text written in your own language into an English version.

5.13 Locate formulas, code, procedures etc between 'easy-on-the-eye' slides

Slides with minimal text tend to be the most effective. However, sometimes you will inevitably have to have slides that show a formula, a piece of code, a procedure etc.

The key is to ensure that your whole presentation isn't made up of such slides. Audiences need a visual break when they are being asked to concentration on understanding mathematical concepts. So precede and follow your 'hard' slides with some slides that are instantly understandable and that contain little or no text. Basically you are rewarding your audience for the attention that you have demanded from them during your 'hard' slides.

5.14   Be aware of the dangers of presentation software

If you buy twenty tubes of paint you don't automatically have a painting. Likewise, if you create a set of PowerPoint slides you don't automatically have a presentation. You just have a set of slides.

A presentation is slides plus a lot of practice.

Try practicing your presentation without using any slides. If you find it difficult, it means you are relying too much on your slides.

PowerPoint templates encourage you to

1. create a series of similar looking slides
2. use bullets on every slide
3. have the same background, which may include your institute's logo
4. have a title for each slide

The first three can lead to a very tedious and repetitively visual presentation. There are a limited number of PowerPoint backgrounds, and most audiences will have already seen most of them. Try to invent your own background, or if not use a very simple background color.

But the fourth, titles, is very useful. Titles are like a map for the audience guiding them through the presentation.

Having similar looking titles (i.e. same color, font, and font size) throughout the presentation should be enough to give it a sense of cohesion and consistency. This means that you can vary the other three - the look, the use or not of bullets, and have a changing background where appropriate.

5.15 Only use animations if they serve a good purpose

Some features of presentation software often seem to be used solely to impress the audience. No matter how clever and how new an animation is it will never disguise a bad presentation. If you think that your presentation needs animations, then there is probably something wrong with the presentation itself.

Animations that introduce a slide or bullet (fade in, peek in, dissolve, fly in etc) are distracting, and often extremely annoying. Anyone who has been to a conference before will have seen practically all the animations that PowerPoint (and other software) have available.

If you use an animation to build up a process / sequence on a diagram, it is very likely that the diagram in itself is too complicated. It may be better to just simplify the process—the audience doesn't need to see or understand every step.

However, animations are occasionally useful, particularly if you have to do a very long presentation (which is likely in the business world, but not at a conference).

In any case remember that animations

- may not convert from your laptop to the conference PC

- typically and inexplicably go wrong during the presentation itself

5.16 Introduce items in a list one at a time only if absolutely necessary

Presentation applications allow you to introduce items in a list one at a time. This can be useful if it is crucial to delay information, for example when giving your conclusions in order to get the audience to focus on one conclusion at a time.

Otherwise, show all the items at once and give the audience three to five seconds to absorb them before you start talking. This means that

- you don't have to keep hitting the mouse to introduce the next item. Your hands are thus free and you can move away from the laptop and keep your eyes focused on the audience

- the audience doesn't have to constantly keep changing where they are looking (you or your slides), and they are not waiting for the next item to appear. They can do all their reading at once

- you won't inadvertently introduce two items at the same time (and thus lose the whole point of delaying the information)

5.17 A few tricks provided by presentation software

PowerPoint and other presentation software have thousands of features that increase exponentially with each new version. This book focuses on what you say and write but not on presentation software itself. So this section simply lists a few tips that I personally think are useful.

My philosophy is to keep things as simple as possible. The slides should be able to stand alone by themselves without you needing any special effects. Also any effects you use will probably be old hat (i.e. seen a thousand times before) to some of the audience and possibly annoying or distracting to others.

Four things that I do find useful are:

- 'presentation mode' where you can see both the current slide, the next slide, your notes

- the B button - use this to blank the screen (and attract attention)

- the option to be able to pre-set moments where you might need to skip one or more slides

- duplicating slides - for instance you can have duplicate copies of your final slide so that you don't inadvertently 'go out' of the presentation mode; or you can duplicate one slide several times and turn it into a sequence of slides with minor changes between them (this often works better than the official animations of PowerPoint)

However, if you are interested in the latest techniques there are various YouTube 'experts' who have dedicated inordinate amounts of their free time to showing you how to use them.

5.18   Final checks

Frequently you will import diagrams from other presentations or documents, including presentations and docs that were originally written in your own language. Because you are so familiar with these diagrams, tables etc you may not notice that they contain words from your own language. Double check everything to make sure there are no 'foreign words'.

Check that all your text is visible, and that is visible in all types of light. The bottom 10% of a slide tends to be difficult to see by all the audience, so consider shifting text higher up in the slide. In any case, test your presentation in similar conditions to the one at the conference (use the main conference room at your institute). Position yourself in various parts of the room (imagining some tall guy is sitting right in front of you) and check what you can see.

The visibility and colors on your slides will change massively depending on how much sun is in the conference room and where this sun is coming from. Ideally you need a totally "sun-friendly" presentation. Test your presentation at various times of day, in various rooms (e.g. east, south facing), and with various window configurations (i.e. windows directly opposite the screen, to the left, right.

Chapter 6

Ten Ways to Begin a Presentation

Ten Facts or Fiction?

1. It rains more at weekends than on weekdays.

2. Although it is often claimed that no matter its size or thickness, no piece of paper can be folded in half more than seven times, high-school student Britney Gallivan folded a piece 12 times.

3. Cars were first started with ignition keys in 1949.

4. The two highest IQs ever recorded on a standard test both belong to women.

5. The first washing machine was marketed in 1907.

6. Sugar was first used an ingredient in chewing gum by a dentist (William Semple in 1869).

7. Leonardo da Vinci invented an alarm clock that woke the sleeper by rubbing their feet.

8. Only 1 in 20 children are born on the day predicted by the doctor.

9. Tomato ketchup was once sold as a medicine.

10. There are no clocks in casinos in Las Vegas.

© Springer International Publishing Switzerland 2016
A. Wallwork, *English for Presentations at International Conferences*,
English for Academic Research, DOI 10.1007/978-3-319-26330-4_6

6.1 What's the buzz?

1) Choose three factoids from the previous page (they are all true) that you think you could possibly use at the beginning of a presentation. Alternatively find some factoids yourself that are relevant to your field. Find at least three factoids that you think you could use in a presentation. Answer these questions.

   1. What criteria did you use to choose them?

   2. Which factoids did you immediately reject and why?

   3. How might you use the ones you selected?

   4. How would you expect the audience to react to them?

   5. Do you think audiences generally like learning new and unusual facts?

Note that what you think is an interesting factoid might not coincide with the opinion of the majority. So show your factoids to a colleague, explain how you think you will use them, and then solicit your colleague's opinion regarding whether:

- the factoid is actually interesting and is likely to capture the audience's attention

- your intended use of the factoid is the most effective way of using it

2) Giving the audience an interesting statistic is just one way to begin a presentation. Think of at least three other ways to begin a presentation. If you need inspiration, look at a sample of presentations on TED.

3) An editor of a British TV news program once said: *The best news presenters are people who have something in common with the best television presenters – you feel like you are watching a human being, not just someone delivering prepared lines. Unless you make that emotional connection with the viewer, I don't think you can succeed.*

In what ways can presenters set up an 'emotional connection' with their audience?

****

How you introduce yourself and how the audience react to your introduction determine at least 30% of the success of your presentation. Audiences form their impressions of a presenter within approximately 90 seconds, after which it is difficult to change their opinion. This chapter outlines how to gain an audience's attention and how to connect with them on an emotional level.

6.2 Basic do's and don'ts at the beginning of your presentation

DO:

- Try to look as if you are enjoying yourself. Many presenters only start to enjoy themselves after the first 10–15 minutes, but you should try to get into this mode as soon as possible and this means being as relaxed as possible.

- Help the audience to like you.

- Gratify the audience's natural self-interest - immediately give them the impression that you presentation is going to be useful for them.

Do NOT:

- Lower audience expectations by apologizing for the quality of your presentation or of your knowledge of English.

- Put your hands together and locate them as they covering a fig leaf, or rub them together as if you were a magician.

- Say "I am happy to be here" but look as if you can't wait to leave the room

- Look down and speaking in a halting voice.

- Confuse being professional with being detached from the audience and adopting a particular tone and voice.

6.3 Decide how you are going to begin

How you introduce yourself and how the audience react to your introduction determine at least 30% of the success of your presentation. Audiences form their impressions of a presenter within approximately 90 seconds, after which it is difficult to change their opinion.

Many of the best presentations, or certainly the most enjoyable ones, are those where the presenter simply chats to the audience and tries to connect with them immediately. You can watch TED.com and see hundreds examples of this.

You can do this by using one or more of the following techniques:

a) say what you plan to do in your presentation and why (6.4)

b) tell the audience some general facts about where you come from (6.5)

c) show a map (6.6)

d) give an interesting statistic that relates to your country (6.7)

e) give an interesting statistic that relates directly to the audience (6.8)

f) get the audience to imagine situations (6.9)

g) ask the audience a question or get them to raise their hands (6.10)

h) say something personal about yourself (6.11)

i) mention something topical (6.12)

j) say something counterintuitive (6.13)

If you are an inexperienced presenter the easiest way to begin is the first (i.e. point A above), but the second, third and fourth are also not difficult to manage. The beginnings described in the other points are advanced tips and require more confidence and creativity. However, they are worth trying because they deviate from what the average non-native speaker does and thus tend to attract audience attention.

Whichever beginning you chose, when you get up try to smile and keep your eyes on the audience—don't look up at the ceiling or down at the floor as this gives the impression that you can't remember what to say. Have a quick glance (look) at your notes, rather than looking behind you to remember what is on your slide. Audiences like positive enthusiastic presenters, so don't joke or say anything negative about the location of the congress, the organization, or about the local people, and the local infrastructure. This may amuse some members of the audience but alienate others—particularly those who live locally.

6.4   Say what you plan to do in your presentation and why

A good standard introduction while showing your title slide is to say some or all of the following:

- what hypotheses you wanted to test

- why you chose this particular method for testing them

- what you achieved

- what impact this might have on your field

ORIGINAL	REVISED
Hello everyone and thank you for coming. First of all I'd like to introduce myself, my name is Ksenija Bartolić. As you can see, the title of my presentation is *Innovative Methods of Candidate Selection in Industry.* I work in a small research group at the University of Zagreb in Croatia. We are trying to investigate the best way to select candidates for a job and we hope our research will be useful not just in the field of psychology but also for human resources managers in general.	Hello, I am here to talk about a new way to select candidates for a position in a company. I'd like to tell you three things. First, why I think the current methods for selecting candidates are not effective. Second, my radical alternative, which is to let the receptionist of the company make the decision. And third, how trials proved that even against my own expectations this solution reduced recruitment costs by 500%. Moreover, it was as effective as traditional interviews in more than 90% of cases. I believe that human resources managers …

Both versions are perfectly acceptable. Both are clear and reasonably succinct and you can obviously choose the one you feel most natural/confident with. The revised version has the following advantages:

- it avoids giving information that can be easily deduced from the title slide (i.e., the name of the presenter and the title of the presentation)

- it immediately tells the audience what they can expect to hear, without having to show an outline slide

- it covers the main messages of the presentation

- it includes the main result of the research at a point in the presentation where audience attention is likely to be high—the audience doesn't have to wait to the end of the presentation to hear what the outcome of the research was

However, the original version also has an advantage. By delaying important information (i.e., the overview of what the presenter is planning to say) it gives the audience a few moments to settle into their seats and tune in to your voice. Even if the audience are not listening or concentrating, and even if they have an initial problem with the presenter's accent or voice level, they will still be in a position to follow the rest of the presentation. So the revised version is good provided that the audience are already focused on you, which is generally the case if you are not the first presenter of a particular session.

The other nine beginnings outlined below are designed to immediately attract audience attention, but delaying key information by 30 seconds to a couple of minutes on the basis that the audience are not generally at their most alert during the first 60 to 90 seconds. The advantage of such introductions is that understanding the rest of the presentation does not hinge (depend) on the audience hearing and absorbing every word.

Note: The "original" versions are perfectly acceptable but are generally less effective in attracting audience attention than the "revised" versions.

6.5   Tell the audience some facts about where you come from

Audiences are often interested in learning new information about countries that they are not familiar with. For example, if you are at a conference in Europe or North America, and you are from a country outside these areas, then exploit your uniqueness and tell the audience something about your country.

This information should not last more than 30 seconds.

Also, it must be clear to the audience that there is some connection with the topic of your research.

ORIGINAL	REVISED
Good afternoon everyone, my name is Cristiane Rocha Andrade and I am a PhD student at the Federal University of Paraná in Brazil. I am here to give you a presentation on some research I have been conducting on allergies to cosmetics and to propose a way to use natural cosmetics.	I come from Brazil. It took me 30 hours to travel the 9189 km to get here, so please pay attention! In Brazil we have two big forests, the Amazonian and the Atlantic with around 56,000 species of plants. More than 90% of these species have not been studied yet. This is why I decided to study natural cosmetics with raw materials from Brazil.

In the revised version, Cristiane cleverly gets the audience to pay attention, by explicitly telling them to do so (but in a humorous way). She uses many numbers, including the exact number of kilometers between her home town in Brazil and the location of the conference. She could have said "about 10,000 km" but that would not have had the same dramatic and humorous effective. She then connects where she comes from with the aim of her studies.

6.6   Show a map

Maps are often used in presentations to show the location where your research was carried out, or to show your country of origin, particularly for those people coming from less well-known countries.

Bear in mind that the audience's knowledge of geography will very much depend on where they come from. You may need to use two maps: one to show the big picture (i.e., where your country is in relation to countries that the audience will certainly know the location of) and another bigger map to show where your country/region is.

Maps seem to have a positive psychological effect on presenters. If the presenter is proud of where he/she comes from, he/she becomes animated and passionate when talking about his/her homeland. This elicits a good reaction from the audience and thus boosts the presenter's confidence.

For example, I watched Elena Castenas, a presenter from Visayas State University in the Philippines, begin her presentation with a map of her country, and say the following:

> I come from the world's twelfth most populated country - the Philippines - where about 92 million people live. About a tenth of the population live, like me, abroad. What many of us miss the most is our country's seven thousand one hundred and seven beautiful islands - if you get a chance go there, they are really amazing. So we have the benefits of a truly wonderful archipelago and a mass of natural marine resources, but land resources are very limited. Because of the population pressure, we need to increase crop production by maximizing land utilization through crop diversification for example by intercropping and crop rotation. So in my research I am trying to evaluate the allelopathic potential of grain legumes on corn, rice, and barnyard grass. By doing this I hope to make a contribution to improving living standards in my country.

This introduction had a very positive effect on the audience because Elena smiled while she was talking (particularly when she said the words *beautiful*, *amazing* and *wonderful*), and this made her seem both credible and convincing. By giving the exact number of the islands she managed to show not just statistical accuracy but also passion. She also tried to relate directly to the audience (*if you get a chance ...*). But she wasn't showing the map and talking about her country just for fun: she linked the geography of her country to the topic of her presentation. Her reasons for doing the research were also very convincing—increase crop production and thus raise living standards. At the same time the audience learned something about one of the world's biggest (but probably not very well known) countries.

6.7 Give an interesting statistic that relates to your country

Imagine that you are studying how soil erosion affects farmers and food production in your country. A typical but not very interesting way to start would be

> Today I am going to present some results on the problem of soil erosion and how it affects food production in my country.

But you could begin much more dramatically with a statistic:

> Ten thousand tons of soil are lost through erosion in my country every year. This means that fertility is lost and desertification ensues.

Or you could begin in a much more personal way:

> Two months ago I went home and saw the devastation caused by the floods [shows picture of floods]. I have an uncle whose land has been almost completely eroded. This means that his crops will fail this year. So why is this a problem? It means that in the world today ...

Another possible beginning of the same presentation could have been to say, "*In my country 30 tons of soil per hectare is lost due to rain every year.*"

But the problem is that 30 tons of soil are not something your audience can easily visualize. However, if you say, "*Imagine if this room was filled with soil. Well, after a single rainstorm on a small field in my country, three quarters of the soil would have disappeared.*" In this case you are giving the audience a statistic that they can relate to. It may not be completely accurate, but it is accurate enough for them to see that you are talking about a catastrophe. If you then say what the consequences would be if this process isn't stopped, again using something the audience can relate to (*the equivalent of Iceland would disappear in less than a year*), then you will have a captivated audience.

For more on statistics, see 12.9.

6.8 Give an interesting statistic that relates directly to the audience

A very effective introduction is to show the title slide while the audience is coming in. Then when it is time to start, blank the screen and tell the audience a fundamental and recent statistic in your field or a key result in your research. After giving your statistic, you introduce yourself and say why the statistic relates to what you are going to tell the audience.

Of course, you know why you are mentioning a certain statistic and the relevance that it has, but the audience might not. Help them make the connection. If possible use statistics that they can relate to their personal experience or that they can easily understand or visualize.

Your statistics need to relate to your audience's capacity to understand them. Which of these statistics do you find easier to understand/visualize or has the greatest impact on you?

- 73 million papers have been completed in the last 10 years.

- Last year 7,300,000 papers were completed.

- Every day 20,000 scientific papers are completed.

- 14 papers are completed every minute.

- In the 10 minutes that I have been talking to you this morning 140 papers will have been completed around the world.

- Hands up those of you who have finished writing a paper in the last seven days. Well around the world, in the last week about 140,000 papers will have been produced, that's an incredible 14 papers every minute.

- By the year 2050, eight hundred million papers will have been written, that's enough paper to fill this conference room thirty three thousand times.

Statistic 1 is probably too high for audiences to comprehend—if possible reduce statistics from millions, billions, and trillions to something more manageable. Statistics 2–4 are all fine, but they lack impact. Statistic 5 is more interesting because the timescale is now (the very moment that the presenter speaks), rather than a generic day or year. Statistic 6 directly involves the audience and motivates them to listen to the answer. Statistic 7 makes an unusual comparison to physical space.

6.9 Get the audience to imagine a situation

Without introducing yourself or the topic of your presentation, make your first word of your presentation "Suppose ...." and then give the audience a hypothetical situation which relates both to the audience and to the topic of your research.

ORIGINAL	REVISED
My name is Minhaz-Ul Haque and the title of my presentation is Using Protein from Whey-coated Plastic Films to Replace Expensive Polymers. As you can see in this outline slide, I will first introduce the topic of ...	Suppose everyone in this room had brought with them today all the food packaging that they had thrown away in the last year. I have counted about 60 people here. Given that the average person consumes 50 kilos of food packaging a year, then that is three tons of packaging. Over the next 4 days of this conference, we will produce about 450 kilos of packaging, including plastic bottles. My research is aimed at increasing the recyclability of this packaging by 75%. How will we do it? Using protein from whey-coated plastic films to replace expensive polymers. My name is Minhaz-Ul Haque and ...

6.10 Ask the audience a question

An effective way to start a presentation is to get the audience to think about a question. If you use this technique, ask your question, wait for a maximum of two seconds, and then continue.

You do NOT want the audience to answer your question otherwise that will take up time and ruin the flow of your presentation.

Let's imagine you are at a conference on rare diseases. There is little point in beginning your presentation by showing your audience a slide with the following definition:

Rare Diseases are a heterogeneous group of serious and chronic disorders having a social burden.

Your audience will probably already know what a rare disease is. Instead you need to tell them something they don't know and something that will attract their interest. So, cut the text completely and write the following on the whiteboard (but have a slide as a backup in case there is no whiteboard):

1:50,000

1:2,000

The audience will be immediately curious to know what the numbers refer to. This is what you could say:

> Do you know anyone who has a rare disease? [*Two second pause*] Well if you are from the United Kingdom, the chances are that you don't. But if you are from Spain, then you might know someone who does have a rare disease. Does that mean that here in Spain we have more rare diseases? No, it simply means that our definition of what constitutes a rare disease is different from that in the UK. A rare disease in the UK is something that affects 1 in 50,000 people. In Spain we follow the European Union definition of 1 in 2,000. That's a very big difference. Well, my research group has been looking at …

The technique is to immediately tell the audience something that they may not know, rather than giving them an abstract definition of something they already know. Notice that each sentence is short—this makes the sentences easy for you to say and easy for the audience to understand. The two-second pause after asking the question may seem like a long time to you (when you are on the podium) but for the audience it is a chance to think about the question you have just asked, and to them it doesn't seem long at all.

An alternative to asking a question is to get the audience to raise their hands in response. As with the question technique, give the instruction (hands up if/raise your hands if), then wait for a maximum of two seconds before you continue.

ORIGINAL	REVISED
Hello everyone, I am Rossella Mattera, a PhD student in Molecular Medicine. I am here today to tell you about the ExPEC project, in particular about a vaccine against ExPEC. What is ExPEC? ExPEC or extra-intestinal pathogenic Escherichia coli, is a microorganism that causes a large spectrum of diseases associated with a high risk of death. The commonest extra-intestinal E.coli infection that is caused by these strains is cystitis, in fact 80% of women have this "experience" during their lifetime, with a reinfection in less than 6 months …	Hands up the men who have had cystitis. [*Pause*] I bet many of the men here don't even know what cystitis is [*said in jokey tone*]. In this room there are 20 women and 16 of you women will experience cystitis during your lifetime. You men are lucky because cystitis mainly affects women. It is a horrible infection that makes you feel you want to go to the toilet every two or three minutes. Cystitis is caused by ExPEC or extra-intestinal pathogenic Escherichia coli. This infection affects 80% of women. Cystitis, pyelonephritis, sepsis, and neonatal meningitis are common infections caused by these strains. Most ExPECs are resistant to the antibiotic therapy, therefore we need a vaccine. I am a PhD student in Molecular Medicine. I am here today to tell you about a vaccine against ExPECs.

6.11 Say something personal about yourself

Tell an anecdote about yourself—how you first became interested in the topic, what you particularly like about this area of research, where you work, and what is special about it, a particular event that took place during the research, for example an unexpected problem, a counterintuitive result. Show the audience your enthusiasm for the topic—tell them what amazes and excites you about your research. When you talk about your passion for your work your face will automatically light up and you voice will be animated—the audience will thus be more engaged.

ORIGINAL	REVISED
I am going to describe the creation of strawberries with a strong consistency in the pulp. In our research we modified strawberry plants with agrobacterium and we obtained 41 independent transgenic plants. On the basis of yield and fruits firmness, we then selected six different varieties of strawberry.	I became interested in agronomy and biosciences completely by accident. One summer holiday while I was a student I was working in an organic ice cream shop. Every day we got crates of fresh fruit, and every day we had to throw away kilos of strawberries because the ones at the bottom were completely squashed and had already started to mold. The pears, on the other hand, were always fine. So I thought, what if we could mix the succulent look and delicious taste of a strawberry with the strong consistency of the pulp in a pear?

In the original version, the presenter launches into her topic without giving the audience time to switch their brains on. If the audience miss what she says now, their understanding of what she says later may be impeded. In the second version, she answers a question that many people have—how did someone choose to do the job they do? The audience enjoy comparing their experiences with that of the presenters.

Here is a true story told by Professor Maria Skyllas-Kazacos from the University of New South Wales, of how she became a chemical engineer.

One of the choices in the industrial chemistry degree, I think when you got to the third year, was whether to do the mainstream industrial chemistry subjects or to do polymer science. A friend a year above me said, "Oh, you should do the polymers. Polymers is a really big, important industry." So I decided to try polymers. I went along to the first class—only five or six of us had chosen this, and I was the one girl—in a polymer engineering laboratory. The lecturer started to talk about grinding and milling and adding carbon black to rubbers, and he said, "When you come in the lab, you've got to wear dirty clothes because we use a lot of carbon black in here and you're going to get covered in it. And tie your hair all the way back and make sure it's all covered, because any loose hair can get jammed in the machine and you'll be scalped." I had very long hair! A friend told me later that this lecturer did not want girls in the lab and deliberately went out of his way to scare me off doing polymer engineering—and he succeeded—I dropped polymer engineering immediately and took up the industrial chemistry option instead.

Note how she

- uses colloquial language and sounds like she is talking to a friend

- gives interesting details

- quotes from other people (i.e., uses their words)

- mixes long sentences with short ones

- obviously enjoys telling this story

6.12   Mention something topical

Try to relate your beginning to something that is already in the audience's mind, a recent news story or something connected to the conference.

ORIGINAL	REVISED
My name is Horazio Perez and I work at the Center for Transportation Research in … In my presentation today I would like to tell you the results of an experimental study on real time bus arrival time prediction using GPS data.	I know that a lot of you, like me, have been getting to the conference each day by bus. I don't know about you, but I have had to wait about 10 to 15 minutes each time. And it's been great fun. In fact, not only have the buses been late, but as soon as one comes, then another two quickly follow. And that's made me even happier. Why? Because my research is investigating why this happens— why do buses come in threes? And if it happens here in Geneva, where Rolex have their headquarters, then clearly no one else has solved the problem yet, and I am going to get in there first. My name is Horazio Perez and …

Horazio takes a very banal situation, catching a bus, and relates it both to the audience's experience and the topic of his research. He also adds an element of suspense by talking about "fun" and "happy" in a situation which for most people would simply be frustrating. By doing this he attracts and holds the audience's attention.

6.13   Say something counterintuitive

People like to have their views challenged, as long as these views are not related to things they feel very strongly about such as religion, ethics, and politics. If your research has proved something that goes against commonly held opinion, then this is a perfect opportunity to gain the audience's attention.

ORIGINAL	REVISED
In this presentation a comparative analysis will be made of some investigations into the proficiency in the use of the English language on a world scale. The parameters and methodology used to make the analysis, along with some of the results will be presented. I will begin by giving a brief overview of the background ...	Who speaks and writes the best English in the world? The British maybe, [*Pause*] after all they have the Queen, and that's where the language originated? [*Pause*] Or do you think it's the Americans? Or the Canadians or Australians? [*Pause*] Actually it's the Scandinavians, the Danes, and the Dutch. And if you have been attending most of the presentations here in the last few days, I guess it's these guys who you understood the best. Does this mean that the native English speakers can't even speak their own language? Of course not. But ...

6.14   Moral of the story

The secret is to experiment. Try adapting your topic to one or more of the ways outlined above. Be creative. Have fun. And keep trying until you find the best approach. But before using it at the conference, test it out on colleagues to make sure that it gets the reaction you hoped for.

The more fun you have preparing your presentation, the more fun you will have when you give the presentation, and the more fun the audience will have listening to you.

It is fundamental to connect with the audience. If you don't connect with them, they will not give you the attention you deserve. This is particularly true if your presentation is scheduled just before lunch, after lunch, or at the end of the day, i.e., at times of the day when the audience's attention is very low.

Finally, it is not only at the beginning of your presentation that you can use these techniques. They are also excellent ways of regaining attention later in the presentation.

Chapter 7

Agenda and Transitions

Factoids

What do you imagine were the answers of the following research questions:

1. Are people born on the same day (and time) more likely to have something in common, than those born some days later?

2. Is there a link between a person's level of optimism and how long they will live?

3. When telling a lie, is it easier to control your body language or to control the words that come out of your mouth?

4. Can non-experts recognize which is the fake smile and which is the genuine smile in two very similar photographs of the same person?

5. Are people in the US superstitious when it comes to buying a house numbered 13? And do sellers consequently have to lower the price of such houses?

6. Do 'lucky' people perform better when choosing lottery numbers than 'unlucky' people?

7. Do people become more superstitious during periods of economic crisis?

8. Are women more likely to laugh at a man's joke, than a man at a woman's joke?

9. Do more right-handed gloves go missing than left-handed gloves?

10. When a family has an annual income of around $75,000 (US dollars), will any additional income raise their level of happiness?

© Springer International Publishing Switzerland 2016
A. Wallwork, *English for Presentations at International Conferences*,
English for Academic Research, DOI 10.1007/978-3-319-26330-4_7

7.1   What's the buzz?

1) An 'agenda' slide, also called an 'outline' slide, summarizes for the audience what you are going to tell them during your presentation.

Think about these questions:

1. How important is it to have an agenda slide?

2. Agenda slides typically consist of four or five bullets. What information is typically given in these bullets?

3. How effective are the things that presenters write on their agenda slide – wouldn't most of the bulleted items be obvious to the audience?

4. Is it possible to manage without an agenda slide, i.e. simply by giving your agenda verbally?

2) A 'transition' is when you move from one topic to another. What can you do to make the audience aware that you are now moving on to a different topic? How can you use a transition to regain your audience's attention?

****

Although the logic of your presentation is clear to you, it won't necessarily be clear to your audience. Having an agenda slide and using the right transition phrases will help to guide your listeners.

In this chapter you will learn how to

• move from your first slide into the main part of the presentation

• introduce each new section and thus highlight the logical structure of your presentation

KEY TO FACTOIDS: all yes except for 1, 4, 6 and 10.

7.2   Consider not having an "agenda" slide

Scientific presentations tend to follow the same structure—introduction, method, results, discussion. Unless you intend to radically deviate from this structure then you do not necessarily need to use an outline slide as a transition into the main part of the presentation.

A poor outline slide like the ones below is a signal to the audience that they will hear the same old things again.

OUTLINE

➢ Introduction

➢ Methodology

➢ Results

➢ Conclusions

AGENDA

➢ Overview

➢ Aims and purposes

➢ Theoretical framework

➢ Research methods

➢ Empirical analysis

The slides above simply tell the audience that your presentation follows the standard procedure and that surprises are highly unlikely. They are a series of abstract words that act as an invitation for the audience to go to sleep—the slides give no information to the audience that they could not have imagined or guessed for themselves. It also encourages the presenter to say things that add no information for the audience (see original version below which refers to the first outline slide above).

However although you do not need to show the audience a slide like this, you <u>do</u> need to tell your audience verbally what you plan to do, i.e., your main messages. So don't forget to do this.

You need to do this in a way that really gives them useful information that will help them to understand the context and structure of your presentation (as in revised version).

ORIGINAL	REVISED
First I will give you a brief introduction to my work. Then I will outline the reasons that led me to conducting this research. Next I will explain my methodology before discussing my results.	First, I'd like to tell you about why I am interested in incompetence in the workplace. Then, I'll be showing you how we managed to investigate this potentially embarrassing area in 10 different multinational companies. And finally, I'll show you our results that indicate that around 80% of middle managers have been promoted into a position for which they simply don't have the skills.

7.3 Use an "Agenda" slide for longer presentations and for arts, humanities, and social sciences

An agenda may be more useful when you are giving a longer presentation (20 minutes, 45 minutes) or for topics outside physical and life sciences. In this case the audience may need a slide showing the conceptual framework to help them understand the rest of your presentation. Keep it down to a maximum of four points, otherwise the audience may think that the presentation will be covering too much for them to readily assimilate. As always, you should focus on your main messages.

An agenda is also useful when you are not describing some research project, but are talking more generally about a certain issue. In this case, the sequence of your presentation may not be immediately obvious and an outline might help to orient the audience.

In some disciplines, presenters begin with a slide containing a question. This question encapsulates the reason for their research, it is the question that they hope their research will answer. For example,

To what extent does Iran's foreign policy include realism?

Would online voting solve election fixing?

How has the Internet affected parent/child relationships?

The presenter then needs to have another slide in which he/she indicates the approach or context used to answer this question. This helps to give a structure to the presentation and to alert the audience to what they can expect to hear.

The outline slide for the last question could thus be

The Internet has

➤ replaced time previously dedicated to family interactions

➤ replaced educational role of parents

➤ given parents a mass of info on good parenting

➤ provided opportunities for shared entertainment

The presenter's commentary on the above slide could be

> When I posed the question "How has the Internet affected parent/child relationships?" I began by focusing on the negative factors, such as how families spend less time together given that most kids today have their PC in their bedroom. And, as a mother myself, I also thought about how parents are being used less and less as a source of information to help kids with school work. But then I realised that parents today can use the Internet to learn about the behavior of their children and how they can improve their relationships with them—there is so much useful information out there. So that was one positive factor. Another positive factor is that there is a lot of fun stuff on the Internet, particularly videos on YouTube that families can actually share together, in the same way as they might watch a TV show together. So these are the four factors that I have been studying, and today I would like to focus on the first and fourth points.

Note how the presenter

• does not read the four bullets but comments on them using different words

• involves the audience in the story of her decision-making process

• uses an informal but nevertheless professional style

• tells the audience that she is only going to talk about two of the points—she wouldn't have time to talk about all four, and this enables her to talk about two in more detail

7.4   Use an agenda to introduce key terminology

An "Agenda" slide is a useful way of introducing key terminology, as in the words in italics in the slide below.

AGENDA

➤   Modification of *polymeric* materials

➤   *Bioreceptor-surface coupling*

➤   Characterization of *functionalized surfaces*

So you could put up the slide and say,

> So here's what I will be talking about. [Pause for two seconds so that audience can absorb the content of the slide] I first became interested in modifying *polymeric* materials because .... Then one day we decided to try *coupling* the *bioreceptors* with the activated *surfaces*. So those are the two things that I will be looking at today, along with some approaches to characterizing *functionalized surfaces*.

The benefits are the audience will

• see and hear you say the key words and thus be able to connect your pronunciation with the words on your slide

• familiarize themselves with your voice without missing any vital information (you have simply told them why you are interested in this topic).

If you are still worried that people will not understand your pronunciation, you can point to the key words on the slide as you say them.

7.5   Only move to the next slide when you've finished talking about the current slide

If possible spend less than a minute on each slide, and certainly no more than two minutes. And vary the time you spend on each slide - 10 seconds maybe enough for some slides.

Audience soon get bored looking at the same slide and start thinking about something else.

Don't move on to the next slide before you have finished talking about the current one. Otherwise the audience will stop listening to you and start absorbing the information on the next slide.

7.6   Use transitions to guide your audience

You know two very important things that the audience does not know:

- what you did and found in your research

- the sequence of your slides and why they follow a particular structure

You need to help the audience follow your presentation. You cannot jump from one slide to the next at great speed. If the audience misses one particular point, they may lose the thread (i.e., the links, logical flow) of the rest of the presentation.

The way of moving from one slide to another, and from topic to topic, is crucial. For the audience it should be like following a map, and you need to make it very clear to them whenever you make a turn. Also, at each turn it is helpful if you summarize for them what you have told them so far. Those in the audience who missed a previous turn now have an opportunity to get back on the right road. This is a different from a paper, where readers can, if necessary, just retrace their steps.

In a presentation, these moves or turns are called transitions.

Before you move to the next section or group of slides

- pause for two seconds. This signals to the audience that you are going to say something important

- look at the audience and give a quick summary of the most important things you have said so far. Repetition may seem boring to you because you know the subject so well, but it gives the audience a chance to check their understanding

- move on to the next section explaining how it relates to the previous one

This whole process should take about 20 seconds, so don't think it is unnecessarily increasing the length of your presentation.

7.7 Learn how to signal a move from one section to the next

Imagine at the beginning of your presentation you say something like, "*I am going to give you the three most important findings of our research*." Then the most obvious transition from the introduction to the main part of your presentation would be to say "*Okay, let's look at the first result*." Then later when you introduce the other two results you can introduce them numerically, *the second, the third*.

If your structure is methodology, results, and discussion, then between the methodology and results you could say, "*Okay, so that covers the methodology, now I am going to outline our results, one of which was really quite unexpected*." This reassures the audience that there is a plan to your presentation, and that they are being guided from step to step.

The second part of the above transition—*One of which was really quite unexpected*—highlights another benefit of transitions. You can use transitions to regain audience attention by getting them interested in hearing what you are going to say next.

7.8 Exploit your transitions for other purposes than simply moving to the next topic

A transition is a good opportunity for

- you to slow down or change the pace of the presentation

- the audience (and you) to relax a little—remember that the audience cannot assimilate vast quantities of information in quick succession

- you to regain the audience's attention by making them curious about what is coming next.

7.9 Only use an introductory phrase to a slide when strictly necessary

When the sequence of slides within a section is logical, you often don't need any expression to introduce the next slide. The transition shouldn't need any introductory explanation.

Instead of saying "*In this next slide we have a diagram of X which shows how to do Y*" you can simply say "*Here is a diagram of X which shows how to do Y*," or even more succinct "*Here is how to do Y*." By avoiding unnecessarily long introductory phrases the impact of your slides will be more dramatic.

7.10   Be concise

If you don't practice what to say when making transitions, you will probably improvise and say something like

> OK, that's all I wanted to say at this particular point about the infrastructure. What I would like to do next in this presentation is to take a brief look at the gizmo. This picture in this slide shows a gizmo. As you can see a gizmo is a ...

Instead of attracting the audience's attention, the above phrases are full of redundancy, add no information, and are likely to send the audience back to sleep.

Try to make your transitions memorable.

> OK, here's something that you may not know about a gizmo: blah blah blah. In fact you can see here that a gizmo is ...

7.11   Add variety to your transitions

Try to vary your technique for making transitions, so do not always use the same phrase. Here are some alternatives:

Turn the screen off: This immediately regains the audience's attention. You can then write something on the whiteboard or say something orally.

Ask a rhetorical question: For example, you can say, "*Have you ever wondered why it is impossible to predict when your PC is going to crash? Well, after I have summarized what we have just looked at, I am going to tell why experts think it is impossible but how we think we have actually managed to solve the problem.*"

Give the audience something to look forward to: The example above shows how you get the audience to concentrate now by telling them you will be giving them interesting information later. Another example: *In the next slide I will be showing you some fascinating data on xxx, but first ...* or *Later on, we'll see how this works in practice ...*

Signpost: Tell the audience where you are in the structure of your presentation. For example if you say "*And now to sum up briefly before the Q&A session*" you are alerting the audience that you presentation is nearly over.

Chapter 8

Methodology

Factoid: Life spans of garbage items (in years)	
Wool socks	1-5
Paper boxes	2-20
Plastic-coated paper	5
Polyurethane	10-20
Polyester cloth and nylon	30-40
Leather footwear	50
Plastic jars and bottles	50-80
Aluminum cans	80-100
Radioactive waste	25,000-500,000 (or forever?)

© Springer International Publishing Switzerland 2016
A. Wallwork, *English for Presentations at International Conferences*,
English for Academic Research, DOI 10.1007/978-3-319-26330-4_8

8.1 What's the buzz?

This part of the presentation is where the audience is most likely to get lost, so clear explanations are fundamental. Bear in mind that your audience will only absorb about 20% of the information you give them.

1) Write simple explanations of how to do one of the following:

- set up a cell phone account

- wire an electric plug

- pass a written examination with minimal study

- survive three years of doing a PhD

- get an internship in a top professor's team

2) Show your explanation to your partner. He / She has to improve it (e.g. by changing the order, adding details, deleting steps).

****

In this chapter will learn how to:

- explain a process / methodology

- bring diagrams and figures alive for the audience

There are many examples from presentations in this chapter. As in the rest of this book, you will see the original version and the revised version. The original versions are all perfectly acceptable and if you are an inexperienced presenter you may find them more suitable than the revised versions. The revised versions should enable more experienced presenters to connect with the audience more effectively.

8.2   First, regain the audience's attention

Most modern movies switch from scene to scene far more frequently than in movies made 20 to 30 years ago (and further back in the past). On the web, videos of three minutes or less tend to be watched far more frequently than those of ten minutes.

This means that our concentration span is getting shorter and shorter, so your audience need to be constantly stimulated if their attention is to be held.

When you describe your methodology, you are probably already three minutes into your presentation and thus your audience's attention will be decreasing.

You have to find ways of regaining it.

See Chapter 12 *Attracting Audiences and Keeping their Attention.*

8.3   Give simple explanations and be careful when giving numbers

This part of the presentation is where the audience is most likely to get lost, so clear explanations are fundamental. Bear in mind that your audience will only absorb about 20% of the information you give them.

Explain things in a way that the audience does not have to make a big mental effort. Your audience will probably only be able to absorb about 40% of what you are saying. So it helps if you repeat anything complex for them—do not expect them to understand everything the first time.

If you use numerical examples, make sure the numbers appear on the slide as it is very difficult for audiences to mentally translate numbers at great speed into their own languages and then be able to follow the example.

8.4 Give examples first, technical explanations second

The methodology part should be one of the highlights of your presentation and you should have fun explaining it. It helps the audience to follow a technical explanation if you give examples and intuitions first and then explain the process. If you begin with theoretical aspects you will probably lose the audience and maybe get lost yourself. If you begin with a simple example you gain the attention of the audience and gain confidence yourself.

8.5 Be brief and only talk about what is strictly necessary

Only spend extra time in an explanation if *how* you did something is more important than *what* you achieved, i.e., if your methodology is more important than your results or if at this stage in your research you have no results. In this case, explain the steps clearly and why your chosen methodology was suitable (or not) for what you wanted to do. But again only mention what the audience really needs to know in order to make sense of what you did.

Reduce any introductory phrases when describing diagrams and examples:

Here I present a panoramic view of the architecture. = This is the architecture.

Now you can see here an example of an interface. = Here is an interface.

We shall see two examples in the following slide. = So here are two examples

In conclusion we can say … = Basically, …

8.6 Show only the key steps in a process or procedure

If you are showing your audience a process, it is tempting to show them all the steps of the process. The typical way to do this is to cut and paste a complex diagram from a book or paper, or to begin with a skeleton diagram and then gradually add new parts to it either via animation or a series of overlapping slides. This has three major problems:

• audiences can recognize a cut and paste—it gives the idea that you couldn't find the time to create something specifically for them

• the animation may not work (due to the transfer from your PC to the conference PC)

• gradually building up a diagram may take too long and can be very tedious for the audience. Also, if you realize that it is taking too long, you will probably speed up your explanation and your audience may not grasp what you are saying.

The solution is to ignore any pre-existing graphics and start from scratch. This does not have to be a laborious process, because you only need to highlight the essential. Your aim is to guide the reader through the highlights of the process. If something is quite complex, then break it up into manageable steps over two or three slides— but occasionally go back one slide or two, to highlight to the audience the various connections. If it takes more than three slides, then consider that you are probably entering into too much detail.

8.7   Use slide titles to help explain a process

When the main purpose of your presentation is to explain a process or how a piece of equipment works, it is a good idea to use your slide titles to explain each step in the process. Here are titles of the first six slides from an engineering presentation. Each slide simply has a title and then a diagram or picture, which the presenter then explains.

Slide 1: Title slide: 3D Laser milling modeling: the effect of the plasma plume

Slide 2: Laser Milling: a process well suited for mold manufacturing

Slide 3: Laser Milling Centers consist of various sub-systems

Slide 4: The laser beam is controlled by a Laser Beam Deflection Unit

Slide 5: A valid estimation of the Material Removal Rate is required

Slide 6: Many parameters affect the Material Removal Rate

Notice that there is no "Outline" slide. The presenter used slide 1 to introduce himself and his research area. Then slides 2 and 3 provided some background information. And then the later slides described how the laser worked. The audience was guided step by step and even a non-engineer like myself was able to follow.

8.8   Explain why you are not describing the whole process

If you include too many details the audience will have to hear complex explanations that cover all possible cases, and look at complex tables and graphs.

If you think people will criticize you for not explaining the whole process, you can say,

> We don't have time to look at the complete process, so I just wanted to show you this part. If you are interested in the whole process then I can explain it at the bar or you can look it up on my web page.

If you are worried that someone in your audience will want to see absolutely every detail in your diagram, chart, table, or graph, then as you show your slide say,

> This is a very simplified version of ... This is what the prototype looks like in very general terms ... The full diagram is on my web page. I will give you the address at the end of the presentation.

You can also use phrases that indicate that you are only talking in general terms, such as

For the most part … Broadly/Generally speaking … With one or two exceptions … As a general rule …

Then you can

- show a diagram of the complete process but magnify one or two parts of the process that you would like to focus on. Magnify means making those particular parts bigger so that the audience's attention is only drawn to those points. The other parts will in any case be deliberately too small for the audience to see

- just show three consecutive parts of the process and focus on the one in the middle, showing how it connects to the previous part and the next part

- highlight using a circle or a particular color the aspect (e.g., a row or column of a detailed table) that you want the audience to focus on so that they will ignore the other information

- use a different font and a bigger font size

8.9 Indicate where you are in a process

Clearly when you are describing a process, such as recycling paper (see example above), you cannot always maintain full eye contact with the audience. You may occasionally need to point at the diagram. You can do this in various ways:

- use a telescopic pointer pen—they range in length from about 500–1000 mm and are relatively inexpensive. You can then stand to the left or right of the screen and use the pointer to indicate the item you are talking about

- use the pointer on PowerPoint (to turn it off, press the A key)

- draw on the screen. To show the pen, press *ctrl* or *cmd* + P (to turn it off, press the A key)

It is best to avoid using the laser pointer on the remote as it can be difficult to manipulate.

8.10 Tell a story rather than sounding like a technical manual

You can make a very technical explanation more interesting if you tell it like a story.

ORIGINAL	REVISED
The method was carried out as follows. Initially, X was done which led to a failure as a consequence of ... The next attempt involved ...	First I tried this, but it didn't work because ... so I tried that ... unfortunately that failed too probably because ... finally, one of the members of research group had a brainwave and ...

If you insist on giving a very technical explanation, keep it as short as possible. Also, give frequent summaries so that the audience can understand how each step is related. You can then say "*In other words ...*" and give a simpler summary.

In other types of presentations you may need to explain for example how you chose patients for a clinical trial, how you chose people for a survey, or how you selected specific data from a databank. You can involve your audience much more if you

• talk about the selection process like a story

• use active verbs rather than passive verbs

• exclude nonessential details

Below are two examples. The first example is a medical study involving laser vision correction:

ORIGINAL	REVISED
The protocol, approved by the University Internal Ethics Committee, was carried out in accordance with what was outlined in the Declaration of Helsinki, and eligible patients were enrolled in the study during a screening visit after providing informed consent. The study comprised 100 patients that is to say 200 eyes, with various levels of impaired vision who had been referred to the Department of Ophthalmology and Neurosurgery. The inclusion criteria covered ages between 20 and 50 years, ... Patients were not included if any of the following conditions were found to be present: corneal astigmatism =1D, surgical complications ...	Basically, we selected 100 patients that members of our department had seen over the last year. We decided to study patients with an age range between 20 and 50, as those are the types of people who tend to opt for laser treatment. They had various levels of impaired vision. For obvious reasons we excluded any patients who had had any of these conditions *[shows list on slide]*.

Note how the revised version leaves out some of the details of the original (Declaration of Helsinki, ethics committee, informed consent, university department name). Although getting the approval of an ethics review committee (ERC) and informed consent from patients are cornerstones in medical research, the audience knows this already and does not need to hear it. It would only be interesting if an ERC had not given approval or if the patients had no idea what the research was about. The name of the university department was probably on the title slide and/or in the conference proceedings and is not relevant here.

This second example is from a survey on Vietnamese students' ability to write scientific English:

ORIGINAL	REVISED
The research was conducted at two departments at Hanoi University of Technology, hereafter referred to as departments A and B. Ninety-four postgraduate male and female students took part in the experiment and survey. All had studied English for at least 7 years ...	For my survey I needed Vietnamese students with a sufficient knowledge of English to be able to write technical English. Initially I started with some undergraduate students, as they were the easiest to find and had the most time available. But it soon became clear that postgraduates would be a better option, as the undergraduates did not have many assignments in English. Then another problem was that many Vietnamese PhD students actually study abroad, so it was quite difficult to find a sufficient number all studying in the same place, and all with a good knowledge of English. In the end, I discovered two departments at the Hanoi University of Technology ...

Both of the original versions would be possible in a presentation, but audiences might find the revised versions more interesting because

- the original versions sound like they were lifted directly from a paper. People do not usually talk in such a way. The use of the passive form (except when describing a process, see Section 13.7) is generally a sign of formality and is more often found in writing

- the revised versions make the presenter the protagonist (the main actor), the presenter talks the audience through the decision-making process in a way that makes the presenter seem like a real human being rather than an anonymous provider of information

8.11 Bring your figures, graphs, etc., alive

Constantly think to yourself "Why should the audience be interested in what I am saying?" If you show a figure, bring it alive to the audience. Try and transmit some of that energy you had when you were doing your research and you got your great/ unexpected results.

Compare these two versions of a presenter's commentary of a slide showing a diagram of how a software application (BlogScope) works. This application is designed to reveal how big businesses manipulate blogs in order to promote their products.

ORIGINAL	REVISED
As you can see, this picture shows the framework of our software and how it is able to reveal whether a blog is subject to hidden sponsorship, whether the blog was originally started by a private individual and was then taken over by a company, and whether consumer-followers and leavers of comments are genuine consumers or have been 'planted' by the company.	So here's the framework. BlogScope has loads of features. *[pause for two seconds while audience looks at the diagram]* I particularly like three things about it, which really reveal how big business is conditioning how consumers react to their products. First, it tells us if the blog is really being operated by an individual or whether a company is secretly sponsoring it. Second, we can find out how the blog began - was it originally set up by an individual, or was a company involved from the start, or was it hijacked by the company? And finally, we can see whether the blog's followers have actually been planted by the company and are working to insidiously promote the company's products.

Note how the revised version

- numbers the three features, thus making it easier for the presenter to list them and easier for the audience to assimilate them

- gives the audience an idea of the big picture first (i.e. how big business is conditioning how consumers react to their products) before moving on to talking about the three individual points

- prefers verbs to nouns (e.g. *sponsoring* vs *sponsorship*)

- uses the active rather than the passive

- uses personal pronouns (*I, us, we, you*)

- uses questions

- uses more emotive words (*secretly, hijacked, insidiously*)

- uses more words than the original, but this is compensated for by its high digest-ibility factor (six short sentences versus one long sentence)

For more on preparing and describing figures, graphs etc see Chapter 5.

8.12 Minimize or cut the use of equations, formulas, and calculations

Equations, formulas, and calculations are difficult and time consuming to explain. They

- rarely interest the audience and often confuse them

- may distract the audience—they start deciphering the equation and stop listening to you

If you show the formula below on a slide, the temptation for you is to explain each of the symbols. This would take several minutes and by the time you have finished the audience will probably have forgotten what you said at the beginning.

$$kV(s) = \frac{q_1 S(s) + \sigma_2 T(s)}{\beta_3 U(s)}$$

Instead of explaining the math in detail, just talk about its importance and how it relates to your study. You can then give details in a handout. For example you could say,

I am not going to explain the details of this formula—you can find them on my website, which I will give to you at the end of the presentation. Basically the formula says that if you want to analyze how easy it is to understand a written sentence, then you shouldn't just concentrate on how many words are used, but also the stress (S) and the time (T) involved in trying to understand it. So U stands for level of understanding. Using this verbosity index we found that scientific papers are 37 times more difficult to read than advertisements for products.

If you must use math, talk slowly, and go through everything step by step. Remember that people normally study equations on paper; it is not easy for an audience to absorb a formula in a very short space of time.

8.13 Use active and passive forms effectively

You can use active and passive verbs even when describing a process in which you were/are not directly involved. Look at this extract explaining how ink is removed from magazines so that they can be recycled.

> When the magazines first arrive at the de-inking plant, they go through the wire cutter, which is this thing here *[indicates the wire cutter on the diagram in the slide]*. The blade of the wire cutter slips under the baling wire, cuts it and releases loose magazines onto the conveyor. Now here you can see how the magazines then move up the conveyor to a pulping machine, which stirs the paper until a thin pulp is formed. After the magazine pulp has been thoroughly cleaned, it is piped to the final step—the paper machine, which you can see here.

Where she can, the presenter has used the active form (in the first part of the description: *arrive, move, cuts, releases*, etc.). In the last sentence she decides to use the passive (*is formed, has been cleaned, is piped*, etc.). This is because the recipient of the action, i.e., the pulp derived from the magazines, is a more relevant subject than the machinery used to move it around, since it is this pulp that is the subject of the whole process and also the subject of this part of the presentation. Moving from active to passive also creates variety in the description, and not using the passive all the time gives energy and dynamism to the description.

Note also how the presenter guides the audience by indicating on the diagram where they are in the process and by explaining technical vocabulary by pointing at the relevant item (*the wire cutter, which is this thing here*).

Chapter 9

Results and Discussion

Factoids

1. A survey of the general public carried out in 1998 found that the top five 'inventions' in history were: 1) the toilet system, 2) the computer, 3) the printing press, 4) fire, 5) the wheel.

2. People generally associate green with spring, yellow with summer, brown with autumn, and white with winter.

3. The common cold *can* be prevented - those taking daily doses of vitamin C were found in a study to have almost 50% fewer colds than those taking a placebo.

4. Cognitive skills are only weakly related to earning power.

5. On a dating site, if you are rich and handsome man but don't post your photo you will receive fewer responses than an unattractive balding man who has a low income and poor education but who does post a photo.

6. There are more fatalities due to boating incidents than to plane crashes.

7. 50% of a child's personality and skills is determined by their genes.

8. 50% of resumes written in the USA contain lies.

9. Beautiful people (as judged by panelists shown photographs) earn 5% more than less good-looking people.

10. Doing athletics at school increases a child's chances of getting a higher-than-average paid job.

© Springer International Publishing Switzerland 2016
A. Wallwork, *English for Presentations at International Conferences*,
English for Academic Research, DOI 10.1007/978-3-319-26330-4_9

9.1 What's the buzz?

1) Do you think that for an audience the Results and Discussion might be the most interesting points in the presentation? Why, why not?

2) Look at the first factoid. Conduct a survey among your class and see if you get the same results as in the 1998 survey.

3) Choose three of the factoids and discuss (in a written form) their most important implications. Then think of ways that you could present this information to an audience.

4) What are your most important results so far? [If you have no results yet, what results are you expecting?]. Think of three reasons why they are important.

5) Imagine you have finished your research. What would have happened if you had not carried out your research? What important findings would not have been brought to light, and what consequences for the scientific community might this have had?

****

Unless describing the methodology (see previous chapter) is the main purpose of the presentation, the results are usually given in the middle of the presentation. In the middle means in terms of time, not the number of slides. You may in fact be towards the end of your slides, as you will go through the first slides more quickly.

This chapter is designed to help you to:

• explain your results using graphs

• show how your results fit in with the wider context

• be open about your results and their difficulty of interpretation

• be honest about apparently 'negative' results

• encourage the audience to collaborate with you

When discussing your results, you will often need to talk about graphs, figures, tables etc. See Sections 5.2-5.4 to learn that the easier a figure is to understand, the less time you will have to spend on explaining it.

9.2 Focus only on the key results, and keep the explanation short

This is the part of the presentation that may be of most interest to the audience, but it comes at a point when audience concentration is likely to be at its lowest.

An audience will forget more than 75% of what they hear within 24 hours, so informing them of all the details of your results is a waste of time.

Your findings and results should generally be the highlight of your presentation. The audience just need brief answers to the following questions:

• what did you find?

• was it what you expected?

• what does it mean?

• why should we be interested?

In a 10-minute presentation, this part should be just a couple of slides. It is not advisable to introduce interesting side issues, as they might confuse the audience.

Try to avoid the temptation to give the audience the full Wikipedia explanation. If you present a slide full of information, you yourself know what is important and where to focus your eyes, but the audience doesn't.

To make it clear that you are generalizing about your results, see 8.8.

9.3   Communicate the value of what you have done—put your results in the big picture

For you it may be clear how your results fit in within the current state of the art, but for your audience it may not. Tell the audience how your findings contribute to knowledge in your specific field. Show and tell them the benefits. Use expressions such as

> What this means is that ... The key benefit of this is ... What I would like you to notice here is ... What I like about this is ... Possible applications of this are ... I would imagine that these results would also be useful for ...

9.4   Explain graphs in a meaningful way

The statistics that you give the audience (whether your own statistics or those of others) will be very familiar to you, so there is a natural tendency to explain them too quickly and in too much detail. The secret is just to select a few and explain them in a way that the audience can understand.

If the statistics are in the form of a graph, it helps the audience to understand better if you explain what the quantities are on each axis and why you chose them. This gives the data a context and also allows you to add some personal details about how and why you selected them. Obviously, however, if the axes are self-explanatory there is no need to comment on them.

Think about how you might explain and comment on the graph below.

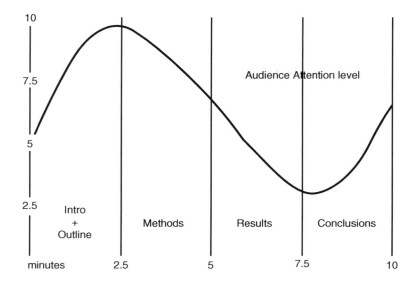

Would this be a helpful commentary for the audience?

> In the graph that can be seen in this slide, which delineates the typical attention curve of an audience during a 10-minute presentation at an international conference, the x-axis of this two-dimensional plot represents the number of minutes, and the y-axis the amount of attention paid by an audience. The graph highlights that at the beginning of a presentation the level of attention is relatively low. Then it rises rapidly, reaching a peak at about two minutes. After approximately three minutes it begins to drop quite rapidly until it reaches its lowest point at around seven minutes thirty seconds. Finally, it rises quite steeply in the ninth minute and reaches a second peak in the last minute.

The problem with the above is that it contains no information that the audience could not have worked out for themselves. Basically all you have done is describe the curve in a rather abstract and tedious way. What you really need to do is to interpret the curve and point out to the audience what lessons can be learned from it. You could say something like this:

> OK, so let's look at the typical attention curve of an audience during a 10-minute presentation. *[Pauses three to five seconds to let audience absorb the information on the graph].* What I'd like you to note is that attention at the beginning is actually quite low. People are sitting down, sending messages on their Blackberry, and so on. This means that you may not want to give your key information in the first 30 seconds simply because the audience may not even hear it. But very quickly afterwards, the audience reach maximum attention. So this is the moment to tell them your most important points. Then, unless you have really captivated them, their attention goes down until a minute from the end when it shoots up again. At least it should shoot up. But only if you signal to the audience that you are coming to an end. So you must signal the ending, otherwise you may miss this opportunity for high-level attention. Given that their attention is going to be relatively high, you need to make sure your conclusions contain the information that you want your audience to remember. So stressing your important points when the audience's attention will naturally be high—basically at the beginning and end—is crucial. But just as important is to do everything you can to raise the level of attention when you are describing your methodology and results. The best ways to do this are ...

Note how the presenter

- does not describe the line, but talks about the implications

- does not mention what the x and y axes represent because they are obvious in this case

- highlights for the audience what they need to know

- repeats his/her key points at least twice (i.e., give important information at the beginning and end, signal that you are coming to an end)

- addresses the audience directly by using *you*

Note also how the graph helps the audience to understand which part of the presentation the minutes correspond to. The graph thus shows that audience attention is dropping considerably around the fifth to seventh/eighth minutes, which correspond to when a presenter is normally giving his/her results. Consequently, given that the results are often the most important part of a presentation, the presenter needs to do everything possible to recapture the attention of the audience and ensure that they actually hear the results.

NB: The information on this graph is only a very approximate idea of how much time to spend on each part of a 10-minute presentation. In some cases, your methodology may be much more important/interesting than your results, in which case you will dedicate more time to it.

For more on describing figures, graphs etc see 5.2-5.4.

9.5 Avoid phrases that might make you sound overconfident, arrogant or critical of others

When you talk about your results, it is generally a good idea to leave your discussion open to other interpretations. Compare the two versions below:

ORIGINAL	REVISED
These results *definitely prove* that plain ethylene-vinyl acetate and cellulose are incompatible. *Our results also demonstrate* that cellulose fibers *are* more effective fillers for ... *No other researchers* have previously managed to find evidence of this effectiveness. *Cellulose should therefore be used* in preference to ...	These results *would seem to indicate* that plain ethylene-vinyl acetate and cellulose are incompatible. *We believe that our results also highlight* that cellulose fibers *may* be more effective fillers for ... *To the best of my knowledge,* no other researchers have previously managed to find evidence of this effectiveness. *I would thus recommend using* cellulose in preference to ...

Note how in the revised version you are not removing the strength of what you are saying. In fact, you gain more credibility if you stress that you are open minded. You show the audience that you are aware that new discoveries are being made all the time and that there may be different ways to achieve the same result.

This means of communication is called "hedging," and in presentations it should prevent the audience from seeing you as too arrogant or presumptuous.

You can protect yourself from such criticism by not stating things too categorically:

- put *would seem to/would appear to* before verbs such as *prove, demonstrate, give concrete evidence, support* (as in the revised example above)

- consider replacing verbs such as *prove* and *demonstrate* with less strong verbs such as *suggest, imply,* and *indicate*

- hedge strong affirmations using modal verbs (*would, might, may, could*) for example *this could possibly be the reason for ... this may mean that ...*

- replace adverbs that appear to leave no room for doubt, such as *definitely, certainly, surely, undoubtedly, indisputably,* with more tentative forms such as *probably, possibly, likely* or *it is probable/possible/likely that ...*

- avoid preceding categorical statements such as "*No data exist in the literature on this topic*" or "*This is the first time that such a result has been achieved.*" You can replace such expressions with *to the best of our knowledge, as far as I know, I believe, I think.*

- be careful not to sound like you want to impose your ideas—the phrase *Cellulose should therefore be used* is very strong, as in this case there is little difference between *should* and *must* (they are both often found in sentences describing obligations)

If you were Jim Smith and heard the original version below, imagine how you would feel.

ORIGINAL	REVISED
I completely disagree with Jim Smith's interpretation of his own findings. He clearly misunderstood the significance of the outliers and failed to take into account the results of the third study.	I found Smith's interpretation of his findings very interesting, though I do think there could be another reason for the outliers. Also, it might be worth analyzing the results of the third study in a different light.

Even if what the presenter said was true, you wouldn't be very happy to hear it expressed in such a negative way. As highlighted in the revised version, the secret is again to "hedge" what you are saying, and to always be polite and constructive.

For more on hedging see Chapter 10 in *English for Writing Research Papers.*

9.6 Tell the audience about any problems in interpreting your results

Don't worry if there is not necessarily one unique or clear way to interpret your results. Again you can use a "hedging" technique, and admit such difficulties:

Interpreting these results is not straightforward primarily because the precise function of XYZ has not yet been clarified.

Although the physiological meaning *cannot be confirmed* by any direct observation, I believe that …

Despite the fact that *there appears to be* no clear correlation, I think/imagine that …

One way of explaining these contrasting results could be …

One of the possible interpretations for such discrepancies might be … but our future work should be able to clarify this aspect

The results did not confirm our hypothesis, nevertheless I think that …

Note how many of the phrases above include modal verbs (*might, could, should*), adverbs of concession (*although, even though, despite the fact, nonetheless, nevertheless*), and verbs that express a hypothesis rather than 100% certainty (*think, believe, imagine*). Such phrases are all useful for making what you are saying sound more tentative.

Also, look at the words in italics in the first three sentences: the subject of the verbs (*interpret, confirm, appear*) is impersonal, the speaker does not say, for instance, "*when I tried to interpret these results.*" This allows speakers to distance themselves from their results, to give the impression that the results do not depend strictly on them personally.

9.7 Explain whether your results were expected or not

If your results were not what you were expecting the audience will be curious to know why. Try to present the reasons in an interesting way, rather than as cold facts:

ORIGINAL	REVISED
The research failed to find agreement with our initial hypotheses. The results indicated X and not Y. Further analysis of the data revealed the necessity to effect a modification of a fundamental nature in our perspective.	I was surprised at the results, to say the least. It was actually the middle of the night, and I remember phoning the others in the team to tell them the news ... The results were not what we were expecting at all. In fact they indicated X rather than Y. And now that we have examined the data in more detail, what we found is now beginning to cause a fundamental change of view.

When, as in the revised version, you comment on your feelings and you use a narrative style, you inevitably use more words. This is not a problem, as in this case if you were concise (like I have suggested you should always try to be) you would lose the drama and thus the interest of the audience.

9.8 Be upfront about your poor/uninteresting/negative results

As stated in the popular journal New Scientist:

Science rarely delivers what scientists set out to find.

A problem for researchers in some fields is that they agree to give a presentation at a conference that is scheduled 6–9 months later, hoping they will be able to present the results of some ongoing research. But they end up with unexpected, uninteresting, or seemingly inexplicable results.

Dr Ben Goldacre is a British medical doctor who has spent much of his career trying to get medical scientists, the pharmaceutical industry, and the mass media to be more transparent in publishing negative results. He talks about the dangers (including the death of innocent patients) of suppressing negative data. This is what he says in his fascinating and very readable book "Bad Science":

'Publication bias' is a very interesting and very human phenomenon. For a number of reasons, positive trials are more likely to get published than negative ones. It's easy enough to understand, if you put yourself in the shoes of the researcher. Firstly, when you get a negative result, it feels as if it's all been a bit of a waste of time. It's easy to convince yourself that you found nothing, when in fact you discovered a very useful piece of information: the thing that you were testing *doesn't work*. ... Publication bias is common, and in some fields it is more rife [widespread] than in others. In 1995, only 1 per cent of all articles published in alternative medicine journals gave a negative result. The most recent figure is 5 per cent negative.

Moral of the story: don't hide any negative results, they might actually benefit the community.

9.9 Turn your 'negative' results into an opportunity for collaboration

The aim of a congress is to share experiences—both good and bad. If you have, or appear to have, negative results the audience will certainly be sympathetic, and probably relieved, because most of them will have been in the same situation. So

- admit to the audience that the results were not what you were hoping for

- never hide the poor results or invent anything to make them more interesting

- say what you plan to do next to resolve these problems

- ask the audience for help—have they experienced this, what did they do? Encourage them to come and talk to you later.

If you don't do the above, you risk giving a bad presentation because you won't be motivated to prepare well, thinking that your results are not interesting, and thus your presentation is unlikely to be inspiring.

In any case, consider asking your professors and colleagues about how they resolve the problems of presenting negative or unexpected data.

9.10 Encourage discussion and debate

Conferences tend to me much more interesting when the presenters speak convincingly about their topic, but they leave the door open to other possible approaches and interpretations. Also, they are willing to discuss any limitations in their research. If you follow this practice you will

- sound more credible. You will seem confident enough to give the audience space to suggest alternative interpretations

- sound less arrogant. Your aim is not to lecture to the audience like a university professor, but rather to discuss your ideas with them. It is important that your tone of voice is friendly and not hard. You do not want the audience to be passive listeners but to be active in asking questions, both in the Q&A session and after the presentation at the bar or social dinner

A series of presentations where ideas and results are presented in a way that there is no room for debate does not make for a stimulating conference.

Chapter 10

Conclusions

What the experts say

Murphy: Anything that can go wrong will go wrong.

******

Niven: If the universe of discourse permits the possibility of time travel and of changing the past, then no time machine will be invented in that universe.

******

Occam: Explanations should never multiply causes without necessity. (*Entia non sunt multiplicanda praeter necessitatem.*)

******

Papert: Many crucial steps in mental growth are based not simply on acquiring new skills, but on acquiring new administrative ways to use what one already knows.

******

Pareto: For many phenomena, 80% of consequences stem from 20% of the causes.

******

Parkinson: Work expands to fill the time available for its completion.

******

Peter: In a hierarchy, every employee tends to rise to their level of incompetence

******

Sturgeon: Ninety percent of everything is crud.

******

Wallwork: The length of a research manuscript tends to be in inverse proportion to the utility of the results outlined therein.

© Springer International Publishing Switzerland 2016
A. Wallwork, *English for Presentations at International Conferences*,
English for Academic Research, DOI 10.1007/978-3-319-26330-4_10

10.1   What's the buzz?

Follow these four steps:

- Do a Google Images search for 'conclusions slides'. This will bring up thousands of slides taken from various presentations.

- Scroll down about twenty rows of images. Copy and paste: i) three slides that are standard but not effective; ii) three slides that are standard and effective; iii) three slides that you think are both original and effective.

- Compare your slides with a fellow student's choices.

- Write a slide summarizing the conclusions that can be drawn from the slides you found on Google Images.

****

The conclusions are an essential part of a presentation - you want to remind the audience of your most important points / messages and leave them with a positive final impression, which will then encourage them to read your paper and contact you in the future.

In this chapter you will learn how to:

- state your conclusions clearly and succinctly

- talk about your future work

- elicit feedback from the audience

10.2 Be brief and don't deviate from your planned speech

The conclusions are an essential part of a presentation—you want to remind the audience of your most important points/messages and leave them with a positive final impression, which will then encourage them to read your paper and contact you in the future.

In a ten-minute presentation, your conclusions should probably last around one minute—in fact, you should only need three or four sentences. If you are not brief you will lose the audience's interest and they won't be able to remember what you have said.

It is vital to prepare your closing and know exactly what you are going to say (every word) and do. Ending suddenly by saying *"that's it"* or *"thank you"* does not create a good impression.

First, stand confidently and look directly at your audience. Signal that you are coming to an end. This is important as it will wake them up and get them to concentrate on the final points that you want them to remember.

Like the beginning, it is worth trying to memorize your last 60 seconds so that you do not have to look at your slides, laptop, or notes—but just at the audience. This will give the audience the sensation that you are confident and professional.

State your conclusions clearly and a little bit more slowly than in the previous part of the presentation—try not to be in a rush to finish!

10.3 Show your enthusiasm and remind audience of key findings

Presentations are most effective when the speaker uses simple language, talks to the audience as if they were a group of friends, and sounds convinced (and if possible enthusiastic).

Compare these two versions of conclusions to a presentation on the conversion of organic waste into energy.

ORIGINAL	REVISED
Well, we have arrived at the end of this presentation now. In conclusion, from these results the following considerations can be drawn. Using the methodology outlined in this presentation, we have given a demonstration that the interview technique commonly used by social scientists and economists has a number of serious drawbacks. The responses of interviewees tend to be phrased in such a way as to appear to assume a certain level of social responsibility. In addition, there is an inherent flow in the questionnaires themselves. And last but not least thank you for your attention.	So, just a quick summary. In three different studies, researchers have found that 52% of US citizens believe in angels, 80% recycle their waste, and 93% consider that they have above average common sense, just to list a few of the rather dubious findings I have mentioned in this talk. We found three key problems with interviewing people. Firstly, people respond in what they consider to be a socially acceptable way. For example the amount that they recycle. We proved in a random sample, that most of those who claimed to recycle, did not. Secondly, the questionnaires are flawed. For instance, there is a very big difference between an angel and a guardian angel, someone who is just looking out for us. And finally we … So thanks for listening. If you would like a copy of our recommendations for interviews, and our suggested alternatives, here is the link. And here's my email address. Please contact me if have any fun - or serious - interview findings that you would like to share with me. I am sure you have plenty!

Note how the original version

- takes 34 words before reaching the phrase *interview technique*, which is the first time that the audience hear key information.

- uses a preponderance of nouns (*given a demonstration* vs *found*, *response* vs *respond*).

- gives no examples and leaves out key facts that in the revised version are used to remind the audience about what the researchers had discovered

- doesn't allow the presenter to sound enthusiastic

- ends with no connection with the audience

- gives no contact details and thus misses opportunities for collaboration

By the way, the same poll that found that more than half of Americans believe in angels, also found that 39% believe in the devil, 37% in precognition, 29% in astrology, and 10% in ghosts and witches.

10.4 Make sure your final slides give useful information

Look at the slide below. If the presenter deleted it, would the audience still be able to follow what he/she says? Very probably, yes.

FUTURE WORK

➤ We want to perform experiments using the prototype gizmo

➤ We will enhance the prototype so that we can produce an industrial version

➤ We will trial the industrial version in hospitals

When you use a slide to summarize your main points, you really want the attention of the audience, so don't write full sentences. By using short phrases you force the audience to think about what they might mean, and this should lead the audience to being more attentive. So the above slide could be rewritten as

---

FUTURE WORK

➤ Experiment using gizmo

➤ Enhance prototype to industry

➤ Trial in hospitals

Such a slide should help you to remember the three points and make the audience more alert to hear the full meaning behind the three words.

However, as mentioned in 4.9 using full sentences may be appropriate if you have an audience with poor English listening skills.

Alternatively, you could avoid having a conclusions slide. Instead, you move to the whiteboard and write your three key words—*experiment, enhance, trial*. Simply by getting the audience to move the focus of their eyes will catch their attention and then they are more likely to listen to what you say.

10.5   Five ways to end a presentation

Below are some ways to end your presentation, which are similar to the ways suggested to begin your presentation, see 6.4-6.13.

1. use a picture
2. directly relate your findings to the audience
3. give a statistic
4. ask for feedback
5. talk about your future work

As you read them, note how they try to do some or all of the following:

- announce to the audience that the speaker is about to give his/her conclusions and do this using just two or three words (e.g., *in conclusion, to sum up*). Audiences tend to have a higher attention if they know something is about to finish

- repeat the key points of the presentation in order to give the audience a clear message to take home and remember

- try to address/involve the audience directly—again this helps to capture audience attention

Use a picture

This is probably the easiest way to end your presentation. There are many ways to use pictures in your final slide:

- if you had a key picture that you used earlier in the presentation, you can re-exploit by superimposing your conclusions on it. This picture should be chosen so that it reminds the audience of an important point that you mentioned earlier

- if you focused on your country when you were introducing yourself at the beginning of the presentation, you could use another photo or a collage of photos depicting scenes from your country and suggest that the audience travel there some time

- if the basis of your conclusions is your future work, you could create a picture that illustrates your concepts or simply gives the idea of future work or work in progress. A typical picture people use is a "men at work" road sign—if possible customize it in some way to differentiate yourself from the thousands of other researchers who use such a slide

- if you are feeling creative you can design an amusing slide (e.g., a cartoon or photo) that sums up your message. You can get ideas for this by looking at the endings of presentations on ted.com

It is worth investing some time in creating a good final slide which the audience will find memorable. And you will be able to exploit or adapt this slide in many future presentations too. For example, I live and work in Pisa, Italy. I had an artist draw a funny cartoon of me holding up the Leaning Tower. I have been using this cartoon for many years during my presentations and it always gets a smile from the audience thus helping to end the presentation on a warm and positive note.

Directly relate your findings to the audience

You can relate the implications of your research directly to the audience—tell them what impact it might have on them personally if your findings were, or were not, put into action. For example

> In conclusion, our comparison of inner city schools in poor areas and private schools in richer areas highlighted that kids from private schools achieve about 20% better results. What we found to be critical was what children do during their summer holidays. The parents of the children from richer families tended to give their kids access to more books and to encourage them to visit museums and so on. Kids from the inner schools simply didn't have this extra boost from their parents. And just to remind you what I said during my discussion of the results, this means that having access to more computers or to better teachers does not seem to make much difference. So if any of you have kids, I think there are four lessons to be learned. First encourage them to be as proactive as possible, second tell them not be afraid of authority, third get them to engage in critical thinking, and finally don't let them spend the whole of the summer holiday lying on the beach or surfing YouTube and Facebook.

Give a statistic

I watched a researcher give a presentation on an alternator for an automobile engine. An alternator converts power from the gasoline engine that drives the car along. In his conclusions he told us that using his alternator would reduce our consumption of gasoline by 2–3% a year, thus saving us 90 euros.

The problem is that 90 euros doesn't sound like a big saving. A more effective way of communicating this information might have been to say

> So, to sum up, I think there are three advantages of my design for an alternator. The first two advantages, as I showed you when I was explaining the design and development, are that it costs less to produce than traditional alternators, and a massive 80% of its parts can be recycled. But I think the third benefit is the one that will interest you the most. My alternator will reduce gasoline consumption by about 2–3%. That may not sound very much. But if everyone in this room used it—I have counted about 50 people here—then we would save nearly 5000 euros a year. If every car driver in this country used it, we would save about 1.8 billion euros a year. That's a lot of money saved on importing gasoline from abroad. And that's without even thinking about the reduced environmental impact.

Using interesting statistics is a great way to end a presentation. But

- relate them to the audience in some way

- if necessary, multiply them to get a number that is powerful and evocative

Ask for feedback

You can use your conclusions to get help from your audience. In the following example, the presenter uses the three points in his conclusions to stimulate interest in the audience:

> What would be great for us is to have your feedback on these three points *[points to his slide which contains three key conclusions]*. First, it seems to us that our Gizmo has solved the problem of overheating—what do you think? Second, our results would appear to show both P and Q—so what is the reason for this apparent contradiction? It would be really useful if any of you could give me some ideas on this. Third, we are pretty sure that our Gizmo could be used in hospitals—but maybe you know of other possible applications.

Talk about your future work

Your plans for the future are actually one of the main reasons you are at the congress. This is a fantastic opportunity to do some self-promotion. You may have up to 100 people listening to you. One of them might be interested in helping you or collaborating with you. Tell the audience that you would welcome speaking to anyone who could suggest ways of continuing your line of research. If you have done a convincing presentation and have showed that you are the kind of person other people might like working with—not just because of your scientific knowledge but equally importantly how you seem as a person—then you might find that you get an invitation to work in another laboratory that might have more equipment or funds than your current one.

Talking about future work is particularly appropriate when you have presented negative findings, when you have told the audience that your research did not go as you expected. You can also use your conclusions to talk about the limitations of your work. In both cases, your future work will probably thus involve rectifying the problems you encountered and telling the audience how you plan to do this.

> A possible limitation of our work is that we have used two rather simple datasets. Unfortunately, due to computational constraints we couldn't use larger networks. But as I hope I have highlighted, we are still only in the first phase. So we are more interested in the methodology. But in the next phase, we are planning to implement the code using other programming languages. In any case, I think that there are two main benefits of our methodology compared to previous ones. First, …

10.6 Write/Show something interesting on your final slide

About 95% of scientific presentations seem to end with a slide that says one of the following:

- Acknowledgments

- Thank you *or* Thank you for your attention

- Questions? *or* Any Questions?

- Contact details: adrian.wallwork@gmail.com

The first, *Acknowledgments*, is not a memorable way to end a presentation. The people you acknowledge are not likely to be of interest to the audience, and so their final impression will be of a very uninteresting slide containing no useful information. However, it may be important to acknowledge people or funding, but just a much smaller font and locate at the bottom of the slide.

The second, thanking the audience, is a standard way to signal that the presentation is over. One of my students said that she always uses it because "*It seems impolite not to do it because everybody else does it.*" This could in fact be a good reason not to use it as it is very much overexploited, and will probably not be appreciated by an audience who may have already seen 20 presentations in the last 24 hours that end in such a way.

The third one is an effective, though again overexploited, way to begin a question and answer session.

The last one (contact details) gives vital information. But it could be expressed in a way that will really encourage people to contact you, for example

> Please get in touch! adrian.wallwork@gmail.com

If you use the second, third or fourth solutions, either individually or in combination, it's nice to superimpose the words on a photo in one of the ways suggested in 10.5 (*Use a picture*).

I have seen many great 'thank you' slides in which the 'thank you' appears to be being said by the person or animal shown in the background photograph. For example, I watched a medical researcher from Kenya do a presentation on possible treatments for diseases that affect millions of African children. Her 'thank you' was a bubble coming out of the mouth of an African child. Another presentation was on planting wildflowers in the middle of roundabouts. In this case the 'thank you' was 'said' by some butterflies that were fluttering above the flowers!

10.7   Prepare a sequence of identical copies of your last slide

Typically if you hit the advance button while showing your last slide you drop out of the presentation program. This then means the audience will see the smaller window of the presentation and your desk top—this does not look very professional. Duplicate two or three copies of your last speaking slide so that if you accidentally advance one too many times at the end of your presentation, the slide looks like it has not changed.

After these slides, you should include some slides that answer questions that you expect to be asked. These slides will be useful during Q&A sessions after the presentation.

10.8   Learn what to say before you introduce the Q&A session

Some things you might want to say before the question and answer session (see Chapter 11) are:

- tell the audience where they can find the relevant documentation, handouts etc.,

- tell them whether they can/should contact you (give your details) or someone else

- thank the audience

- ask them if they have any questions. Note: if you are at a conference and the chairperson is present, then he or she will generally invite the audience to ask questions

Chapter 11

Questions and Answers

Questions

1. Do aphrodisiacs really work? e.g. rhinoceros horns, oysters, peppers, hard-boiled eggs, truffles.

2. Do bananas grow on trees? Are bananas technically a type of berry?

3. Are primitive languages more simple than 'advanced' languages?

4. Does the exception prove the rule?

5. Are gorillas fierce belligerent animals?

6. Does the hair on a man's chest indicate virility?

7. Does lightning never strike twice in the same place?

8. Do man-eating plants exist?

9. Did Darwin either say or imply that man is descended from the ape?

10. Whenever you continue to engage in a potentially hazardous activity (e.g. flying), do the chances of an accident increase?

© Springer International Publishing Switzerland 2016
A. Wallwork, *English for Presentations at International Conferences*,
English for Academic Research, DOI 10.1007/978-3-319-26330-4_11

11.1   What's the buzz?

1) Did you know the answers to the questions on the previous page?! They are all 'no'!

2) Think about these questions.

- How can you prepare for the Q&A session? Is it possible to predict what questions you will be asked?

- If you already knew what questions you would be asked, what could you do to prepare the answers?

- If someone asks you a question and you don't understand what they have said, how do you typically react? What is the best solution?

****

The Q&A session is NOT as difficult as many people imagine. In this chapter you will learn how to:

- anticipate questions from the audience

- deal with difficult questions

- react when you don't understand a question

- exploit 'useful phrases' to extricate yourself from difficult situations

If you know you have prepared well for this difficult part of the presentation, it will give you confidence. In addition, the questioners may be the same people that could help you clarify important points about your research or who may want to collaborate with you or invite you to their lab.

Sections 2-11 deal with how to handle your nerves, how to prepare for the questions you might be asked and how to answer them. Section 12 is a list of questions typically asked at conferences (not necessarily only in a Q&A session) - it is worth taking the time to study the questions and prepare answers to them.

11.2   Learn to deal with your anxiety about the Q&A session

In their lists of what they fear most about giving presentations, in first position my PhD students nearly always put 'not understanding the questions from the audience'.

Most presenters are anxious the Q&A session because they feel they have no control. However you have much more control than you think. You can:

- prepare for all the questions in advance (see 11.12)

- simply tell the questioner that you don't understand the question (see 11.7) - if you didn't understand the question then it is highly likely that most of the other non-native speakers will not have understood it either. You should never feel stupid or humiliated just because you don't understand

- ask members of your research team or friendly people that you have met at the conference to ask you a question (make sure they tell what the question is! or better, suggest what question they should ask). The idea is that your 'friends' are the first people to ask questions. You will answer the questions calmly and confidently. Then if you don't understand one or more of the other questions at least you will have shown the audience that you were capable of answering some questions, so you will not use your credibility

For more on handling your nerves see Chapter 13.

11.3   Prepare in advance for all possible questions

The Q&A session may be the part that you are worried about the most, as it seems that you have no control over the questions the audience might ask you. In reality you do have some control, as long as you give yourself time to prepare before the presentation.

Practice your presentation in front of colleagues, friends, and relatives, and get them to write down three questions that they would like you to answer. Choose the ones that you think are the most relevant, then prepare answers to them.

If you have thought of all the questions your audience are likely to ask, it will enable you to

- seem professional in your immediate ability to answer a question

- stand a better chance of understanding (in terms of the words the questioner uses) such questions when they are asked

- prepare in advance extra slides to answer such questions

- prepare yourself mentally for difficult questions from difficult people, and during the session remain calm and polite

11.4   Give the audience time to respond to your call for questions

It is normally the chairperson's job to ask if anyone has any questions. If he/she doesn't, then you can ask the audience yourself.

When you say, *"Does anyone have any questions?"* give the audience more than just a few seconds, even if you secretly hope that no one will ask you anything so that you can finish and return to your hotel room!

On the other hand, if you are worried that no one will ask you a question, you can

- arrange for one of your colleagues to ask a question that you have already prepared for him/her

- ask yourself a question, e.g., *One question I am often asked is …*

11.5 Get the questioner to stand up. Reply to the whole audience

Sometimes the reason you or the audience can't understand the question, is because the questioner is sitting down and he/she cannot be seen or heard very easily. Simply say

Do you think you could stand up and speak a bit louder? Thank you.

This has the added advantage that you have a second chance to hear the question yourself!

Answer not only the questioner but the whole audience. Good presenters tend to maintain eye contact with all the audience, but keep going back to the questioner to check from their body language (e.g., nodding, positive smiling) that he/she is satisfied with the answer.

Be careful of your own body language. For example presenters who fold their arms may be perceived as being defensive.

11.6 Repeat the questions

If your audience is quite big, repeat any questions from the audience so that

* the rest of the audience can hear the question clearly—this is particularly true if the question comes from someone in the front row, as the back rows will not be able to hear it

* you can reformulate any contorted questions

* you have time to think about an answer

* the questioner can check that you have understood his/her question

In any case, give yourself two to three seconds to formulate your answer before responding.

11.7 Remember that it is not just your fault if you can't understand the question

Your ability to understand the questions depends not just on you. It is also the responsibility of the questioner to phrase and enunciate the question in a way that you will understand it.

So, if you don't understand a question, particularly from a native speaker of English, simply say

> I am sorry, but I am not sure I have understood your question. Could you speak a little more slowly please? Thank you.

Alternatively you could say:

> Would you mind emailing me that question, and then I will get back to you?

> Do you think you could ask me that question again during the coffee break?

> Sorry, I really need to check with a colleague before being able to answer that question.

To learn what to do when you don't understand, see the companion volume *English for Interacting on Campus*.

11.8 Don't interrupt the questioner unless ...

Most people don't appreciate being interrupted when they are asking a question. However, if they are clearly having difficulty in expressing themselves and you feel it would be right to help them, you could say, "*So you are asking me if ...*" Basically you are anticipating what they want to say, and saying it in your own words for them.

If their question is taking a very long time to ask (particularly if it seems that they are just using the opportunity to talk themselves), you can say

> Sorry, I am not exactly sure what your question is. I think it might be best if you asked me at the bar.

If you realize that the question has limited interest for the rest of the audience, respectfully say to the questioner,

> For me this is a fascinating topic, but I think it might be best if we discuss this during the break. If that's okay with you. Now, does anyone else have any questions?

11.9   Be concise in giving your answers

When answering a question it helps to be concise, particularly as you might otherwise forget what the original question was.

If the question only requires the answer yes or no, you can be suitably brief and move on to the next question.

Sometimes you will get two-part questions. It's generally the best option to choose the part of the question that is simplest to answer first. If you forget the other part of the question, you can ask them again, or move on to another question, and then go up to the person after the presentation and talk to them directly.

There are some questions that you could discuss for hours, but the questioner is not asking you to tell them everything you know about the topic, but just what is relevant to now. If you are tempted to begin a long conversation with someone in the audience, offer to meet up later.

11.10   Always be polite

Very occasionally questioners in the audience seem to want to provoke us, and one natural tendency is to become defensive. However, if you watch professional presenters they never say anything negative about other researchers or their findings. Likewise, you don't need to take any criticisms or objections personally. Simply say

> I think you have raised an interesting point and it would be great if we could discuss it in the bar.

> I was not aware of those findings. Perhaps you could tell me about them at the social dinner.

Be aware that some people just ask questions to demonstrate their own knowledge. In this case, you can say,

> You are absolutely right. I didn't mention that point because it is quite technical/because there was no time. But it is covered in my paper.

For more on understanding native English speakers, see the companion volume *English for Interacting on Campus.*

11.11 If you are attending an important professor's presentation, think about the value of asking her / him a question?

One of the reasons for going to a conference is not just to present, but to network (see Chapter 16) and set up collaborations. A typical situation is when you are looking for a PhD or Postdoc position. Imagine that there is a professor at the conference whose team you would love to join. You can of course simply email him/her, but there is a chance you will receive no reply. A much more effective way is to introduce yourself to the professor in person, which either entails arranging an appointment or interrupting the prof while he/she is talking to someone else.

A great way to get yourself noticed, is by asking the prof a question at the end of his/her presentation. This makes it much easier to make an appointment or interrupt the prof in a conversation, as you can simply say: "I was the person in the Q&A session who asked you a question about ...".

If you don't have the courage to ask a question during the Q&A, then you could go up to the professor at the end of his/her presentation.

Whichever solution you adopt, you need to think of an appropriate question to ask.

See Chapter 17 for various strategies for interacting with key professors.

11.12 Think about how you might answer (or ask) generic questions

Below are some generic questions that I have heard at international conferences at the end of presentations, during seminars and workshops, and at social dinners.

You can use them:

- while you are preparing your presentation. If in your presentation you can incorporate the answers to typical questions that audiences ask, then you will be able to reduce the number of questions that you are asked at the end. This is good if you don't feel confident about being able to understand questions or if you think you will be too nervous to answer them

- to ask if you are an attendee rather than a presenter (see previous subsection)

- at social dinners (see Chapter 16)

In some cases I have put two versions of the same question (these are separated by a / symbol). This is important, as the same question might be phrased in various ways. You need to be able to recognize (i.e. hear and understand) such variations.

You also need to be prepared to deal with difficult questions - these are marked with an asterisk (*). It might useful to discuss possible answers with your research team.

REASON FOR RESEARCH / CONTRIBUTION

1. Why did you carry out this research? / What gap were you trying to fill?

2. Are there any other research groups working in this area? If so, are their findings similar to yours?

3. * I am a little bit confused as to why you set out to do this research. Why did you decide to do this research? / I work in a very similar field to yours, but I am not really sure what exactly your contribution is.

4. Have you presented these findings before? / I found your talk fascinating. Thank you very much. I was just wondering whether this was the first time you have announced your findings, or have you presented them at other conferences or in papers?

5. What key papers did you read while preparing your research?

6. What did you enjoy most about doing your research? / What was the most enjoyable aspect of carrying out this research?

IMPORTANCE OF FINDINGS / LIMITATIONS

7. What do you think is the importance of your findings? / I am curious to know where you think the real significance of your findings lies.

8. What do you think your key finding was? / You made a lot of good points during your presentation. I thought it was very interesting. But I am not completely clear about what you believe your key finding to be, or do you think that there is no one finding that stands out above the rest in terms of real relevance?

9. What are the limitations to your research? / What do you think are the limitations to your research?

142

REQUEST FOR CLARIFICATIONS

10. Could you explain the diagram in the fourth slide? / I got a bit lost when you were explaining the diagram in one of your slides. Could you go back to it and explain it again please.

11. What are your recommendations? / I am not entirely clear what your recommendations are.

12. I missed your first slide. Can you just remind me where you work?

13. I wasn't very clear about the true nature of your first conclusion, could you elucidate for me? / Could you tell me your first conclusion again?

14. * Could you repeat your main conclusion please? / I think many of us the audience were a little confused when you outlined your conclusions. Could you recap them for us?

PUBLISHED PAPERS AND FUTURE WORK

15. Have you published a paper on this topic? Are you going to talk more about it at tomorrow's workshop? / I was just wondering, given the high level of novelty of your work, which I would actually consider to be breaking new ground, whether you have actually published any papers on this topic? Also, will you be covering more of what you have said today in tomorrow's workshop?

16. What are you planning for the future? / Your work seems particularly pertinent given the current state of the art in this field. Do you have any idea what your next step will be in this fascinating path that you are following?

COLLABORATIONS

17. We are doing similar research. Would it be possible for us to see your full results? / I found your presentation extremely interesting and informative. At my lab we are working on a similar project. Would you be willing to share more of your results with us?

18. Are you looking for collaborators? / If you don't mind me asking, are you by any chance looking for collaborators to join your team? If so I would be extremely interested.

Chapter 12

Attracting Audiences and Keeping Their Attention

Factoids

1. All the people in the world could fit into the Grand Canyon if stacked appropriately.

2. In New Zealand, Australia and Uruguay there are more sheep than people (10:1, 4.9:1, 3.2:1, respectively).

3. The car color with the worst rate of accidents is black (20.9 accidents per 1000 cars); followed by white, red, blue, grey, gold, silver, beige, green, yellow, brown (13.3 accidents per 1000 cars).

4. Apparently, three per cent of Britons never do housework.

5. On average we spend 90% of our time indoors.

6. You have a greater chance of living longer if you only sleep between 6.5 and 7.5 hours on weekdays

7. Around 66% of women and 50% of men steal items from the hotel room where they've been staying.

8. There is a total area of 28% of a football goalmouth where it is virtually impossible for a goalkeeper to make a save.

9. On average the human brain can only remember four things at any one moment.

10. US residents produce an average of nearly 100g of garbage per hour of every day.

© Springer International Publishing Switzerland 2016
A. Wallwork, *English for Presentations at International Conferences*,
English for Academic Research, DOI 10.1007/978-3-319-26330-4_12

12.1   What's the buzz?

1) According to the presentations expert Shay McConnon: *Juries typically remember only 60% of what they are told.* Why do think this is the case? What does this imply about the way you involve the audience in a presentation?

2) Choose three of the factoids on the previous page. Decide how they might be used by a presenter in his / her presentation. Think about:

   • the topic area of the presentation where the factoid might be used

   • at what point in the presentation it could be used

   • how the audience might react on hearing the factoid (i.e. is there a possibility that you might actually offend them? For example, the fourth factoid might not go down well in the UK and may simply reinforce a stereotype - for more similarly potentially dangerous 'facts' see the factoids on the USA in Chapter 15)

3) Factoids (i.e. interesting statistics) are not the only way you can (re)gain the attention of your audience. What other ways can you think of?

4) Think of ways that you can show the audience how interested you are in your topic and prove to the audience that they should be interested too.

****

In *The McGraw-Hill 36-Hour Course: Business Presentations* Lani Arredondo states that:

> Generally, people are motivated by self-interest. They act on the basis of what they perceive will best satisfy their needs. An audience is more inclined to listen, accept, and act on ideas and information which they find not only relevant to them, but useful and gratifying as well.

This chapter outlines how you can involve the audience by:

   • presenting statistics that are in some way personally relevant to them (e.g. related to their job, country, to the conference itself)

   • giving information and presenting statistics in a way that the audience can easily picture them and absorb them (see next subsection)

   • maintaining eye contact with the audience

You will also learn how to:

   • attract and retain your audience's attention throughout your presentation

   • understand when audience attention is at its highest and lowest

12.2   Ensure you have an attractive title

Your first job in your mission to attract audience attention, is to actually get people to come to your presentation. The title of your presentation is critical.

Look at the title below from a Bangladeshi researcher who presented his work at a congress in Europe:

> Preparation, characterization, and degradability of low environmental impact polymer composites containing natural fibers

It describes some work on composites based on natural fibers, which are materials with a much lower environmental impact. He began by saying:

> Getting ordinary plastic bags to rot away like banana peels would be an environmental dream come true. After all, we produce five hundred billion a year worldwide. And they take up to one thousand years to decompose. They take up space in landfills. They litter our streets and parks. They pollute the oceans. And they kill the animals that eat them.

He had a quick series of slides (with no titles or text) with photos to illustrate his concepts: plastic bags, banana peels, landfills, litter, and polluted oceans. Notice also how he used very short sentences—these were easy for him to say and were dynamic for the audience.

And at the end of his presentation he returned to his original statistic. He asked a few people in the audience how many bags they thought they used a month, and on the basis of that number, he told them them how many years it would take to cover the whole of Italy (where the congress was being held) if everyone in the country used the same number of bags per month.

He certainly managed to attract the audience's attention with this interesting information, but he might have had a bigger audience if he had called his presentation:

> Can natural fibers save the planet?

> Can natural fibers save Italy?

> Europe is slowly disappearing under polyethylene bags

> Bags, bags and more bags

> Will we all be suffocated by plastic bags?

By giving his presentation a very academic title, those people at the congress not specifically interested in polymer composites might have been discouraged from attending his talk.

12.3 Be aware of the implications of the time when your presentation is scheduled

There are good times and bad times in the conference schedule for presenters to give their talks. What are known as the "graveyard slots" (i.e., the worst/dead times) take place

- when attendees would probably rather be having lunch (attendees may focus more on their stomach than on you)

- at the end of the day (the audience have probably assimilated all the information they are capable of assimilating in 1 day)

- at the end of the last day (the worst possible slot, when attendance is always low)

If you have been allocated one of the above slots, you will need to make a special effort to gain and keep the audience's attention. You can do this by

- being a little more informal

- understanding that the audience will be unable to assimilate much new information—therefore consider reducing the number of points you intend to cover and the amount of detail you give

- finishing early and on a high note—the audience will thus go away with a positive impression of you

12.4 Immediately make eye contact with the audience and maintain it throughout

If you don't make eye contact with all your audience throughout the duration of your presentation, they will quickly start thinking about other things.

You can only maintain eye contact with the audience if

- you know exactly what you are saying—if you are not sure what you are going to say next, you will probably start looking up at the ceiling or down at the floor

- your slides are simple—if they are complex you will be very tempted to turn your back to the audience to remember the information on the slide

12.5   Adopt an appropriate level of formality

The style of language you adopt in your presentation will have a huge impact on whether the audience will

- want to listen to you, and their level of enjoyment/interest

- find you approachable and thus someone they might like to collaborate with

There are essentially three levels of formality:

- formal

- neutral/relatively informal

- very informal

Many presenters think they should be formal, but most audiences prefer presenters who deliver their presentation in a relaxed and informal way. In English, this informality is achieved by using

- personal pronouns (e.g., I, we, you)

- active forms rather than passive forms (e.g., *I found* rather than *it was found*)

- verbs instead of nouns where possible

- concrete or specific nouns (e.g., cars) rather than technical or abstract nouns (e.g., vehicular transportation)

- short simple sentences rather than long complex ones

Think about levels of formality in your own language. Do you feel most natural speaking in a very formal way or a friendlier way? The secret in presentations is thus to be not only seen as being both authoritative and competent but also as friendly and warm.

The two are not incompatible—the authoritativeness comes from *what* you say, the friendliness from *how* you say it.

Compare these versions from a presentation on analytical chemistry. Note how the words and phrases in italics in the revised version reflect a much more natural and friendly style of presenting

ORIGINAL	REVISED
The application of the optimized procedure to the indigoid colorants allows their complete solubilization and the detection of their main components with reasonable detection limits, estimated at about 1 ug/g for dibromindigotine. Here the markers are shown—dibromoindigotine for purple and indigotine for indigo.	*When we used* this optimized procedure on the indigoid colorants we managed to completely solubilize them. *We were able* to detect their main components within *quite good* limits, at about 1 ug/g for dibromindigotine. *Here you can see* the markers—dibromoindigotine for purple and indigotine for indigo.
The characterization of organic components was first performed by Py-GC-MS which did not reveal the characteristic compounds of indigo and purple. Quite surprisingly after pyrolysis at 600°C it was still possible to observe the pink color; the failure of the technique was attributed to the massive presence of the silicate clay and research is still in progress.	*We initially characterized* the organic components using Py-GC-MS. *But this did not reveal* the characteristic compounds of indigo and purple. In fact after pyrolysis at 600°C *you can imagine* how surprised we were to still see pink. *We think* this might have been due to the massive presence of silicate clay. In any case, *we are still trying to find out* why this happened.

Note how in the original versions:

- there are no personal pronouns—it sounds like a paper rather than an oral presentation. In normal life, no one speaks like this

- all the verbs are in the passive—this tends to alienate rather than involve the audience

- there is a disproportionate number of nouns

- the sentences are long

The revised version uses lots of personal pronouns. This makes the speech more informal and colloquial and leads to shorter sentences, which are much easier to say. Some of the nouns in the original version have been converted into verbs, and passive verbs have been replaced with active forms. The audience is also addressed directly (*as you can imagine*). The result is that the speech sounds more natural and dynamic.

So when you finish writing your script, check that each sentence sounds like something that you might say to a colleague at lunch time. If it isn't, rephrase it in simpler terms so that the audience will feel that you are talking directly to them. This has big advantages for your English too. The simpler your sentences are the less likely you are to make mistakes when saying them.

12.6 Exploit moments of high audience attention

Audiences tend to remember:

- what is said at the beginning and end of a presentation (when their attention is generally high in any case).

- things that they can relate to personally (see 12.9)

- facts and explanations that they hear more than once.

- curious facts, things that stand out

Ideally you need to state your key points both at the beginning and ending. In the middle go through each key point more in detail. If possible, include an unexpected/counterintuitive/interesting fact for each key point. Try juxtaposing data with quotations, and serious issues with a humorous anecdote.

The point of your presentation is to disseminate information and engage interest for your project. If your audience do not listen, then there is no point in you doing the presentation. So, most ways of getting and maintaining their attention are legitimate provided that they

- are relevant, or in any case interesting and memorable

- do not offend anyone

12.7 Don't spend too long on one slide and consider blanking the screen

Our attention span is affected by how long we look at something that does not change. Most audiences can only look at something static for 30 seconds and before they start thinking about something else. So if possible, reduce the amount of time you spend showing the same slide.

If you have said everything you want to say about a slide, but don't want to move on to the next, then blank the screen (using the B key on PowerPoint).

12.8 Learn ways to regain audience attention after you have lost it

When you are doing your presentation you may be competing for the audience's attention with one or more of the following:

- their mobile phone or laptop—they may be text messaging or emailing

- the person sitting next to them may want to chat

- things happening outside the window

- their hunger (particularly at the end of the morning session)

- their boredom—yours may be the sixth, seventh, or even eighth presentation that they have seen that day

These kinds of distractions do not always depend on the level of interest of your presentation. To regain their attention:

- blank the screen (on PowerPoint you can do this using the B key)

- use the whiteboard—inevitably the audience will want to know what you are going to write. Make sure you write large enough for all the audience to see—this generally means writing very little or only drawing simple diagrams. Make sure you move to the side of the whiteboard so that the audience can see what you are writing/have written

- ask the audience a rhetorical question. Try and predict what kind of questions the audience might be asking themselves at this point of your presentation. Pause. Ask the question. Pause again. Then answer it

- give the audience a statistic. People are fascinated by numbers and they help the audience see the dimension of the situation. See 10.8 on how to present statistics

- produce an object from your pocket and say *"here's something you might be interested in seeing"* or *"I've brought along something to show you ..."* Your audience will be immediately curious to see what the object is. The object has to be big enough for everyone to see, or you have to have lots of them to distribute among the audience—but be careful as they may turn into an even bigger distraction! Objects can also be a good substitute for explanations

- show an unusual slide—this could simply be a slide that breaks with the normal pattern of your other slides. It could be an interesting photo, a clear and effective diagram, or contain a number, a short quotation, or a question

12.9 Present statistics in a way that the audience can relate to them

Compare these ways of stating the same statistics.

ORIGINAL	REVISED
A bird's eye and a human's eye take up about 50 and 5% of their heads, respectively. In our study of the importance of vision in birds of prey, we found that this factor was ...	A bird's eye is huge. It takes up about 50% of its head. Half its head. That's 10 times more space than a human's eye takes up. In fact, to be comparable to the eyes of a bird of prey, such as an eagle, our eyes would have to be the size of a tennis ball. When we studied eagles, vultures, and buzzards, we realized that ...

Note how in the revised version, the speaker gives the same information twice—50% and *half*. This is useful because it is very difficult to distinguish between the sound of *fifteen* and *fifty* (likewise between 13 and 30, 14 and 40, etc). By using the analogy of a tennis ball, the audience gets a much clearer idea of the proportions. Clearly, to be effective it would be helpful to have slides of an eagle's or owl's head and a tennis ball, and maybe a cartoon of a person with tennis ball eyes. Also, you would be guaranteed attention if you pulled two tennis balls out of your pockets!

By the way, a bird of prey's eyes really do take up half its head!

For more on statistics, see 6.7 and 6.8.

12.10   Avoid quasi-technical terms

Compare these two versions. Which one sounds more natural and is possibly easy to understand?

ORIGINAL	REVISED
Engloids are communities gathering scientists of homogeneous thematic areas. They produce and/or consume documents of different types, using different applications and hardware resources.	Engloids are communities of scientists who study the same topic. What happens is that these scientists need to write documents and correspond in English such as in papers, presentations, emails, referees' reports. And to do this they use different applications and hardware resources.

The revised version expresses exactly the same concepts as the original, but in simple English. Avoid quasi-technical terms (e.g., *homogeneous thematic areas*) when you can use something more direct (*who study the same topic*).

12.11   Explain or paraphrase words that may be unfamiliar to the audience

Make sure the audience understand key words—explain/show what they mean, as a multilingual audience may know the concept but not the word in English.

Even if you pronounce a word clearly and correctly, there is still a chance that the audience will not understand the word because they have never seen/heard it before. For example, imagine you are talking about crops and cereals. If you mention *rice* and *maize* and you have an audience of agrarians they will understand. But if you mention specialist or less familiar terms such as *cowpea* and *mung bean* then many people, even agrarians, might not understand even though you have used the correct words. In fact, they may think you have simply mispronounced another word. In such cases you can

- have the word on your slide and say "*a mung bean is a member of the pea family and is grown for forage.*" (*forage*, i.e. food for animals, should be comprehensible as it is sufficiently generic for agrarians)

- have a picture of a mung bean so that people may be able to recognize it

If you use a nontechnical word which you think the audience may not know, say it and then paraphrase it. Example: *These creatures are tiny, they are very small*.

12.12   Occasionally use 'strong' adjectives

If you tell the audience you were "excited" about something, then they are more likely to become excited too, or at least be more receptive to what you are going to tell them. Good adjectives to use, for example, in descriptions of diagrams or when giving results, are *exciting, great, amazing, unexpected, surprising, beautiful, incredible.*

But only use them once or twice, otherwise you risk sounding insincere and their effect will be lost.

12.13   Be aware of cultural differences

In his book *Outliers*, Malcolm Gladwell, a writer at *The New Yorker* magazine, talks about cultural differences in the way we communicate and receive information. In Chapter 8 he makes three very interesting points:

1. many Asian countries are "receiver oriented," this means it is the listener's task to interpret what the speaker is saying

2. the Japanese have much higher levels of "persistence" than Americans. This means that the Japanese can stick to a task for much longer than their American counterparts—they have higher levels of concentration

3. our memory span is correlated to the time it takes in our language to pronounce numbers. Because the words for numbers in Asian languages are quicker to pronounce and are more logical (*ten-one* rather than *eleven*), Asians tend to be able to absorb numbers and make calculations generally far more quickly than those in the West

These three points imply that if you are talking to an audience that includes a good number of people from the West (particularly the United States and Great Britain), you should try to

- work very hard yourself to make it absolutely clear what you are saying, so that it is effortless for the audience to understand

- be aware that your audience may not be used to concentrating for long periods and may thus have a short attention span

- give the audience time to absorb and understand any numbers and statistics that you give them

12.14 Be serious <u>and</u> have fun

Attendees at my courses are often skeptical when I say that audiences are more receptive if they enjoy themselves—my students don't doubt the truth of this, but they think that it is not professional and that their professors would not approve. However, many of the world's top professors do approve.

Professor Chandler Davis, the mathematician and well-seasoned conference attendee, told me,

> Some of us can't help expressing our joy in knowing the facts, particularly those WE discovered; presenters who don't naturally impart the joy should be roused to doing so.

And Nobel Prize Winner in Chemistry, Professor Martin Chalfie, confirmed that

> A professional presentation can be both serious AND fun.

Another professor, psychologist Thomas Gilovich from Cornell University, states that

> Our appetite for entertainment is enormous ... If the listener comes away from the communication either informed or entertained, the interaction has been worthy of his or her time and attention, and the speaker has met one of his or her most basic requirements.

Being entertaining doesn't necessarily mean making people laugh. It means

- occasionally providing standard information in a novel or unusual way

- using examples that your audience can easily relate to

- finding interesting and surprising statistics

- using very simple but unusual graphs and pictures that underline important points in a new way

In any case you may decide to provide a few humorous slides or anecdotes. You can then try one and see what reaction you get from your audience. If it works well you can use the others. If not, skip them.

Be very careful about telling jokes and using 'humorous' slides. They may

- be funny only for you, but not your audience

- not be understood

- be offensive or inappropriate for the culture of your audience

- be completely irrelevant to the topic of the presentation

12.15 Gaining and keeping your audience's attention: a summary

Below is a summary of the other chapters of this book in terms of how you can attract and hold your audience's attention:

1. have a clear idea who your audience are, don't assume that they are naturally going to be interested in your topic

2. have an agenda and a clear structure with clear transitions so that the audience know where you are going

3. make it easy for the audience to follow you and your slides

4. help the audience to understand why you are showing them a particular slide

5. involve your audience and give them lots of examples

6. make frequent eye contact

7. avoid too much text on your slides

8. use simple graphs and tables

9. make your text and visuals big enough for everyone in the audience to see clearly

10. avoid entering into too much detail (i.e., just select those things that the audience really need to know about the topic)

11. avoid spending more than a couple of minutes on one specific detail

12. have a variety of types of slides (not just all bullets, or all text, or all photos)

13. speak reasonably slowly and move from slide to slide at a speed that the audience will feel comfortable with

14. sound interested and enthusiastic about your topic

15. vary your tone of voice

16. move around occasionally rather than being static

Chapter 13

Handling Your Nerves

30 seconds to 4 minutes. The magic time range during which:

❖ An audience forms their opinion of a presenter.

❖ A presenter settles down into their presentation and forgets their nerves.

❖ A researcher should be able to explain their poster to a passerby.

❖ A human resources manager spends on reading a CV that has been selected for them to assess.

❖ Job interviewers form an opinion of a candidate.

❖ Viewers will willingly watch a video on the web.

❖ A professional tea maker allows a cup of green tea to brew.

❖ The red wine in Tolkein's Middle Earth makes its drinker drunk.

❖ The average person spends on a trip to the restroom in a restaurant, cinema etc.

© Springer International Publishing Switzerland 2016
A. Wallwork, *English for Presentations at International Conferences*,
English for Academic Research, DOI 10.1007/978-3-319-26330-4_13

13.1 What's the buzz?

1) Read the two statistics / findings below and answer these questions.

- Do you get more nervous before or during a presentation? Why?

- Are you fears rational?

- Make a list of things that could go wrong during a presentation. Is there nothing you can do about them?

- Can you 'control' your English?

Statistic 1: Although 90% of your nervousness is not actually visible to the audience, if you feel confident rather than nervous this will have a huge impact on the success of you presentation.

Statistic 2: Surveys of the general public, college students, employees in the workplace, and CEOs of Fortune 500 companies have found that what Americans fear most is public speaking.

****

Many times during my presentations courses students have said:

1. I get very nervous when I am in front of a lot of people, so there's nothing I can really do about it ...

2. I am worried that the audience won't understand my accent ...

3. My English grammar and vocabulary are very poor, but if I was doing the presentation in my own language ...

4. My results aren't very interesting so I can hardly create a good presentation around them ...

5. I panic at the idea that I might forget what I want to say ...

Handling your nerves generally comes with practice—the more presentations you do, the less nervous you will become. Sections 13.2-13.6 address the five points above.

Other chapters and sections in this book should also help you to reduce to level of anxiety, as outlined on the next page.

If you have a written version of your speech (Chapter 3) that you can print and use as notes to refer to during the presentation (or upload onto your phone - 13.6 and 15.1), this will help you not to forget what you want to say.

If you know your slides are good (Chapters 4 and 5), this will help you overcome some of your fears. Then during the actual presentation, when you get a good reaction to your slides and to what you say, this will automatically give you extra confidence.

Chapter 15 suggests ways to rehearse your presentation. If you have practised several times, you will feel much more confident and thus less nervous.

In 16.13 you will learn that if you are particularly shy then you can exploit opportunities in your social life to become the center of attention in a conversation.

If you are extremely worried about doing a presentation in English, then you could opt for a poster session (Chapter 18).

13.2   Standing up in public

Few people enjoy standing up in public. But when you have done it a few times, you will actually begin to enjoy it.

If you are very shy then you may be able to overcome using a combination of the following strategies:

- offer to do teaching work at your department or institute. Teaching experience is excellent training for presentations because you have to learn to explain things clearly and engage your students. Also, as a teacher you will naturally be at the center of attention and this will help you to get used to it

- practise presenting in low-risk situations, for example in front of undergraduate students at your department and at national (rather than international) conferences. Presenting in your own language will certainly help you to get the skills you need for presenting in English.

- put yourself at the center of attention in social situations. For example if you typically remain silent while eating with friends, then try to introduce topics of conversation yourself. You can practise these beforehand (both in your own language, or in English when you are at the social dinner at a conference)

- in your free time join a dance, acting, singing club - or any club where you will have to perform in front of others

- if you live in an a tourist area, then try to strike up conversations with foreign passengers on trains and buses - this is also an excellent way to practise your English

- practise yoga and other relaxation techniques that you can do immediately before your presentation

In any case, although you may not be a born presenter, you will probably have an above average knowledge and considerable experience in your field, plus a passion for your research. Try to use these qualities to give yourself confidence and to show the audience that you know what you are talking about even if your English is not perfect. Focus on what makes you unique: your nationality, your background, your specialist knowledge.

A good presentation requires many skills that can only be learned over time. If in the past you did a bad presentation very probably it was because you had not prepared sufficiently. When you then have to do your second presentation you will have that bad memory of the first. It is important to put that bad experience behind you. Do not let it condition you. Concentrate on getting it right the second time by preparing good content and then practicing it in front of as many people as you can.

13.3   Dealing with your English accent and grammar

To learn how to deal with your accent, see Chapter 14 Pronunciation and Intonation.

If your content makes your message clear, a few mistakes in your English (both accent and grammar) will make no difference. The audience is made up of scientists wanting to hear your results, they are not English teachers wanting to assess your linguistic proficiency. The way you relate to the audience and involve them is more important than any grammatical or nontechnical vocabulary mistakes that you may make.

If you don't have the time and/or money to write a speech and have it revised, then try to make your English as perfect as possible:

- in the introduction

- while explaining the agenda

- when making transitions from one series of slides to another series

- in the conclusions

- when calling for questions

These are the points when the audience will notice the mistakes the most and when they are forming their first and last impression of you, i.e., the impressions that will remain with them after the presentation.

If you make an English mistake while doing your presentation

• don't worry (the audience may not even notice)

• don't correct yourself—this draws attention to the mistake and interrupts your train of thought

13.4   Presenting negative or 'uninteresting' results

First you need to understand if your results really are 'negative'. If they were unexpected, then you can tell the audience the story behind your research, what your expectations were at the beginning and how things did not turn out as planned. This 'story' in itself is interesting for the audience, especially if you use a narrative / story-telling format (watch Ted to see how many presenters adopt this technique.

Remember above all that negative results help to promote advances in science (see 9.8 and 9.9). In addition, you can use your 'negative' results to attract collaboration from members of the audience who may be working on a similar (or totally different) area and have ideas that might be useful for you.

What exactly is an 'uninteresting' result? If it's a negative result, then you can do as suggested in the paragraph above. If by 'uninteresting' you think the audience will actually get bored and stop listening, then you have to work hard to turn such results into something interesting. I suggest you enlist the support of your colleagues in this task. You absolutely cannot tell something to the audience that you suspect might be of no interest.

13.5   Handling nerves during the Q&A session

I recently received this email in Italian from an Italian PhD student of mine, Stefania Manetti.

My English is not good. I am used to writing, but not speaking. I can survive giving a presentation because I have time to write and prepare what I am going to say - I've got time to reflect. But when it comes to the Q&A season, I get blocked and can't even speak. At a recent conference, I sometimes managed to understand the questions, but even then I couldn't answer them. This gave the impression that aside from the presentation in itself, I wasn't prepared to deal with any questions concerning my research. At a meeting, where there were both Italian and English speakers present, I was able to understand the questions, but couldn't answer them in English, only in Italian - I was the only person to do this, and I felt ashamed.

I have another meeting on Wednesday, what can I do?

This was my answer to Stefania:

Between now and Wednesday, you should think of all the possible questions that you might be asked at the meeting. Brainstorm the answers to these questions with your colleagues.

Translate the questions (and all the possible varieties of the same question) into English. Then write down the answers.

At the beginning of the meeting make an informal announcement saying that you find rapid spoken English difficult to understand and ask if people could kindly address questions to you slowly and clearly. This might encourage the questioners to be a little more sympathetic towards you.

These approaches should help a lot as a temporary measure, though you do need to have the courage to admit to the audience that you have problems with understanding.

In the long term you need to discover ways to get over this psychological block (it is not a problem with your English, I saw how you were in class). Maybe you could do 1-1 English lessons, but really you need to gain experience in having people's attention focus on you - acting and dancing classes are a good help for this.

I don't have a miracle cure for you, I am sorry, but there are concrete things you can do and you are certainly not the first person to have this problem.

A week later Stefania wrote back to me saying that my short-term solution had worked well, and that she was now going to work on the long-term goals which she believed would help her in life in general, not just for her academic career.

For more on successfully handling your fears at the Q&A session, see Chapter 11.2. To learn how to become more at ease when you are the center of attention see 16.13.

13.6   Prepare for forgetting what you want to say

A frequent problem is forgetting a specific word or phrase that you need to say.

There are three good solutions for this; you can

- look at your notes (either written or on your phone - see also 15.2)

- drink some water, or take out a handkerchief to wipe your nose, and use this time to remind yourself

- say *"I am sorry I can't think of the word. In any case..."* And then you simply proceed with the next point

You may not consider exploiting your smartphone at an international conference to be professional. However, I guarantee that soon it will become common practise and seen as being no different to referring to paper notes in your hand.

The main advantage, apart from the two freedoms outlined above, is that it will boost your confidence.

I have noticed that most of my students who use their smartphones for presenting actually only use them to change slides. However, they know that if they want, they CAN take a quick look at their notes / script to remind themselves of where they are. This fact of being able to look massively increases your confidence - you know you can if you want to, but strangely you don't actually need to!

13.7   Get to know your potential audience at the bar and social dinners

Talk to as many people as you can over coffee breaks and meals. Knowing in advance who is coming to your talk may make you feel more relaxed as they will be friendly faces in the audience.

If the audience has met you before you begin your presentation they will also proba-bly be more motivated to listen to you. In any case, remember that at the beginning of your presentation the audience will be on your side—they will want you to succeed.

Talking to as many people as possible should also enable you to assess their knowl-edge of your topic and also to convince them to come and watch you rather than attend a parallel session.

To learn how to network and socialize, see Chapters 16 and 17.

13.8 Check out the room where your presentation will be

It is a good idea to familiarize yourself with the room where you are going to be doing the presentation. Try to imagine yourself in the room doing your presentation. Then think/find out about

- how loud you will have to speak given the size of the room and how far you are from the audience

- whether you will need a microphone

- where you will position yourself so that the audience can always see you and so that you don't trip over any wires

- how the remote control works e.g., how you can blank the screen without turning the projector off (the button is generally called "blank", "hide", "mute" or "no show"); and how effective the laser pointer is

- where chalk and pens are available for the blackboard/whiteboard

- whether bottles/cups of water will be provided

13.9 Do some physical exercises immediately before your presentation

As you know from taking exams, being slightly nervous actually helps you to perform better. If you are too relaxed you become overconfident. Don't worry about your nerves, they will soon disappear a couple of minutes into the presentation.

Make sure you sleep well the night before. Don't stay up all night rewriting your slides. You should arrive at the presentation feeling fresh, not tired. If you feel stiff and rigid at the beginning of a presentation you may need to learn some relaxation techniques.

Do some physical exercises before you begin:

- breathe in deeply

- relax/warm your neck and shoulder muscles

- exercise your jaw

Another form of breathing exercise is to practice making the phrases you use in your presentation shorter and shorter. Short phrases give you time to pause quickly and to breathe between one phrase and the next—this will slow your speed down if you are nervous.

Chapter 14

Pronunciation and Intonation

Factoids

84% of English words are spelled (and pronounced) according to a regular pattern. Only 3% have a completely unpredictable pronunciation (e.g. *one, two, Wednesday, February, thought*). Unfortunately those 3% are among the most frequent used in the language.

*****

A survey conducted in the 1920s in the US found that only 1 in 100,000 Americans could pronounce all ten of the following words correctly: *data, gratis, culinary, cocaine, gondola, version, impious, chic, Caribbean, Viking*.

*****

A professor at Cambridge University once declared: 'I hold firmly to the belief … that no-one can tell how to pronounce an English word unless he has at some time or other heard it.'

*****

Research has found that people tend to hear only about 50 per cent of what is said to them and retain about 10 per cent of that. … Frequently, more important than the words themselves is how you say them and what you do while saying them.

*****

In 2004 it was reported that some parents in South Korea were forcing their children to have painful tongue surgery in order to give them perfect pronunciation, for example to enable them to pronounce 'l' and 'r' sounds. Cha Kyoung-ae, an English professor at a Seoul university, said: "English is now becoming a means of survival. Entering a college, getting jobs and getting promoted – many things hinge heavily on your mastery of English. The surgery may be an extreme case, but it reflects a social phenomenon."

© Springer International Publishing Switzerland 2016
A. Wallwork, *English for Presentations at International Conferences*,
English for Academic Research, DOI 10.1007/978-3-319-26330-4_14

14.1 What's the buzz?

Think about these questions:

1. Are there some regional accents in your country that you find difficult to understand? Are you acutely embarrassed when you don't understand such speakers? Why (not)?

2. Do you think that speakers of British English sometimes watch US DVDs with subtitles, and vice versa? Do you think the British and North Americans feel stupid when they don't understand each other?

3. The following words have two possible pronunciations, do you know what they are? *contribute, innovative, kilometer, either*

4. Do you know the difference in British and US pronunciation of the following words: *address, adult, detail, frustrated, router, twenty*?

5. What conclusions can you draw from your answers to questions 1-4? How important is it in an international conference to have perfect English pronunciation?

6. What are the typical pronunciation problems in English of speakers of your native language? How can you try to avoid them?

****

In her book *Second Language Learning and Language Teaching*, Vivian Cook writes that an English teacher's aim is not *to produce imitation native speakers, with the sole exception of those training to be spies.*

No one is going to kill you if you cannot pronounce a word correctly: times have changed since the situation over 2000 years ago:

> The Gileadites captured the fords of the Jordon leading to Ephraim, and whenever a survivor of Ephraim said, "Let me cross over," the men of Gilead asked him, "Are you an Ephraimite?" If he replied, "No," they said, "All right, say 'Shibboleth.'" If he said, "Sibboleth," because he could not pronounce the word correctly, they seized him and killed him at the fords of the Jordon. Forty-two thousand Ephraimites were killed at that time. (The Holy Bible, Old Testament, Judges 12.5-6)

However if you do have a very strong accent or particularly poor pronunciation, this could have a negative impact on your audience's ability to understand you. This chapter is designed to help you improve your pronunciation and teach you a few tricks for dealing with the difficulties you may have.

14.2 English has an irregular system of pronunciation

English has a very irregular pronunciation system as highlighted in the table below.

PRONUNCIATION INCONSISTENCY	EXAMPLES
same spelling, different pronunciation	*live /laiv/ as in a live concert; live /liv/ as in I live in London; read, lead, wind*
different spelling, same pronunciation	*would = wood; where = wear = ware; hole = whole; scene = seen*
different spelling of final syllable, same pronunciation	*manage, fridge, sandwich; foreign, kitchen, mountain*
same spelling of vowel sound, different pronunciation	*were / here, cut / put, chose / whose, one / phone*

In addition to the above, there are also many words with silent letters: We(d)n(e)sday, bus(i)ness, dou(b)t, comf(or)table. The silent also letters vary from English speaker to English speaker, so twen(t)y is common in Essex (England) and many parts of the US.

14.3 Dealing with your accent and pronunciation

Your pronunciation only has to be good during the presentation. You are not going to be able to eradicate your accent, all you need to do is focus on pronouncing clearly the words that you need in the presentation itself. These words you should be able to pronounce reasonably well. 'Reasonably' means a close approximation, preferably enunciated slowly and clearly, so that even if it is not 'standard' it is at least comprehensible.

This is fundamental because if the audience cannot understand you, they will have great difficulty in following your presentation.

Don't panic! There are many fantastic presentations given on TED by presenters with a poor English accent (and poor grammar). A great example is the French designer, Philippe Starck, who begins his TED presentation by saying: *You will understand nothing with my type of English* - see 2.9.

A typical ten-minute presentation includes between 300 and 450 different words (depending on the incidence of technical terms and how fast the presenter speaks). The number of different words in 15 or 20-minute presentations does not usually rise by more than 10–20 words compared to a shorter presentation, since most of the key words tend to be introduced in the first ten minutes.

Of these different words, the majority are words that you will certainly be already very familiar with: pronouns, prepositions, adverbs, conjunctions, articles, and common verbs. From my experience in teaching PhD students to do presentations, the average person may need to use between 10 and 20 words that might create difficulty in pronunciation. And learning the correct pronunciation for such a limited number of words is not difficult.

You can identify possible problems with your English if you write a script - see Chapter 3.

14.4 Use online resources to check your pronunciation

Write out your entire speech as suggested in Chapter 3 and then upload it into Google Translate (where you can use the listening feature), ivona.com or Odd Cast (http://oddcast.com/home/demos/tts/tts_example.php). Ivona and Oddcast are good fun because you can also choose the sex and accent (e.g. British, US, Indian) of the speaker. The pronunciation and stress of the automatic reader of these two free applications is accurate in most cases. But not all cases.

If you have any doubts, consult with an online speaking dictionary, which will clearly indicate where the stress should be. You can try howjsay.com, which even gives alternative versions of some words e.g. *innovative* and *innovative*, both of which are now considered correct (note: *innovative*, which is typical of many non-native speakers, is completely wrong and is not given as an option).

Here are some useful online dictionaries:

howjsay.com

wordreference.com

learnersdictionary.com

oxfordlearnersdictionaries.com

dictionary.cambridge.org

By using such online resources you can:

* note down where the stress falls on multi-syllable words (e.g. *control* not *control*)

* listen for vowel sounds, and learn for example that *bird* rhymes with *word* and so has a different sound from *beard*

- understand which words you cannot pronounce. This means that you can find synonyms for non-key words and thus replace words that are difficult to pronounce with words that are easier. For example, you can replace

  ° a multi-syllable word like *innovative* with a monosyllable word like *new*

  ° a word with a difficult consonant sound like *usually* or ***thesis***, with a word that does not contain that sound *often, paper*

  ° a word with a difficult vowel sound like *worldwide* with a word that has an easier vowel sound like *globally*

- make a list of words that you find difficult to pronounce but which you cannot replace with other words, typically because they are key technical words

- understand which sentences are too long or would be difficult for you to say

The sounds you have in your own language will certainly influence the sounds that you can and cannot produce in English.

To find out the English sounds that people of your language have difficulty with you can do an Internet search: "name of your language + English pronunciation + typical mistakes." If possible, find a site that (1) lists the typical sounds, (2) has audio (so that you can hear the sounds), and (3) illustrates the shape that your lips and tongue need to make to produce the relevant sound. If you don't have your lips and tongue in the right position it will be impossible for you to reproduce the correct sound.

14.5 Practise your pronunciation by following transcripts and imitating the speaker

An excellent way to learn the correct pronunciation of words is to use transcripts of oral presentations. Many news and education corporations (e.g. bbc.co.uk and ted.com) have podcasts on their websites, with subtitles in English and / or a transcript. You can thus hear someone speaking and read their exact words in the transcript. You could practise reading the transcript yourself with the volume off. This will motivate you more strongly to listen to the correct pronunciation when you turn the volume back on.

In addition you can learn how to pronounce some phrases that are typically used in a presentation by going to: www.bbc.co.uk/worldservice/learningenglish/business/talkingbusiness/

14.6   Don't speak too fast or too much, and vary your tone of voice

If you speak too fast, particularly when you are nervous, it makes it difficult for the audience to absorb what you are saying. And the impression may be that if you are presenting information very fast then it is not particularly important.

Make sure you pause frequently – do not talk continuously. Stop talking for between one and three seconds not only between slides, but also when giving explanations. The audience needs to have time to absorb what you are telling them, and they need a rest from hearing your voice.

If the sound of your voice never changes or you have a very repetitive intonation (e.g., at the end of each phrase your voice goes up unnaturally or is significantly reduced in volume), the audience will lose essential clues for understanding what you are saying and sooner or later they will go to sleep. You need to vary your

SPEED	how fast you say the words. Slow down to emphasize a particular or difficult point. Speed up when what you are saying is probably familiar to the audience or will be easy for them to grasp.
VOLUME	how loud or soft you say the words—never drop your voice at the end of a sentence
PITCH	how high or low a sound is
TONE	a combination of pitch and the feeling that your voice gives

You can vary these four factors to show the audience what is important about what you are saying. You can create variety in your voice by

- imagining that your audience is blind or that there is a curtain between them and you—you are totally dependent on your voice to communicate energy and feeling

- listening to people who have interesting voices and analyzing what makes them interesting

- recording yourself and listening to your voice critically

Remember that if you don't sound interested in what you are saying, the audience will not be interested either.

Presentations expert Jeffrey Jacobi, in his book *How to Say It - Persuasive Presentations,* recommends reading texts aloud that express strong opinions or are full of colorful language; for example: letters to the editor (of newspapers), children's stories, and advertisements. Initially, you can practice in your own language and then move on to English.

Another way is to practice your presentation using different types of voice and mood: angry, happy, sarcastic, and authoritative.

14.7   Use stress to highlight the key words

English is a stress-timed language. The way you stress words should help to distinguish the non-essential (said more quickly and with no particular stress) from the important (said more slowly, with stress on key words).

Stress also indicates the meaning you want to give. Try saying the following sentences putting the stress on the words in italics.

Please *present* your paper next week. (present rather than write)

Please present *your* paper next week. (your paper not mine)

Please present your *paper* next week. (paper not report)

Please present your paper *next* week. (not this week)

Please present your paper next *week.* (not next month)

Although the sentence is exactly the same, you can change the meaning by stressing different words. And the stress helps the listener to understand what is important and what isn't.

When you stress a word in a sentence you:

- say the word more slowly than the ones before and the ones after

- raise the volume of your voice a little

- may decide to give your voice a slightly different tone or quality

Never put the stress on alternate words or always at the end or beginning of a sentence.

14.8 Be very careful of English technical words that also exist in your language

A lot of English words have been adopted into other languages, often with different meanings but also with different pronunciations. Here are some English technical words and acronyms that are also found in many other languages: *hardware; back up, log in; PC, CD, DVD.*

Note that

- words that are made up of two words have the stress in English on the first syllable: *hardware, supermarket, mobile phone*

- words whose second part is a preposition also have the stress on the first syllable: *back up, log in*

- letters in acronyms have equal stress: *P-C, C-D, D-V-D*

It is a good idea to say the key words and English technical words more slowly.

Give equal stress and time to each letter in an acronym. Remember that an acronym such as IAE is very difficult to understand because it contains three vowels, and vowels (and consonants too) tend to be pronounced differently in different languages. If you use acronyms in your presentation it is best to have them written on your slides too.

14.9 Practise *-ed* endings

When you add -ed to form the past forms of a verb, you do not add an extra syllable. For example the verbs *focused, followed, informed* are NOT pronounced *focus sed/ follow wed/inform med.* The number of syllables of a verb in its infinitive form (*fo cus*) and in its past form (*fo cust*) is the same. The only exceptions are verbs whose infinitive form ends in -d or -t, for example *added, painted*, which are pronounced *add did* and *paint tid*.

14.10   Enunciate numbers very clearly

You can help your audience by writing important numbers directly onto your slides. Also, remember to distinguish clearly between 13 and 30, 14 and 40, etc. Note where the stress is: *thirteen thirty*. Make sure you enunciate clearly the *n* in *thirteen, fourteen* etc.

14.11   Avoid *er, erm, ah*

In order not to distract the audience, try hard not to make any nonverbal noises between words and phrases. You can stop yourself from saying "er" if you

- avoid using words like *and, but, also, however, which,* and *that* because your tendency is probably to say "er" every time you use them (e.g., *and er then er I did the tests but er this er also meant that er ..*)

- speak in short sentences

- pause/breathe instead of saying "er"

In any case if you practice frequently you will know exactly what you want to say, so you will not have to pause to think. Consequently there will be no gaps between one word or phrase and another, and thus no need to say "er."

You may not be aware that you make these noises. To check if you do, record yourself delivering the presentation.

14.12   Practise with a native speaker

When you have practised, ask a native speaker to listen to you giving your presentation and write down every word that you pronounce incorrectly, and then teach you the correct pronunciation. This may be expensive (if you do this with a professional English teacher) and time consuming, but is very useful.

Chapter 15

Rehearsing and Self-Assessment

Factoids

In a paper entitled *Unskilled and Unaware of It: How Difficulties in Recognizing One's Own Incompetence Lead to Inflated Self-Assessments*, the authors cite the case of McArthur Wheeler who 'walked into two Pittsburgh banks and robbed them in broad daylight, with no visible attempt at disguise. He was arrested later that night less than an hour after videotapes of him taken from surveillance cameras were broadcast on the 11 o'clock news. When police later showed him the surveillance tapes, Mr. Wheeler stared in incredulity. "But I wore the juice" he mumbled. Apparently, Mr. Wheeler was under the impression that rubbing one's face with lemon juice rendered it invisible to videotape cameras'. This effect is now known as the Dunning-Kruger effect after the authors of the study. The story was originally quoted by Michael A. Fuoco in the Pittsburgh Post-Gazette under the headline: *Trial and error: They had larceny in their hearts, but little in their heads.*

******

According to an article published in the Washington Post on 17 April 2000, twenty million Americans believe they have been abducted by aliens.

******

In one of former US president George W Bush's speeches on education, available on YouTube, he said: "Rarely is the question asked, is our children learning?"

******

A National Geographic Literacy Survey testing the ability of US citizens aged 18-24 to find certain countries on a world map gave the following results: Afghanistan (83% could not locate the country), the UK (69%), Japan (58%), the US (11%).

© Springer International Publishing Switzerland 2016
A. Wallwork, *English for Presentations at International Conferences*,
English for Academic Research, DOI 10.1007/978-3-319-26330-4_15

15.1 What's the buzz?

1) Make a checklist of five things you need to do or check when you are rehearsing your presentation.

2) Think about the following.

   • What are your weak points? Are you blind to them like Wheeler in the first factoid? Do you think your colleagues would recognize these weak points in you?

   • What typical weak points do your colleagues have? Do you think they would agree with your assessment?

   • If you were with a group of colleagues and you were assessing the presentation of another colleague, do you think as a group you would be fairly unanimous in your assessment?

3) Watch a colleague's presentation or find one on TED (Chapter 2). Decide if their slides were

   • specifically designed to help the audience understand the topic

   • simply prompts for the presenter so that he/she wouldn't forget what to say next

The main task of your slides should to be fulfill point (a), but at the same time to fulfill point (b).

****

I have watched several thousand PhD students and researchers deliver their presentations.

Most of these students don't have a clear idea of what their weak points are. Many tend to focus too much on their English ("*I make a lot of grammar and vocabulary mistakes*"), or on their nerves.

In reality their problems tend not to be language-related, and frequently have nothing to do with their nerves. For example, they fail to notice that:

• they spent much of the presentation with their back to the audience

• when they were actually facing the audience, they weren't looking at them directly, but either above the audience's heads or towards the ground

- there was too much text in their slides

- that they made distracting *um* or *er* sounds between one slide and another

- they showed no enthusiasm

- etc (see 1.4 for a list of other typical defects)

In summary, we are often unable to assess our own weaknesses (and strengths!).

However, although we are unable to recognize our own defects, we are very profi-cient at recognizing those in others. And generally speaking, most people tend to agree on what constitute the defects in another person's presentation.

Moral of the story:

- it is very hard to judge the failings (and merits) of your own presentation

- before doing a presentation at a conference, you should always present in front of your colleagues and ask for their feedback

This chapter suggests what to look out for while you are rehearsing. It then proposes ways to get others to assess your performance, plus means to self-evaluate.

15.2   Use your notes (upload them onto your phone)

If you have prepared a script, as suggested in Chapter 3, then your initial practice could simply be to read your script aloud so that you become familiar with what you want to say. Then, abandon your script completely and just use notes.

As you practice, if any phrase or word does not come easily to you, try to modify it until what you want to say comes quickly and naturally.

Finally, put your notes on a table, and try doing the presentation aloud without look-ing at your notes. Of course, if you forget what to say, then quickly look at your notes.

Even the best presenters make use of notes on the day of their presentation—it is standard practice and no one will think it is unprofessional if you occasionally look down to remember what you want to say. For an example of a presentation on TED where the speaker refers to his notes, see Jay Walker's talk entitled 'English Mania'. Jay's speech is also a great example of how to talking in short sentences helps both the presenter to remember what to say and the audience to follow the presentation (19.5).

As an alternative to using written notes, I strongly recommend you upload your presentation onto your phone (13.6) so that you can see both the slides AND your script.

There are several apps that allow you to control your slides from your phone via Bluetooth. This means that you are free to

1. walk around - you don't have to stand (or worse) sit in front of your laptop
2. glance at your smartphone and read from your script / notes

I have stressed more than once in this book that although you may think that holding your phone during your presentation is not an 'acceptable' practice it is nevertheless becoming increasingly common … simply because it is such a great method for:

• moving from slide to slide

• pointing at particular elements in a graph or table (i.e. like the pointer in a remote control device)

• enabling you to check what you want to say by looking at your script or notes

In my view there is nothing unprofessional about using a device that helps you to deliver a professional presentation in the most effective manner possible.

15.3   Vary the parts you practice

Given time constraints, people often manage only to practice part of their presentation at a single time. The result may be that you only practice the first half of your presentation. So it is a good idea to occasionally begin in the middle, or begin with the conclusions—don't just focus on the technical part. Also, don't forget to practice answering questions—imagine the question, and then answer it in various ways (including imagining that you didn't understand the question).

In any case, practice the opening and the ending again and again and again. These are the two parts of the presentation where you should not improvise, and where it helps considerably if you know exactly what you are going to say. First and last impressions are the ones that remain with the audience.

15.4   Practice your position relative to the screen

Try to reproduce the real conditions of the conference room. So if you are practicing with colleagues don't stand right next to them, but at a distance. Use a desk as a podium, and imagine the screen is behind you. Think about the best place to stand.

If you stand in front of the screen, the beam will light you up and the audience won't really be able to see you. One solution is simply to turn the screen off (using the B key on PowerPoint).

To avoid blocking your slides from the audience's view, stand to one side of the screen. Only move in front of it when it is strictly necessary to point to things on your slides.

Note that if you stand on the left side of the screen, you will probably focus just on those members of the audience on the right-hand side (and vice versa). So you need to keep swapping sides.

Make sure you make eye contact with everyone including those at the back. If you don't give certain sections of the audience regular eye contact, they will start to lose interest.

You can practice this by yourself at home. Stand at one end of the biggest room of your house. Imagine that the items of furniture (chairs, tables, desks, shelves, even windows) in various parts of the room are members of the audience. Practice talking to each item. Spend no more than three seconds on each item of furniture, then move on to another item.

Avoid focusing on a single individual in the audience for more than two seconds, otherwise this individual will feel uneasy.

It also helps if you can project your slides onto a wall. This will help you become familiar with learning not to look at your slides, but at the audience. Of course, if you only have a minimal number of slides that you don't really need to look at (because they are so simple or easy for you to remember) then you will have less temptation to look behind you. In any case, you should be able to deliver your first 60 seconds without looking behind you at the screen, or at your laptop or at your notes.

15.5 Don't sit. Stand and move around

It is a good idea not to sit and talk into the laptop. When you are sitting your voice does not project as well.

You can also make better eye contact with people further back simply by leaving the podium and moving around the room. This will also help you feel more relaxed. It is also an excellent way of gaining the audience's attention, rather than the screen being their focus of attention. But make sure there are no wires in your path as you may trip over them.

If you move in a relaxed, but not repetitive, manner in front of the audience, it will give them the impression that you are at ease and comfortable in the presentation environment. And by implication your ease will make the audience think you are confident about your presentation itself.

Standing in a different position once every two or three minutes will also help you to remember not to focus on just one section of the audience.

15.6 Use your hands

Do whatever comes most naturally to you with your hands and arms. Inexperienced presenters often begin by rigidly holding their arms to their sides, or folding them across their chest. Such positions tend to make the audience feel that you are nervous or maybe a bit hostile. So try and move your hands around as soon into the presentation as possible. A perfect point to do this is in your outline, where you can use your right hand to touch the fingers of your left hand to indicate your three/four main points. For instance, by saying *"first I want to, second ... third."*

Some people find it helps them overcome their nervousness by holding something in their hands, for instance the remote control, a pointer, or a pen. Try only to do this for a few minutes, as it stops you making full use of your hands.

Others find they are more relaxed with their hands in their pockets, but this may make the audience feel that the presenter is not very professional.

In any case, avoid things that may be distracting for the audience such as playing with your ring or scratching any part of your body.

Many good presenters use their hands to add extra emphasis to what they are saying. However, if for cultural reasons you feel that using your hands would be a sign of disrespect or lack of professionalism for the majority of the audience, then do what feels comfortable for you.

15.7   Have an expressive face and smile

If you show interest through your facial expression then the audience will feel it and will themselves become more enthusiastic about what you are saying.

If you just have a blank expression, then you will not transmit any positive feelings to your audience.

The only way that you can show genuine enthusiasm is to feel it. This means that you need to identify areas of your research (or even of your life as a researcher, or about your country or town) which you truly find special, which you think the audience will find interesting, and which you can talk about with passion.

You can practice smiling in front of a mirror, and if you smiling doesn't come naturally to you then you can even attend smiling courses in the USA and the UK! But if you find it difficult to smile, don't worry, you can replace a smile with a passionate delivery and the occasional forceful hand gesture.

15.8   Organize your time

Presentations rarely go according to plan. So allow for

* the previous presenter going over his/her allocated time, meaning that you have less time to do your preparation

* people arriving late

Prepare for this by

* knowing exactly how much time you need for each part of your presentation

* having your most important points near the beginning of the presentation, never just in the second half

* thinking in advance what slides you could cut, particularly those in the latter part of the presentation (see 15.9)

* planning how to reduce the amount you say for particular slides (see 15.9)

* using options in your presentation software that allow you to skip slides

Sometimes during a presentation you are so focused that you can't even remember at what time the presentation is supposed to end (particularly if times have been changed from the original schedule). Write down the finishing time on a piece of paper and have the paper beside your laptop. You should also have your watch beside your laptop—although your laptop has its own clock, seeing your watch on the desk will remind you to check the time.

If you do run out of time don't suddenly say "*I will have stop here.*" Instead, briefly make a conclusion.

If you are ahead of schedule you can have a longer Q&A session at the end of the presentation. In any case, don't feel that you have to fill the amount of time you have been allocated. No one is going to complain if you finish a few minutes early. But they may complain if you go over your allotted time slot.

15.9   Cut redundant slides (but not interesting ones), simplify complicated slides

Once you have practised your presentation a few times (either by yourself or in front of colleagues) you should be able to identify any slides or parts of your speech that

- could be cut

- need to be simplified

The main aim of a presentation is to arouse an audience's curiosity and to stimulate their desire for more information. It is like the trailer to a movie – you only see (hear) the highlights. This then stimulates your desire to watch the whole movie to get the complete picture, or in the case of a presentation to read the relevant paper/documentation, to buy the product, to read the manual.

You will certainly know much more about the topic than your audience needs to know. What comes out of your mouth should only be 10% of the iceberg. The other 90% should remain firmly in your head. So decide which points are *absolutely* essential to include.

Imagine that the length of your allocated time for the presentation was reduced from 60 minutes to 40 minutes. Decide which points

- the audience might already know or not be interested in

- you have included simply because you think you SHOULD include them, because you think it is more professional to cover everything or because you think by putting them in you will make a good impression on your boss

- you could put in the handout as extra information without affecting the main logical argument of your presentation (the audience might prefer to read the details at their own leisure and at their own speed)

- have you included simply because you yourself find them interesting but they are in fact not particularly relevant?

- could be grouped together under one category so that they could be covered together and more quickly?

Would your presentation not succeed as a result? Or would it actually be clearer and more dynamic?

15.10   Prepare for the software or the equipment breaking down

Your presentation will probably be uploaded for you onto the conference PC. Test that everything works correctly as much time in advance of your presentation as possible. This is important as there are different software versions and sometimes incompatibilities between Macs and PCs (particularly regarding animations).

Some of the most successful presentations are done with no slides. If you have a printout of your slides and your computer breaks down completely then you can continue without the slides, and if necessary draw graphs on a whiteboard.

In any case, it is a very good idea to practice for such a breakdown, i.e., to give your presentation without any slides. It will teach you two things: (1) it is possible to do a presentation with no slides (2) it will show you which of your slides are probably redundant.

15.11   Make a video recording of yourself

Getting detailed and objective feedback from your colleagues is difficult unless you adopt the form-filling procedure outlined in the next subsection (15.12). If you are reluctant or too embarrassed to ask for such feedback, then one solution is to video yourself (you can use your phone to do this).

When your replay the video, check that you do:

• not look at the screen, ceiling or floor instead of making eye contact with the audience

• not make hand gestures that might be considered irritating, repetitive or inappropriate

• not inadvertently touch inappropriate parts of your body

• not make distracting sounds: *um, erm, er* etc

15.12   Learn how to be self-critical: practice with colleagues

Learning to be able to evaluate your own presentation and your presentation skills is key to giving an effective scientific talk.

If you are going to a conference with a group of colleagues, this is a perfect opportunity to practice beforehand by doing your presentations in front of each other. If you ask your colleagues *"How did I do?"* or *"What do you think?"* they will probably just give you some vague encouraging comment. Instead it helps to have a check list with which to assess each other.

Bear in mind that the things you find ineffective in your colleagues' presentations may be exactly the same kind of mistakes you make, so you can certainly learn from other people's errors.

On the next page are some points that you may find useful to include.

	Assessment Sheet
STRUCTURE	• Strong beginning - topic introduced clearly
	• Overall topic previewed
	• Clear transitions and links between points
	• Clear conclusions and strong ending
SLIDES	• Clear text
	• Simple diagrams
	• Not too much detail
	• No distracting colors, fonts, animations
BODY LANGUAGE	• Eyes on audience not on screen
	• Moved around
	• Used hands appropriately
VOICE / DELIVERY	• Right speed - did not begin in a rush
	• Clear and loud voice
	• Short clear phrases, individual words articulated clearly
	• No annoying noises (er, erm, um)
	• Good pronunciation
	• Enthusiastic and friendly
	• Sounded credible
AUDIENCE INVOLVEMENT	• Attention of audience immediately gained
	• Topic clearly related to audience
	• Audience personally involved in some way
	• Variety to maintain attention

Ideally, you should do your presentation twice. In one of the two sessions, your audience should stop you every time you

• say a word they cannot understand—this enables you to understand which words you need to practice pronouncing or simply replace with a synonym

• look at the screen or your laptop instead of them

Practising with your colleagues who are also attending the same conference has another advantage: they will know what to expect from you. This means that when you see them sitting in the audience at the conference you know that they are going to react positively and give you encouragement. If they haven't seen your presentation before, you may be unsure of their response and this may make you lose confidence.

15.13   Get colleagues to assess the value of your slides

After you have practice your presentation with colleagues, ask them what slides you could cut and which slides they found complicated to understand.

You could ask them to classify each point in your presentation as follows:

A: absolutely essential

B: important

C: include only if time permits

Your aim is to focus only on what the audience want/need to hear so you don't need to include things simply because you think you SHOULD include them; for example, because you think it is more professional to cover everything or because you think by putting them in you will make a good impression on your boss.

15.14   Email your presentation to your professor
and colleagues

Make sure that your boss and colleagues see your presentation or demo before you actually deliver it in front of your client. The solution is to email him/her the presentation beforehand so that they will then know what to expect. What you don't want is your boss putting their hands in their hair in despair or your colleagues looking confused. However, your boss is likely to be busy and probably won't read the presentation. Instead just say 'Here is my presentation. Could you just check slide 20 as I am not sure how the audience will react'.

This is a good strategy if you are not sure, for example, whether:

- a graph or figure will be clear to the audience

- you have written too much text (or not enough)

- a humorous slide might be inappropriate

- you have covered everything that needs to be covered

15.15   Do a final spell check on your slides

Preferably get someone who has never seen the presentation to do the spell check, you yourself will be unlikely to spot mistakes that give that we generally what we think we have written rather than what is actually written.

15.16   Improve your slides and your speech
         after the presentation

When you do your presentation live in front of a real audience it sometimes reveals faults that did not appear while you were practising. After giving your presentation, look at your slides with a critical eye and ask yourself

- why was this slide necessary? If I cut it, what would change?

- did this slide really support the objective of my presentation?

- why did I include this info? Was it relevant/interesting/clear? What impact did it have?

- could I have expressed this info in a clearer or more pertinent way?

- was this series of slides in the best order? Was there anything missing in the series?

- were these slides too similar to each other? Did they really gain the audience's attention?

After your presentation, write down the questions you were asked, so that the next time you do the same presentation you will have the answers ready.

In future conferences you may be able to use exactly the same presentation, so practicing for it will be much easier if you already have a script.

After each presentation it is worth going through the script to modify it and improve it in the light of the audience's reaction and questions. You will see where you need to add things and where to cut parts that weren't necessary, that the audience didn't understand, or which you found difficult to explain.

Chapter 16

Networking: Preparation for Social Events

Factoids

- Surveys have shown that 87% of people dread having to suffer boring conversations at social events.

- According to the EU, nearly 50% of Europeans speak English well enough to have a conversation, and nearly 70% of European managers have a good working knowledge of English.

- Topics that are acceptable for conversations between people who have just met vary considerably from culture to culture. Whereas in some Asian cultures it might be perfectly acceptable to ask someone how much they earn, in Western cultures this might be considered very impolite and embarrassing.

- Social psychologist Sidney Jourard from the University of Florida investigated how often people touch each other while having meals together in restaurants. In a restaurant in San Juan (Puerto Rico) people touched each other up to 180 times in the space of one hour, in Paris 110 times, in Gainesville (USA) twice, and in London never!

- People with more active social lives are both healthier and live longer. This is even more true, the more diverse your social relationships are.

- Around 55% of workers in the US take less than 15 minutes for lunch. The average lunch is less than 30 minutes. A fifth have no lunch at all up to five times a week.

- In the UK and North America it is considered acceptable to be no more than five minutes late for a business meeting, and up to 15 minutes for a dinner appointment.

© Springer International Publishing Switzerland 2016
A. Wallwork, *English for Presentations at International Conferences*,
English for Academic Research, DOI 10.1007/978-3-319-26330-4_16

16.1 What's the buzz?

1) Which for you is the main reason for going to a conference?

    a) to report the results of your research

    b) to learn about the state of the art

    c) to network and make new contacts for possible future collaborations

2) What skills do you need to be a good networker? Which of the skills do you already have and which do you need to develop?

3) How much more difficult is it to socialize in English rather than in your own language?

4) Have you noticed many differences in the way different nationalities communicate with each other orally? How important is it to be aware of such differences at an international conference?

****

You may find social events much more difficult to manage than work/technical-related events. When you are talking about your research, you will generally have more command over the vocabulary that you need in order to conduct a discussion. However, even in a social situation, you can shift the conversation to topics where you have greater command of English or a wider general knowledge.

In this chapter will learn the importance of networking and how to prepare for a social event at a conference.

16.2 Exploit conferences for publishing your research and for networking

Apart from being an excuse for spending a few days in an exotic location, there are many additional benefits of attending a conference. If you give a presentation or have a poster session, then you can "publicize" your results and give your readers a chance to learn something about you and your work. You will thus gain valuable visibility, and hopefully credibility too. This should give you a good opportunity to then set up new contacts and collaborations.

Those who go to conferences frequently recommend not attending too many events or going to too many presentations. The idea is not just to learn everything you can about your research topic, but to use every moment you can to network (i.e., to meet new people in the hope of setting up new collaborations). Other professors I spoke to recommended going to more marginal workshops rather than the big-name presentations. You are likely to learn more at the workshops (you can read the big name's paper by yourself at home) and will have more opportunity to participate and meet other people.

How you come across as a person both during your presentation and afterwards at the social events is often just as important as the content of the presentation itself. My own studies with PhD students have revealed that after only 10 days most people remember more about what they thought about the presenter and how he / she made them feel, than they can about what the presenter actually presented.

But even if you only attend a conference without giving any presentations, you will still have many opportunities to

- find out what the hot topics are, and what other researchers are working on, and keep up to date regarding technical progress. This is important if you are a member of an international technical working group or if you wish to set up collaborations

- get feedback on your published work

- get new ideas while listening and talking to other people

- network and meet up with old friends, colleagues, and people who until now you may have only contacted via email or telephone

You can do all these things successfully if you feel confident about talking to people in English. It will help you considerably if you have the right English phrases available. This section is designed to help you achieve those goals.

16.3 Anticipate answers to questions that people might ask you after your presentation

If you are going to a conference to give a presentation, there is always a good chance that someone will come up to you after the presentation and ask you questions or set up a meeting for later.

If you want to create a good impression and avoid possible embarrassment, it is good idea to prepare answers to as many possible questions you can think of. You should do that in advance of the conference so that you can create suitable answers in English (see 11.12).

16.4   Learn how to introduce yourself for both formal and informal occasions

Most Anglos today introduce themselves in a very simple way by saying:

> Hi, I'm James.

> Hi, I'm James Smith.

> Hello I'm James Smith.

> Good morning I am Professor Smith.

Anglos say their first name (*James*) followed, in more formal situations, by their family name (*Smith*).

If someone asks *What is your name?* you would normally reply with both first and family names.

Anglos often give their own name rather than directly asking the interlocutor for his / her name. This may take place several minutes into the conversation, particularly if the conversation appears to be worth continuing. A typical introduction is as follows:

> By the way, my name is Joe Bloggs.

> Sorry, I have not introduced myself—I'm Joe Bloggs from NASA.

> I don't think we have been introduced have we? I'm …

At this point you would be expected to reply with your name.

> Pleased to meet you. I'm Brian Smartarz.

If you didn't hear the name of the person you have just been introduced to, you can say:

> Sorry, I didn't catch your name.

> Sorry, I didn't get your name clearly. Can you spell it for me?

> Sorry, how do your pronounce your name?

Don't be reluctant to ask for a repetition of the name, otherwise you will spend the rest of the conversation looking at their name tag! Also, we all like it when people remember and use our name; we feel important and consequently we are more responsive to people who remember it.

If you are too embarrassed to ask someone to remind you of their name, then you could offer them your card and hopefully they will then give you their card. Giving someone your card also means that you immediately have something to talk about:

> Oh, I see you are from Tokyo, I was there last year.

> So you work for the Department of Linguistics, do you know Professor Kamatchi?

> So you work in Italy, but I think you are from China, is that right?

16.5 Use people's titles where appropriate

In English there is only one form of *you*. If you wish to show someone respect, then you can use their title, for example, Dr or Professor. However, many Anglos consider titles as being quite formal, and they might say: *Please call me John*. This means that from that moment on the communication can take place in a more friendly atmosphere. In other words, if you are a PhD student and you are talking to Professor Smith, you should continue to address him as Professor Smith until he suggests otherwise.

In English there are a very limited number of titles; in the academic world there are only Dr and Professor. Your country may have many other titles, for example, lawyer and engineer. Such titles are impossible to translate into English. This means that if you are for example an engineer, you should not address another engineer as Engineer Smith, but simply as Dr Smith or Professor Smith. However, in emails you might wish to address an engineer whose native language is not English using the word engineer in their language, for example, Herr Diplom Ingenieur Weber (for a German).

If you wish to give someone a title and that person is not an academic, then for men you can use *Mr* (pronounced *mister*) and for women *Ms* (pronounced *muz*, like the *cause* in *because*). *Mr* and *Ms* do not indicate whether the person is married or not. The terms *Mrs* (pronounced "misses") and *Miss* are not so commonly used nowadays as they indicate that the woman is married and unmarried, respectively—such information is not considered necessary for the interlocutor.

See Chapter 2 in *English for Academic Correspondence* to learn more about salutations in emails.

16.6 Prepare strategies for introducing yourself to a presenter after his / her presentation

After someone's presentation, you might like to ask them questions at the bar or at the social dinner. First you will probably need to attract their attention and introduce yourself.

> Excuse me, do you have a minute? Would you mind answering a few questions?

> Excuse me, do you think I could ask you a couple of questions about your presentation? Thanks. My name is ... and I work at ... I am doing some research on ... What I'd like to ask you is: ...

Other questions you might like to ask are as follows:

> Could you give me some more details about ...?

> Where can I get more information about ... ?

> Can I just ask you about something you said in your presentation?

> I'm not sure I understood your point about ... Could you clarify it for me?

> Have you uploaded your presentation? If so, where can I find it?

Many presenters are very tired immediately after doing their presentation and just want to get away and have a drink or something to eat. Also, if you are in a line with other people, the presenter will probably want to deal with each person in the line as quickly as possible.

So, when you finally get to talk to the presenter say:

> I don't want to take up your time now. But would it be possible for us to meet later this evening? I am in the same field of research as you, and I have a project that I think you might be interested in.

16.7 Learn how to introduce yourself to a group of people

To avoid having to introduce yourself into a group, you could try to arrive early at any social events. This means when you see your key person entering the room, you can go up to them immediately before they get immersed in a conversation.

If your key person is already chatting to another person or a group of people, then you need to observe their body language and how they are facing each other. If they are in a closed circle, quite close to each other and looking directly into each other's faces, it is probably best to choose another moment. However, if they are not too close, and there is space between them, then you can join them. In such cases you can say:

Do you mind if I join you?

I don't really know anyone else here. Do you mind if I join you?

Is it OK if I listen in? [*to listen in* means to listen without actively participating]

Sorry, I was listening from distance and what you are saying sounds really interesting.

Then you can wait for a lull (pause) in the conversation and introduce yourself:

Hi I'm Adrian from the University of Pisa.

At this point your have their attention. You can continue by asking a question to check that you have correctly identified your key person.

Are you Professor Jonson? Because I have been really wanting to meet you.

If there is no key person in the group, but in any case the conversation seems interesting. You can say:

What you were saying about x is really interesting because I have been doing some similar research and …

So where do you two work?

Thus, you can either immediately start talking about what you do or ask the other people a question. Asking a question is the most polite strategy as it shows that you are interested in them. It also gives you a chance to tune into their voice.

At some point, someone in the group will probably ask you what you do. Rather than stating your position in academia (e.g., *I am a PhD student. I am a lecturer. I am an assistant professor.*), it is generally best to say something more descriptive and specific:

I am investigating new ways to produce fuel efficient cars.

I am doing some research into the sensations people have when beggars ask them for money.

If you are more descriptive, people are more likely to make comments or ask questions. If you just say *I am a PhD student*, then the conversation may then be directed to someone else.

In any case, make sure you do not spend too much time talking about yourself. Find out what the other members of the group are interested in and focus on that.

If you no longer wish to keep talking to the group, you can say:

Wellit's been really interesting talking to you. I'll see you around.

I've really enjoyed talking to you. Enjoy the rest of the conference.

The use of the present perfect (*it has been*, *I have enjoyed*) immediately alerts the rest of the group that you are about to leave.

16.8   Identify typical conversation topics and prepare related vocabulary lists

You will massively increase your chances of understanding a conversation in a social context, if you prepare vocabulary lists connected with the kind of topics that might come up in conversation. It is true that an infinite number of topics could be discussed at a social dinner, but what is also certain is that some topics come up very frequently. These topics include

- the location and how the conference has been organized

- the social events (including tourist excursions) connected with the conference

- the weather

- the food

- other people's presentations

- latest technologies (cell phones and applications, PCs, etc.)

If you learn as much vocabulary as possible connected with the above points, you will feel

- more confident about talking, that is, offering your opinions and responding to others

- more relaxed when listening

The result will be that you will be able to participate in the conversation actively, and thus have a more positive and rewarding experience.

Other topics which are typically covered at social events include family, work, education, sport, film, music, and the political and economic situation of one or more countries. Again, if you learn the words (meaning and pronunciation) associated with these topics, you will be able to participate much more effectively.

16.9 Learn what topics of conversation are not acceptable for particular nationalities

There are some topics of conversation that are universally acceptable, such as those used for breaking the ice (e.g., the ones listed at the beginning of 20.2). As an example, money is a topic that some British people might consider inappropriate for discussion with strangers at a social event—this means that they might find it embarrassing to be asked questions about how much they earn, how much their house is worth, and how much they spend on their children's education.

What is appropriate varies from nation to nation. I spoke to a Japanese researcher who told me,

> In Japan we are hesitant to talk about personal matters. For instance, many British people I have met like to talk about their families and show photographs, but the Japanese don't do that, at least not in depth. We would say "I have a husband. I have a son and I have two daughters." Japanese men like talking about hobbies, golf, for example. We talk about food. Women even like to talk about what blood type they are.

Sometimes you may think that your interlocutor is asking too many questions, which may be also too personal. Most Anglos would not consider questions such as Where do you study? What kind of research do you do? What did you major in? What seminars are you planning to go to? Did you take your vacation yet? to be too personal. Such questions are merely a friendly exploration in a search to find things that you may have in common.

Some questions would be considered inappropriate by most Anglos, for example:

How old are you?

What is your salary?

What is your religion?

Are you married?

How old is your husband / wife?

Do you plan to get married?

Do you plan to have children?

How much do you weigh?

Have you put on weight?

How much did you pay for your car / house (etc.)?

16.10 Think of other safe topics that involve cultural similarities rather than just differences

The social events organized at international conferences provide a perfect opportunity for discussing similarities and differences in culture. If you focus on the similarities, it will generally create a better atmosphere, rather than trying to claim that your country does things better than another country.

This does not necessarily involve having heavy ethical or political discussions but can be centered on more straightforward, but nevertheless interesting, topics such as

- legal age to do certain things (e.g., drive a car, vote)

- dialects and different languages within the same national borders

- the role of the family (e.g., treatment of the elderly, ages people leave home)

- things people do for fun (e.g., bungee jumping, karaoke)

- tipping habits (e.g., hotels, restaurants, taxi drivers)

- holiday destinations

- jobs and how often people change them, how far people commute to work

- national sports

- natural resources

- shop and office opening and closing times

- punctuality and its relative importance

If you prepare vocabulary lists for the above topics and learn the pronunciation of the words, then you will have more confidence to initiate and / or participate in a conversation.

16.11   If you live near the conference location, be prepared to answer questions on your town

If you live in the region where the conference is being held, then you have the perfect opportunity to share your knowledge and practice your English! Here are some typical questions and answers:

> Are there any good restaurants where I can try / sample the local food?

> Yes, there is a good one near the town hall, and another one just round the corner from here on Academia Street.

> What local sites would you recommend that I go and see?

> Well the standard places where all tourists go are .... But I suggest that you visit the museum of ... and if you like food you could go to the market on Academia Street.

> Do you have any suggestions as to where I might buy a ...

> You could try the department store which is on the main road that leads to the mosque.

Note the construction with suggest and recommend: to suggest / recommend that someone do something

If someone is critical of the local services or about the organization of the conference, and if you don't want to enter into a long defense, you can simply say:

> Yes, I know what you mean.

Or if you want to be more defensive you can say:

> Well, to be honest, I just think you have been unlucky.

16.12   Prepare anecdotes that you can recount over dinner

You will probably be able to participate more effectively in a conversation if you initiate the topic area yourself. You could prepare short anecdotes on one or more of the following:

- travel stories (e.g., missing planes, terrible hotels)

- misadventures in the lab

- the worst presentation you ever did

- the best / worst conference you ever attended

These are good topics because they are neutral and everyone in your group is likely to have something to contribute. If you initiate the conversation, it will help to boost your confidence.

An alternative to stories / anecdotes are factoids (i.e., interesting statistics), for example, factoids about your country, about your research area, or about anything you find interesting. I find a good way of collecting interesting facts or quotations is to note them down from any book you are reading. For instance, I have just finished reading Andy Hunt's excellent book *Pragmatic Thinking and Learning*. These are just a few of things that I wrote down:

> The majority of all scientific information is less than fifteen years old.

> You'll be at the peak of intelligence at the very end of the project and at your most ignorant at the beginning.

> We have "bugs" in the way we think—fundamental errors in how we process information, make decisions, and evaluate situations.

> Did you ever sit down and deliberately decide to be liberal, conservative, libertarian, or anarchist? A workaholic or a slacker?

> Because it was fun, the presentation was much more effective. Normally, no one pays any attention to the standard talk.

> Multitasking can cost you 20 to 40 percent of your productivity.

You can introduce a factoid by saying:

> I read in the newspaper this morning that …

> I was surfing the web the other day and I found an interesting statistic that says …

> Did you know that …?

> I read some research that says you can tell the difference …

> I have heard that apparently most people would prefer …

Or you can just slip the factoid or the quote / idea into the middle of an ongoing conversation. Basically, you just need to be curious about the world. So keep a note book of interesting things that you read. And make a list of interesting experiences that you have had. Then you can use such facts and stories on social occasions.

It is also helpful to learn something about psychology and communication skills. Socializing is all about relating to people and communicating well with the other attendees. Learning good communication skills and social skills entails knowing how the human brain receives information, and how we perceive each other.

16.13   Practice being at the center of attention in low-risk situations

Do you like standing up in front of other people or do you feel nervous and self-conscious? If you are the kind of person who usually does not talk much at dinners, parties, and even in everyday banal social situations (e.g., in front of the coffee machine, on the telephone), then try and make an effort to talk more and find yourself at the center of attention.

Don't just listen to people, learn to have the courage to interrupt them and comment on what they have said. For instance you can relate what they have said to your own experience. You could say:

I know exactly what you mean. In fact …

Actually I had a very similar experience to what you have just described.

I was once in exactly the same situation.

I completely agree with what you are saying. In fact, …

I am not sure I totally agree with you. In my country, for instance, …

Tell people things that have happened to you or that you have read or heard about. You can do this in low-risk situations (i.e., where your conversation skills and level of English are not going to be judged), for example, when you are with a group of friends.

You could practise doing two-minute presentations with a group of colleagues. You could do this either in your own language or in English. Possible topics:

- what you enjoy doing most in life

- your favorite movie or book and why you like it so much

- the worst journey of your life

- the best holiday

- your dreams for the future

- your ideal house

Another solution is to offer to do teaching work at your department or institute. Teaching experience is excellent training for presentations as you have to learn to explain things clearly and engage your students.

If you practice being at the center of attention, you will gain more confidence.

Chapter 17

Networking: Successful Informal Meetings

Factoids

❖ The word *protocol* refers to a set of rules governing how communication should take place (e.g., behavior at a conference). Originally, in ancient Greece, it referred to a piece of paper that was glued onto a manuscript in order to identify the author. Similarly, *etiquette* (i.e., acceptable rules for social behavior) had its origins in the French custom of giving a little ticket to those who attended public ceremonies. This ticket gave attendees instructions on how to behave during the ceremony.

❖ A study reported in *How to prepare, stage, and deliver winning presentations* by Thomas Leech was undertaken to determine how executives, professional-society leaders, and university professors viewed the relative importance of the various subjects studied at university. All typical technical skills were ranked after communication skills in importance.

❖ In an essay entitled *How to Listen to Other People*, S.I. Hayakawa, the Canadian-born American academic and politician of Japanese ancestry, wrote that "listening does not mean simply maintaining a polite silence while you are rehearsing in your mind the speech you are going to make the next time you can grab a conversational opening. Nor does listening mean waiting alertly for the flaws in the other fellow's arguments so that later you can mow him down. Listening means trying to see the problem the way the speaker sees it".

❖ Over 80% of the outcome of a meeting is already decided before the meeting actually happens.

❖ A survey of the way meetings are conducted revealed that the main causes of ineffectiveness were (in order of negative impact): deviating from topic of meeting, insufficient preparation by participants, attendees talking too much or too little, length of the meeting.

❖ The Greek-speaking Stoic philosopher Epictetus is reputed to have said: "We have two ears and one mouth so that we can listen twice as much as we speak".

© Springer International Publishing Switzerland 2016
A. Wallwork, *English for Presentations at International Conferences*,
English for Academic Research, DOI 10.1007/978-3-319-26330-4_17

17.1 What's the buzz?

1) Imagine you have set up a meeting with a professor from a foreign institute who you hope might be interested in offering you an internship at his / her department. You have already communicated via email and have briefly explained who you are and what you would like to do. Now you are face to face having a coffee at the conference bar. Write a dialog between you and him / her in which you introduce yourself and explain your proposal for carrying out research at his / her department.

2) Re-read what you wrote in Exercise 1 and answer the questions.

   • Who speaks the most, you or the prof? Might it be better if you spoke a little less at the beginning? Is it important in such situations to have a balanced conversation?

   • Have you highlighted the benefits just for yourself or have you also explained why the professor would also benefit from your proposals? Is it important to balance the benefits between the two parties?

****

Research shows that three factors determine a successful career: performance 10%, image and personal style 30%, and exposure and visibility 60%. The more visible you are as a researcher, the more likely you are to find interesting and remunerative research positions. If you use a conference as an opportunity to introduce yourself to as many people as possible, you will help to widen your opportunities for new collaborations. However, merely introducing yourself is not sufficient. You also need to create a good first impression on your interlocutors and engage with them in small talk.

Peter Honey, chartered psychologist and creator of Honey & Mumford Learning Styles Questionnaire, says:

> So far as other people are concerned, you are your behavior. Although there are other things which go towards making you the person you are—your thoughts, feelings, attitudes, motives, beliefs and so on—your behavior is apparent to everyone.

This chapter focuses on typical ways that Anglos introduce themselves and set up meetings. I am not suggesting that this is the best way to conduct such activities, but simply that this would be the norm if you were visiting countries where English is spoken as the first language.

You will learn how to:

- introduce yourself face to face in a variety of situations

- walk up to a complete stranger and ask to arrange a meeting

- set up and conduct informal meetings with key people

- ensure the best possible outcome of the meeting

- follow up on the meeting

17.2 Decide in advance which key people you want to meet

People do not go to conferences just to watch presentations. One of the primary reasons is networking, that is, finding people with whom you can set up collaborations or who can give you useful feedback on your work. Networking is much simpler if you have a clear idea in advance of who you would like to meet (hereafter "your key person"). A simple way to do this is to

- look at the conference program and find the names of key persons

- find information about them from their personal pages on their institute's website

- find a photograph of them so you will be able to identify them in a room from a distance

Then you need to prepare questions in English that you wish to ask them.

You should also predict how they might answer your questions. This will increase your chances of understanding their answers and will also enable you to think of follow-up questions.

17.3 Email your key person in advance of the conference

You will massively increase your chances of having a conversation with your key person if you email them before the conference to say that you would be interested in meeting them. Here is an example:

> Subject: XYZ Conference: meeting to discuss ABC
>
> Dear Professor Jones
>
> I see from the program for the XYZ Conference that you will be giving a presentation on ABC. I am a researcher at The Institute and I am working in a very similar field. There seems to be a lot of overlap between our work and I think you might find my data useful for … I was wondering if you might be able to spare 10 minutes of your time to answer a few questions.
>
> There is a social dinner on the second night - perhaps we could meet 15 minutes before it begins, or of course any other time that might suit you.
>
> I look forward to hearing from you.

The structure is as follows:

1. say how you know about the key person (i.e., they are attending the same conference as you)

2. briefly describe what you do

3. show how what you do relates to what they do

4. indicate how long the meeting might last (keep it as short as possible)

5. suggest a possible meeting place and time, but show flexibility

Of course, there is no guarantee they will even open your email, but if they do you will have created an opportunity for a meeting. Such an email requires minimal effort. It also helps to avoid the embarrassment of having to walk up to a complete stranger and introducing yourself in English.

17.4 Consider telephoning your key person in advance of the conference, rather than emailing

In an era in which many people communicate via email or various phone messaging systems and apps, you can gain a lot of attention by adopting a traditional means of communication: a phone call!

By making a phone call you massively increase your chances of meeting someone, especially given that they may never read your email, or read it too late.

Professor Susan Barnes at the Lab for Social Computing, Rochester Institute of Technology, wrote to me confirming that email is not necessarily the best way to initiate communication with someone you don't know:

> If you have something important to say to someone with whom you have never previously had contact, then use the phone rather than email. Through an initial phone call people become real to each other. This sets up a positive relationship which can then be continued via email. On the other hand, a rushed email may contain errors and create the wrong first impression. People pay more attention to a phone call than they do to email. Future communication will be more successful, if you start the relationship in a positive manner.

The level of success of your phone call can be enhanced considerably if you have a very clear idea of what you want to say before you actually make the call. Write down some notes about what you want to say, and then make sure you know how to say everything in English.

You should also find out as much as possible about the person who you want to talk to. What level of formality will you have to use? What is their level of English? Are they a native speaker? Have any of your colleagues spoken to this person? What can you learn from their experience: for example, does this person have a reputation for speaking very fast? If so, you need to learn appropriate phrases for encouraging them to slow down.

Think about what the other person might ask you, and prepare answers to such questions. If you do so, you are more likely to be able to understand the question when it is asked.

Give that this would be a very important call for you, you may find it useful if you simulate the call with a colleague, and ask the colleague to ask you pertinent questions.

If you take notes during the call, it will help you to paraphrase what the other person has said so that you can check your understanding. Obviously, notes will also help you to remember what was said and this will be useful if you decide to send your interlocutor an email summarizing the call.

At the end of the call, in order to check that you have not missed anything, make a mini summary of what has been said. This gives your interlocutor an opportunity to clarify any points. You can say:

> Can I just check that I have got everything? So we have decided to meet at the end of the first session on the second day. We will meet at the coffee bar near the main entrance. We will both remember to wear our name badges. Thanks very much. I am really looking forward to meeting you.

17.5 Think of how the meeting could be beneficial not only to you but also to your key person

Although we sometimes do things purely for altruistic reasons, we are generally more motivated to help people if it seems that there might also be some benefit for us. It is thus a good idea to think of how a collaboration with you could benefit your key person—what knowledge do you have that would be useful for them, what part of their research could you do on their behalf, what contacts do you have that might be useful for them too?

17.6 Find out as much as you can about your key person, but be discreet

If you think that the meeting you have arranged could help you significantly in your career, then you need to do everything you can to ensure a successful outcome. Find out everything you can about the person—read their papers, find them on LinkedIn or Facebook, locate their personal website, or find about their academic achievements on their department's website. Find out what is important for them and what they are interested in aside from their research work. Look for things that you might have in common.

> I read in one of your papers that …
>
> I was looking at your profile on your university's website and saw that …
>
> Diego mentioned that you are doing some research into …

Most people will be flattered that you have taken the time to read their papers or looked at their work profile. However, although most people will not mind if you have investigated a little about their professional life, they may find it creepy (i.e., weird and disturbing) if you have been looking at their holiday photos on Facebook and know all about their hobbies. So be extremely careful how you refer to the things that you have learned about the person.

You can make your meeting much more beneficial if you determine to find any person that you meet interesting. This will make you more animated and thus appear more interesting to your interlocutor. You will also be less distracted as you will be focusing totally on the other person.

During the conversation restate and / or summarize the key points to check that you have understood. This is also a way to keep your mind alert and at the same time proves your appreciation of your interlocutor's remarks.

17.7   Encourage your key person to come to your presentation or poster session

The more people who come to your presentation, the more people are likely to come up to you directly (or contact you via email) to discuss your work. To increase your chances of people coming, particularly your key person, you can do some self-publicity. To everyone you meet at the social events, at the bar, at the coffee machine, or wherever, you can say:

> I am doing a presentation on X tomorrow at 10.00 in Conference Room number 2. It would be great if you could come.
>
> If you are interested in X, then you might like to come to my presentation tomorrow. It's at 11.00 in Room 13.
>
> I don't know you would be interested, but this afternoon I am presenting my work on X. It's at three o'clock in the main conference hall.

Then you give the person your card, with a previously handwritten reminder on the back of the card stating the topic of the presentation, the time, and the location.

17.8   Exploit opportunities for introductions at the coffee machine

If your key person is alone by the coffee machine, this is a great opportunity as you will hopefully get their undivided attention.

First you need to attract the key person's attention. Here are some phrases you could use:

> Excuse me. I heard you speak in the round table / I saw your presentation this morning.
>
> Hi, do you have a couple of minutes for some questions?
>
> Excuse me, could I just have a word with you? I am from …

I am X from the University of Y, do you think I could ask you a couple of questions?

Second, it is generally a good idea to say something positive about the person and / or their work:

I really enjoyed your presentation this morning—it was certainly the most useful of today's sessions.

I thought what you said at the round table discussion was really useful.

Third, suggest you move to somewhere where you can sit.

Thank you, shall we go and sit in the bar?

Shall we go and sit over there where it is a bit quieter?

If you see that they are in a hurry, then it is best to arrange to meet later. Show that you understand that the person is busy and that you don't want to take up much of their time. In fact, tell them the exact amount of time involved, this is more likely to get them to accept.

Would after lunch suit you?

Shall we meet at the bar?

When do you think you might be free? When would suit you?

Would tonight after the last session be any good for you?

Could you manage 8.45 tomorrow? That would give us about 10 minutes before the morning session starts.

I promise I won't take any more than 10 minutes of your time.

If they agree to your proposal, then you can say:

That would be great / perfect.

That's very kind of you.

17.9 Be prepared for what to say if your proposal for a meeting is not accepted

If they don't agree to your proposal, then you can say:

> Oh, I understand, don't worry it's not a problem.
>
> That's fine. No problem. Enjoy the rest of the conference.
>
> OK I have really enjoyed speaking to you in any case.
>
> In any case, maybe I could email you the questions? Would that be alright?

17.10 Prepare well for any informal one-to-one meetings

Your meeting will be far more beneficial if both parties prepare for it. It is a good idea to let the person know in advance exactly what information you need. For this reason, setting up meetings for the following day is a good tactic as it gives the other person time to think about the answers. In such cases you can say:

> Would you mind giving me your email address, so that I can email you my questions?
>
> I have prepared a list of three questions that I would like to ask you—they are here on this sheet. If perhaps you could take a look at them before we meet, that would be great.

Having questions prepared indicates that you are a serious person who is not going waste the person's time.

17.11 Be positive throughout informal one-to-one meetings

The outcome of an informal meeting often depends on how well it begins. If your key person is late for the meeting, reassure them that it is not a problem:

> Don't worry, I am very grateful you could come.
>
> No problem, it doesn't matter.
>
> Can I get you a coffee?

If you are late:

> I am so sorry I am late—I got held up paying my bill—have you been waiting long?

First, acknowledge that you are grateful that the person has found the time to meet with you.

First of all, it is very kind of you to come.

Thank you so much for coming. I really appreciate it.

Did you have time to have a look at the questions I sent you?

Ensure that you only make positive comments about the conference, its location, and its organization. People respond much better to positive-thinking people and are more likely to listen to them and consequently to consider future collaborations. So avoid negative comments such as:

Last year's edition of this conference was much better don't you think?

I have been so bored by some of the presentations.

I have been surprised by the total lack of any decent social events.

Instead, find something positive to say:

I really enjoyed the first presentation yesterday.

The trip to the museum was very interesting I thought.

I am enjoying trying out all the local food.

There is always a chance that the person provides you with no useful information at all. Nevertheless, it is always best to show interest and take a few notes.

Give your key person time to express themselves, but be sure you respect the time-frame that you arranged, and then conclude by saying:

OK, I don't want to keep you any longer.

Well, I don't want to take up any more of your time.

Well I think we've covered all the questions … but would it be OK if I email you if I need any further clarifications?

Well, it was really kind of you to spare your time / of you to come

What you said has been really interesting and useful, thank you.

I am sure there are other people you will be wanting to meet.

17.12 A verbal exchange is like a game of ping pong: always give your interlocutor an opportunity to speak

It is fundamental never to dominate any verbal exchange, particularly if your interlocutor is someone who could potentially help you.

An exchange should be like a game of table tennis (ping pong). You speak for a few seconds, then you send the "ball" to the other person by finding a way to let him / her speak, then he / she speaks and passes the ball back to you.

Compare the following two dialogs, in which a researcher, Carlos, is interested in collaborating with an expert in neurolinguistics, Professor Jaganathan. Carlos hopes the professor might offer him a position in her laboratory.

Dialog 1

> Carlos: Good morning Professor Jaganathan. I saw your presentation this morning and in my opinion it was very good. My name is Carlos Nascimento and I work at the Brazilian National Research Council. My field of interest is neurolinguistics applied to second language learning. Last year we began some experiments on blah blah blah blah ... [*talks continuously for another three minutes*]. I believe our fields of interest have much in common. I was wondering if you might be available to discuss a possible collaboration together. Would you be free for dinner tonight, or tomorrow evening? It would be very useful for me if we could meet. And also ...
>
> Jaganathan: Um, sorry I am rather busy at the moment, could you send me an email?

Professor Jaganathan's reaction may be to think that an evening with Carlos would be hard work. She would have to listen to the constant flow of Carlos's incessant talking. The impression might be that Carlos is only interested in himself and that for him Professor Jaganathan is just a means to his end. Also, his comment about Professor Jaganathan's presentation being "very good" sounds like he is the expert rather than her.

Carlos's perspective may be very different. He may think that by talking in this manner he will be creating a good impression because it shows that he is confident.

Another possible reason for him talking so much is that he is nervous. When we are nervous we often talk a lot more and at a faster speed than we would normally do. This usually does not create a good impression on our listener.

Dialog 2

> Carlos: Good morning Professor Jaganathan, my name is Carlos Nascimento. (1) Do you have a minute?
>
> Jaganathan: Er, yes. But I have to be at a meeting in ten minutes.
>
> Carlos: (2) Well, I promise I won't take more than two minutes of your time. (3) I thought your presentation was really very interesting. (4) I am just curious to know how you set the last experiments up. It must have been quite challenging.
>
> Jaganathan: You are right it was. In fact, we had to ... and then we had to ... and finally we ...
>
> Carlos: That's really interesting. Well, my group in Rio did a very similar experiment, and I think our results and our project in general might be (5) very useful for you in terms of speeding up the test times.
>
> Jaganathan: Really?
>
> Carlos: So I was wondering if you might be free for a few minutes at the (6) social dinner tonight, or tomorrow evening? (7)
>
> Jaganathan: Sure, that sounds great. Let's make it tonight.

The second dialog is much more successful because Carlos

1. gives the professor an opportunity to say that she cannot speak now; this is also a sign of respect

2. tells her how much of her time he requires (i.e., *two minutes*)—this will reassure her that she will not miss her meeting

3. compliments her on her presentation in a way that makes him sound genuinely appreciative

4. asks her a question about her work and makes a supposition about the difficulties involved (*challenging*)—this gives her an opportunity to talk and also puts her at the center of attention rather than just him

5. gives a reason why she should be interested in talking with him.

6. does not ask her to have dinner alone with him but in the context of a social event—this means that she doesn't feel any embarrassment or pressure

7. makes an arrangement without mentioning anything about a "collaboration" — Carlos will then delay mentioning a collaboration until he has given the professor enough valid reasons to be interested in such a collaboration

The result is that Professor Jaganathan is happy to meet with Carlos.

To be able to communicate in the way I have suggested in Dialog 2, you really need to practice beforehand. You need to think carefully about what you are going to say. But just as importantly you must think about how you can avoid dominating the exchange by finding ways to encourage your interlocutor to speak. Given the importance of such exchanges, I strongly recommend that you simulate the exchange with a colleague. Try it first in your own language, and then in English.

The same principles are also true when you say goodbye—either at the end of a conversation, or at the end of the conference itself. Again you play ping pong, as highlighted in the dialog below in which Carlos says goodbye to Professor Jaganathan on the last day of the conference.

Dialog 3

Carlos: Professor Jaganathan, I just wanted to say how much I enjoyed meeting you the other night. The food was great wasn't it?

Jaganathan: Yes, it was really delicious and the location was great too.

Carlos: So, when I get back to Rio I will discuss what we said with my professor and then he will contact you. Is that still OK with you?

Jaganathan: Yes, of course.

Carlos: And finally can I just thank you again both for your presentation and particularly for finding the time to speak with me—I really appreciate it. Have a great trip back to Bombay.

Jaganathan: Thank you.

Of course, the professor doesn't participate as much as Carlos in the exchange, but at least she feels she is being considered.

Again, if you simply improvise such exchanges, rather than preparing for them in advance, you may give a rather negative impression on your interlocutor.

Carlos also takes the opportunity to summarize what has been decided (*I will discuss ...*). Making such summaries of important meetings is vital for both sides to ensure that there are no misunderstandings.

17.13   Ensure that you follow up on your meeting

One of the most important aspects of networking is to follow up on a face-to-face meeting. Many of the potential benefits of the meeting will be lost if you don't take advantage of them by sending an email, such as the one below.

Dear Professor Kisunaite,

I am the student in Social Psychology from *name of institute / country*.

Thank you very much for sparing the time to meet with me last week. Your comments were particularly useful.

As I mentioned at our meeting, if by any chance a position arises in your laboratory I would be very grateful if you would consider me - my CV is attached.

I am also attaching a paper which I am currently writing that I think you will find of interest.

Once again, thank you for all your help and I do hope we will meet again in the near future.

Best regards

This email acts as a reminder to the professor of

- who you are

- what you discussed

- what decisions were reached and / or what offer was made

Chapter 18

Posters

Factoids

One of the first ever scientific poster sessions was organized for the annual meeting of the American Society of Clinical Oncology in 1981.

A conference poster is typically A0 size (841 mm × 1189 mm) portrait style. Experts recommend that it should be clearly visible from at least 1 m away (the title and summary from 3 m; 80 pt font) and that the key message should be clear within 5-10 seconds of reading.

Posters have been around for centuries but it wasn't until the invention of lithography in 1796 that they could be mass produced.

Initially used for advertising (e.g. railway companies advertising their routes), posters became an art form during the *Belle Époque* (1871-1914), producing the *Art Nouveau* style, which began in France and then flourished throughout Europe and the USA.

Posters were first used for propaganda and recruitment during the First World War, with two famous campaigns: "Lord Kitchener Wants You" in the UK, and "Uncle Sam Wants You" in the USA.

Pinup posters (i.e. pictures of attractive women) first became popular in the 1920s.

A site called Busy Teacher offers over 300 posters for English language classrooms, their most popular being "English is a crazy language".

The world's biggest (and most expensive) film poster was created in 2015, and measures around 4650 square meters. The Bollywood movie it promoted was called *Baahubali*.

© Springer International Publishing Switzerland 2016
A. Wallwork, *English for Presentations at International Conferences*,
English for Academic Research, DOI 10.1007/978-3-319-26330-4_18

18.1 What's the buzz?

1) Think about these questions:

   a) How many (types of) posters do you see every day? What are these posters for?

   b) What are the most effective advertising and political poster campaigns that you have ever seen? Why were they effective?

   c) What connection is there between a poster at a poster session at a conference and a poster advertising some product on a billboard?

   d) What techniques from commercial posters could you incorporate into a conference poster?

   e) What is the purpose of a conference poster? What are the qualities of a good poster?

   f) What are the typical faults of a poster at a conference? What defects do you need to avoid?

   g) Do you think there might be a correlation between how attractive a poster is and the quality of the scientific results depicted in the poster?

   h) When you see a poster at a conference, how many seconds/minutes would you be willing to dedicate to understanding the basic concept of the research covered?

2) You can get an idea of the variety of poster types by typing "academic posters" or "conference posters" into Google Images. Choose a few examples, and with colleagues compare which work and which don't and why.

****

A whole book could be written about the art of designing posters for conferences. This chapter focuses on the purpose (and opportunities) of a poster, the content, and your role in explaining your poster. Design issues are crucial but are outside the scope of this book.

Part 1 focuses on how to create a poster, and how to talk it through with people who are showing interest in it. Part 2 outlines what sections to include and what to put in each section.

18.2   PART 1: CREATING A POSTER AND KNOWING WHAT TO SAY

18.2.1   Purpose

The main purpose of a poster is exactly the same as a presentation:

- inform others about the key results of your research

- get yourself noticed

- get others interested thereby increasing your chances of acquiring more funds to enable you to continue your career in research

Posters have some advantages over presentations:

- you meet people face to face ... and these people could potentially collaborate in your research, or even offer you an internship

- you will be less nervous; in fact your professor may recommend a poster as being your first approach with a conference

- presentations typically last just for 10-15 minutes, with a poster you potentially have longer to explain your work

- there are more opportunities for exchanging ideas

- posters are generally on display throughout the whole conference - so a lot of people can potentially read and hear about your research and get your contact details

18.2.2   Types of research that might be better presented in a poster rather than a formal presentation

A poster may be a better way to present:

- complicated or conceptually difficult methods and results

- very specialized or esoteric work that may have a limited (yet nevertheless interested) audience or would be lost on a big audience

18.2.3 Deciding what to include

As with a formal oral presentation, the key is not to tell the audience all you know, but only what they really really need to know.

In an oral presentation, you might decide to present three key points.

In a poster, if possible limit yourself to one essential concept. This will have massive advantages:

- you won't be tempted to crowd your poster with text and diagrams - you will produce a much more attractive-looking poster

- you will just have one story to tell, which will make organizing the structure of your poster much easier

- the poster will be much easier explain to people

The result will be that people will appreciate your clarity of mind and may be more likely to contact you and / or collaborate with you.

The way you present your poster could help define your future career!

See the final subsections (18.3.1–18.3.6) to learn how to structure your poster in terms of textual information.

18.2.4 Using bullets to describe your research objectives

Decide whether some blocks of text might be better to be broken up into bullets (see 4.18 to 4.21).

Note: the research described below is fictitious and was written purely for the purposes of this book.

For example, instead of writing:

> Research objectives: The purpose of this research was threefold. The first aim was identify the top 10 websites offering advice on alternative treatments for depression. Secondly, we compared the alternatives offered by these sites with traditional medical practice. Thirdly, we interviewed a set of 25 parents whose children (aged from 16-26) had suffered as a consequence of opting for the alternative medicine when they had already been prescribed traditional medicines.

You could write:

Research objectives

- identify top 10 'alternative medicine' websites for treating depression

- compare 'alternatives' with traditional medical practise

- interview parents whose children (aged from 16-26) had suffered as a consequence of opting for the alternative medicine when they had already been prescribed traditional medicines

Note how the bullets:

• are more like Tweets or telegrams, i.e. not totally grammatical, but enabling the word count to be reduced

• stand out much more clearly than a block of text

• the third bullet is much longer as this also covers the key result of the research (i.e. that patients who have been prescribed traditional treatments who then opt for alternative approaches may suffer as a consequence)

In order to make your research objectives and key findings stand out, use a much bigger font than the other text. You can also put key words in bold.

The idea is to enable people passing by to assess within a few seconds whether it is worth their time to stop, read more, and ask you questions.

18.2.5   *Other points in the poster where you can use bullets*

You can then use the same system described in 18.6 for one or more of your sections dedicated to:

• hypotheses / predictions

• methods

• findings

• significance

• recommendations

However, don't base your entire poster on bullets. Your aim is to make your poster attractive, and that means creating variety for the reader's eye.

Put the bulleted statements in big, bold letters. Your audience will then understand within seconds what you set out to do, how you did it, what you found, and how it fits in to the wider picture. Use additional text to provide some detail. However given that you will be physically present to answer questions, bulleted text may be sufficient.

18.2.6   Checking your text

Once you've written the text, check for the following problems. The chapter references are to *English for Writing Research Papers*.

- long sentences (Chapter 4)

- redundancy (Chapter 5) - cut as much as you can, pretend you actually have to pay the conference organizers for every word you use!

- ambiguity (Chapter 6)

- results not highlighted clearly (Chapter 8)

18.2.7   Quality check

Check that dimensions conform to the specifications given by the conference organizers.

Have friends or family view your poster for typos, clarity, readability, and power of attraction.

Once you've made your poster look its best, ensure it presents the key point of your research in the most convincing light.

Make sure the colors you've chosen work in all types of lighting (position of windows, time of day, brightness of bulbs).

18.2.8 What to say to your audience

You can have a hundred people come and stand in front of your poster, but if you don't interact with them then you have failed in your mission. Some people may just read the summary, and then expect you to take them through the rest. Others may read it carefully and then ask for more details.

So, first practise explaining the whole poster clearly and concisely. You may have to give such an explanation repeatedly throughout the session (for some useful phrases see 20.10).

Second, prepare a list of all possible questions you might be asked (in the same way as for the Q&A session, see 11.12).

Third, revise the relevant literature on the topic and remind yourself of why you chose certain methods and statistical tests. You might be asked questions on these factors.

Fourth, be prepared for non-technical 'visitors' - you need to be able to explain any technical vocabulary and concepts as if you were talking to a member of your family rather than a colleague in the same field.

Fifth, be prepared for important 'visitors' e.g. professors who might be able to offer you work in their lab. You can do this by memorizing the names of key people who you would like to meet, and then checking their name tag (which they should be wearing at all times) or by asking their name. These people are key to your future, so you really need to be able to 'sell' your research to them. And remember they may even be dressed quite informally - you can't tell a prof from his / her clothing!

Sixth, have a business card and handout to give people. The handout should be a one-page summary of your research. It should also include the title of your presentation, your name plus the other authors, the name of the conference (year and location), the university / institute where you carried out the research, and your email address.

Now look at the above six points again. Would they have been easier for you to read (and remember) if you had used numbered bullets? Or are there enough bullets in this chapter already, so it actually creates variety not to use bullets everywhere?

18.3 PART 2: WHAT SECTIONS TO INCLUDE AND WHAT TO PUT IN THEM

The rest of this chapter outlines some research investigating how the language you speak affects the quantity and quality of the information you can extract when using a search engine. Although the research is fictitious, most of the data are accurate.

A typical poster will cover some or most of the points outlined in this subsection and have a similar structure.

18.3.1 Title

One or two lines (depending on how long the lines are!) concisely indicating the key issue investigated. The idea is to attract as many people as possible, you never know how your research may transfer well into a very different field.

Never use ALL CAPS in titles; emphasize titles in one way: boldface, italics, or underline, but never all three.

See 4.2-4.4 to learn ways to write titles.

Example titles for the research in question (i.e. language and web searches):

> If you are born and live in Italy, does your websearch return the same quality of information as a person born in the US?

> Italy vs US: the digital divide in terms of quality of information gleaned through websites.

18.3.2 Summary

Having a brief summary in the form of mini-sections increases the chances of pass-erbys to understand whether they wish to read more.

Example:

> Aim: 62 % of websites worldwide are in English, only 2 % in Italian. Does this mean that a non-English speaking Italian is at a disadvantage when searching, for example, for medical information or a movie review?

> Example finding 1: 4,200,000 hits for *anorexia* nervosa; 110,000 for *anoressia* nervosa. No. 1 hit for google.com: a Wikipedia entry on anorexia. No. 1 hit for google.it (i.e. Italian Google): a Nestlé advert on dietetic products.

Example finding 2: 20.9 million hits on google.com for *Roman Empire*, in the top 10 returns no mention of movies, videogames, or books. 589,000 hits on google.it for *Impero Romano*, a YouTube video is at No. 6, and the top 20 includes four pizzerias/restaurants named 'Impero Romano'.

Conclusion: Which is better - info on health and history, or the address of a great place to eat?

The particular research given above lends itself very well to graphic illustrations e.g. a picture of a Nestlé advert on dietetic product, a screenshot of the Wikipedia entry, a picture of a famous Roman site in Italy.

18.3.3   Introduction

Provide minimum background information, plus any definitions you think that non-expert readers may need to know (remember that unless you are at a very small conference, many of your 'audience' will not be experts in your field).

Put your research into the context of the state-of-the-art, and explain the 'gap' you are filling (as you would in a research paper, but this time in a much more user-friendly format).

Here is an example of how NOT to write your introduction:

Now that Google virtually controls the information we have access to, on the basis of previous searches (thus serving up the most recent and most eye-catching info, rather than necessarily the most pertinent), we decided to investigate what the various Google search engines around the world return to the websurfers, focusing on Italy (where our research team is based) and the US. Following on the work of Jatowa [2018] we ...

The first sentence above could also be written in much shorter sentences - four sentences rather than the original one sentence. Shorter sentences are generally easier for 'readers' to absorb, and also enable you to insert literature references more easily. So a much clearer version is:

Via search engines, governments virtually control all the information we have access to [Orwell, 1984]. Returns are made on the basis of previous searches [Deja Vu, 2016]. This provides the most recent and most eye-catching info [I Candy, 2017], rather than necessarily the most pertinent. We investigated what the various Google search engines around the world return to the websurfers. We focused on Italy (where our research team is based) and the US (where we would all like to work - offers please!).

Note also the level of informality, i.e. the humorous reference to 'offers please'. Your poster doesn't necessarily have to be more informal than a presentation, but there is no reason why it shouldn't be.

Again, consider inserting a graphic. To provide variety, in this case rather than a photo, you could have a pie chart.

18.3.4 Materials and methods

This should be a brief description (i.e. minimal detail) of your approach, procedure, equipment, statistical analysis etc.

> Searches were made using google.com and google.it on five topics: medicine, history, tourism, social networks, food recipes. (Topics chosen at random from a collated list of the 50 most searched for topics in the US and Italy).
>
> Within each topic, five specific areas were chosen (using same randomized method - e.g. for medicine: anorexia, bipolarism, motor neurone disease, dyslexia, Alzheimer's).
>
> To avoid locational bias, identical searches were conducted from 20 different PCs located in 20 different countries (plus 5 locations in US and 5 in Italy).
>
> The top 20 returns generated by each PC and on each topic were inputted into a database.
>
> The results were processed using GooStat vers. 2.1. and ScattiStat 3.1.

In the example, note the use of short sentences (some in a telegraphic style, i.e. some articles and verbs are missing), all in the passive form. Note also that each sentence is contained on a separate line to aid rapid reading.

Try to replace the detail that you would normally provide in your paper with a diagram, flow chart or such like.

18.3.5 Results

Your results section is likely to take up the most space on your poster. It should answer some or all of the following:

- did your procedure / methodology work?

- did it produce the expected results? did your results tie in with your research hypothesis?

- what were the main results and what do they mean?

This is the place to include tables, figures and graphs, with very clear legends, all just containing essential information. The more info you can put in a pictorial form the better - the people who look at your poster will want to get info in the clearest form possible.

18.3.6 Conclusions

Your conclusions should contain a one or two sentence statement about what your results imply. In the example below, the conclusions end in a fun way to leave the 'reader' with a positive impression and also offer the opportunity for an image of a pizza with pineapple (apparently invented in 1960 by a restaurant owner in Ontario, Canada).

You are certainly not obliged to end your poster in such an informal way, but you should perhaps assess the benefits of not doing so before you dismiss such an approach.

Our results indicate that if your first language is not English then you are probably being denied a lot of key information, irrespectively of the country where you make your search in your language. This is confirmed by the literature which states that ...

Future work will repeat the same procedure using Spanish and Chinese (i.e. two major languages) and Swahili (60-150 million speakers, Italian: 65 million).

Key question arising from our research: can a people (i.e. North Americans) that put pineapples on a pizza and think it tastes great, really be taken seriously?

If you think the approach in the last two lines above is flippant or unprofessional, then obviously you could end your conclusions in a much more serious way, which you may consider to be more appropriate. For example:

Key question arising from our research: Why is the quality of info returned by google.it in Italian inferior to that returned by google.com in English? Is it simply due to a kind of international digital divide which saw Italians writing content for the Internet (e.g. Wikipedia pages) around 10 years later than their native English speaking counterparts in the USA, and so they just need to catch up? Or is it more serious: will non English-speaking people never have the same access as, for example, US and UK citizens?

Note: As mentioned at the beginning of this chapter, the research on what Google returns on a language/location basis has never actually been done (as far as I know). However, I would like to think that someone reading this book might do the research for real. I am concerned that English speakers may have another source of unfair advantage over their non-English speaking counterparts.

18.3.7 Your contact details

In a large font give your readers:

1. your contact details (one email address is enough, no phone, no Skype etc)

2. one website where they can learn more about you (this could be your webpage at your institute, a LinkedIn page, a ResearchGate page etc, but one link is enough)

3. if not the same as in Point 2, a link to where readers can download the poster and the related paper

18.3.8 Other things to include (in a much smaller font)

Include a bibliography with any references that you have used in your text or diagrams. The conference may have its own rules with regard to how you cite the literature.

Acknowledge those who helped you, suppliers of equipment etc.

Disclose any conflicts of interest.

Chapter 19

Advice for Native English Speakers on How to Present at International Conferences and Run Workshops

Factoids

1. Less than 8% of the world's population speak English as their first language, by 2050 this figure will drop to around 5%. The British Council claims that 25% of the world's population has some understanding of English.

2. According to Professor David Crystal, 96% of the world's languages are spoken by 4% of the people.

3. The average European non-native speaking researcher may spend up to €20,000 learning English at various points in their life.

4. One of the world's biggest selling non-fiction books (over 15 million copies) published by a British publisher is a book on English grammar for foreigners by Raymond Murphy. It was first published in 1985.

5. English has nearly one million words (including technical and scientific words). Most native speaking adults use no more than 10,000 words in their daily communication. It is possible to make yourself understood using 1-2,000 words, providing that those words coincide with the listener's word set. Non-native speakers will generally have a similar set of technical words specific to the field that you work in, but their extent of general vocabulary will be much less than a native speaker's.

6. In 1997 the ten most popular words on the Internet included *sex, chat, nude, porno* and *weather*. In 2015 only *weather* from the 1997 list was still one of the most searched for words.

7. In 1997 English was used for 84.3% of websites globally, 15 years later this figure was down to 62%.

8. In 1994 the English language teaching industry in Britain alone was worth €700 million per year. Twenty five years later it was worth five times as much. It is now forecast to grow by 25% per annum.

© Springer International Publishing Switzerland 2016
A. Wallwork, *English for Presentations at International Conferences*,
English for Academic Research, DOI 10.1007/978-3-319-26330-4_19

19.1 What's the buzz?

In an early edition of a best-selling book on how to give presentations, the author wrote:

Have you ever been to an international conference where speakers from different nationalities were giving talks in foreign languages? Do you remember a presentation where it was only half way through that you realised it was actually in English? I certainly do.

This is obviously a very damning statement of non-native speakers, probably typical of the early 1980s when the book was published (the author subsequently cut this comment in later editions). However, what the author failed to mention, is that it is equally true that some native speakers are particularly difficult to understand!

In my experience many non-native speakers find communicating orally with, for example, American and British research groups, more stressful than working in English with for instance Europeans, Asians and South Americans.

The reason has nothing to do with personalities or levels of efficiency and collaboration, but with language.

Many break out into a cold sweat at the thought of conducting a Q&A with native English speaking counterparts because they know that they will understand only a small percentage of what they hear. They feel that seminars, workshops and meetings in general are often unproductive because the native English speakers tend to dominate the discussion and thus have an unfair leverage.

When learners of English fail to communicate successfully, they frequently assume it is because of their English ability. Such failures can be demotivating at best, but are often also embarrassing, frustrating and even humiliating. The reason for this lack of understanding is that native speakers often make no concessions for their interlocutor.

This is not a deliberate policy on the part of the native speakers, but simply because many are unaware that their spoken English is difficult to understand.

This means that they often speak too fast, use inappropriate language (e.g. colloquial structures and expressions), and may also have a strong regional accent that that their interlocutor has probably never been exposed to before.

In addition, many native speakers 'swallow' their words when speaking. This means that even a non-native speaker with a good command of English grammar and vocabulary cannot hear / identify the swallowed words, irrespectively of the accent.

If you find this chapter useful, and you are a reviewer or editor, then you might also like to read Chapter 11 *Writing a Peer Review* in the companion volume *English for*

Academic Correspondence. You will pick up some tips for reviewing the work of non-natives without risking offending or demoralizing anyone.

****

This chapter is designed to make native English speaking readers of this book more aware of the difficulties that their non-native counterparts have at international conferences. It focuses on how native speakers should deliver presentations and conduct workshops with non-native audiences.

Sections 19.2-19.6 describe what it's like to be a non-native speaker when listening to a native speaker.

Sections 19.7-19.11 outline things to be aware of when preparing your presentation.

Sections 19.12-19.15 focus on vocabulary issues.

The final sections suggest ways for chairing / running workshops and seminars.

19.2   Learn from seasoned speakers

I have conducted many surveys with British and American academics and business people to discover the problems they had when dealing with foreign clients. Whilst many of these people were aware that there was a communication problem, they did not realize there was anything concrete they could do about it, other than trying to speak more clearly.

However, my interviewees that regularly met with non-native speakers, were well aware of the problem and always took pains to make their communication clear. Below are three examples of what such experts have told me.

I have spent much of my career speaking publicly and privately with a broad range of audiences, from the ultra-technical to the general public. When speaking to and with people for whom English is not a native tongue, I have found it nearly universal that speaking more slowly and distinctly helps more than vocabulary changes, although I avoid special terms and acronyms when the audience is not expected to have command of the topic-specific argot.

Vint Cerf, Chief Internet Evangelist at Google,
one of the founding fathers of the Internet

I was born in Morocco and moved to England when I was seven, so I had to learn English when I arrived. During my life I have also learned French and Spanish. This has helped me enormously in communicating with foreign customers, as I am fully aware of the difficulties that they have in terms of understanding native English speakers. So when, for example, I am explaining something orally to scientists and subject matter experts I might say: "We are able to screen all open reading frames of any disease-causing agent." But to a potential foreign investor I know that if I say the sentence above quickly it will just sound like a series of noises. Instead, I have to speak in a way my 11 year old son can understand - that doesn't mean dumbing down what I want to say, but speaking more slowly, giving examples and frequently checking that they have understood me. The result is that clients really appreciate the fact that I am making an effort to help them understand me. In my work experience, I have seen so many presentations given by Americans and Brits that left the non-native element in the audience completely frustrated because they only managed to understand a quarter or less of what was said. This has a serious negative effect on future collaborations, as clearly everyone needs to feel that they are being given equal consideration.

Mustapha Bakali, President of the Bill Clinton Health Access Initiative

The citation was written when Bakali was Chief Business Officer of Intercell Biomedical Research & Development AG

What I'd hope is ... that native English speakers are sensitive to this new role which English is taking on, and use their own language in such a way that it is easy for people who are non native speakers to understand them. Very often non-native speakers speak better English than native speakers.

Hamish McRae, British journalist and author

19.3   Understand what it feels like not to understand

It helps if you can put yourself in the shoes of a non-native speaker and really feel what it's like not to understand. The best way is to try and learn a foreign language. But a simpler and more immediate way is to listen to music lyrics.

There are several websites that help music lovers decipher the lyrics of songs. Even for a native speaker, it's tough to hear the difference between:

The sky's in love

This guy's in love

Disguise in love

Try listening to Sia (the Australian singer) performing her song 'Distractions' live. You can make out the odd word or phrase here and then, but most of it is a mystery!

Then there's the classic song *Alice* by the Cocteau Twins. Trying listening to it before reading the paragraph below.

According to metrolyrics.com, the song begins as follows:

When I lost him ache
Shudder shock of pale
My, my true love
Niccol Donati, these days are
Smoking days

The lyrics to *Alice* reported on that site and many other sites are of course gibberish. The vocals of Elizabeth Frazer, the singer, don't actually rely on any recognizable language, so the only word said distinctly in this song is 'Alice'.

But the lyrics reported above are very representative of how it feels to be a non-native speaker listening to a native speaker – you just get snatches of what you think they have said and try to construct a logical thread between one snatch and another.

19.4 Watch TED to understand how it feels to be a non-native speaker

One of my favorite TED talks is 'Design and Destiny' where the French designer, Philippe Starck, talks about his work for 17 minutes with no slides at all.

His beginning highlights an obsession of many non-native speakers:

You will understand nothing with my type of English.

One of the funniest (at least for me!) presentations on TED is by the Swiss comedian and cabaret artist Ursus Wehrli, who according to the introductory blurb on the TED website 'shares his vision for a cleaner, more organized, tidier form of art — by deconstructing the paintings of modern masters into their component pieces, sorted by color and size'.

However, this presentation is not simply about modern art. It works on many levels. First it is a non-native English speaker's revenge on a native speaker audience.

It is best to watch the first few minutes of Wehrli's presentation before reading the rest of this subsection.

234

http://www.ted.com/talks/ursus_wehrli_tidies_up_art?c=193562

Wehrli manages to make fun of the audience by saying:

> I'm a little bit nervous because I'm speaking in a foreign language, and I want to apologize in advance, for any mistakes I might make. Because I'm from Switzerland, and I just hope you don't think this is Swiss German I'm speaking now here. This is just what it sounds like if we Swiss try to speak American. But don't worry – I don't have trouble with English, as such. I mean, it's not my problem, it's your language after all. I am fine. After this presentation here at TED, I can simply go back to Switzerland, and you have to go on talking like this all the time.

He also speaks for a few seconds in German: the audience laugh both because it's funny, but also because they feel a little out of their comfort zone (they, this time, are the ones who don't understand).

19.5   Watch TED to understand how to talk to non-natives

A great way to gain insights into how English is being learned around the world is to watch Jay Walker's talk entitled 'English Mania'.

> *http://www.ted.com/talks/jay_walker_on_the_world_s_english_mania?language=en*

Jay Walker is head of Walker Digital and was named by *Time* magazine as one of the fifty most influential leaders in the digital age.

Not only will you learn about global English, but Jay's speech is a great example of how to talk to non-native speakers (though most of his audience I suspect were actually native speakers).

Let's analyse the opening minute of his speech:

> *Let's talk about manias. Let's start with Beatle mania: hysterical teenagers, crying, screaming, pandemonium. Sports mania: deafening crowds, all for one idea -- get the ball in the net. Okay, religious mania: there's rapture, there's weeping, there's visions. Manias can be good. Manias can be alarming. Or manias can be deadly.*
>
> *The world has a new mania. A mania for learning English. Listen as Chinese students practice their English by screaming it.*

72 words. 10 sentences. 60 seconds. That's an average of 7.2 words per sentence – much less than 100 words per minute. Jay chooses to:

- use short sentences

- use simple language

- speak very slowly and clearly

Does Jay launch straight into his topic? No. He introduces the theme i.e. manias, but not the key topic i.e. English. This gives the audience (particularly the non-natives) time to tune into his voice. So consider having a 30 second introduction to your presentation where the audience hear something interesting and relevant, but not crucial.

Jay does not use any written slides, only images. This may work if your message is incredibly clear and requires little or no mental effort on the part of the audience.

However, international audiences generally appreciate slides with at least some text on them. This means that if they can't understand what you are saying, they can at least follow your slides.

To learn some more factors that you need to be aware of when talking to non-natives see Steve Silberman's talk on TED (2.5, but read 2.4 first to understand the context).

19.6   Learn another language!

You will quickly realise what a humbling experience learning another language can be – but fun too!

19.7   Have two versions of your presentation

You could have two versions of your presentation. The one that you show the audience, and a more detailed version with additional texts and notes which the audience can download and watch

- before they come to your presentation so that they are prepared for what you are going to tell them (OK, this might ruin the impact of any great statistics or images that you have used, but the benefits for an audience whose English is poor far outweigh such issues)

- while you are giving your presentation – in fact many of the people in your audience will have a laptop, iPad, tablet or smartphone with them, so they can upload your slides + notes

- after your presentation to enable them to recap

19.8   Ensure you adapt a presentation that you have given to native speakers and make it suitable for non-natives

I once watched an informal presentation on a web application framework called Ruby on Rails. The presenters were from the US, but the conference was in Europe. They had slides titles such as:

Yep, even scaffolding works

Some sorta cool aspects of fixtures

Preeeeetttty!

What the hell is RSpec?

Such titles are fun, but not very informative for non-natives.

19.9   Focus on what non-natives actually like about native speakers

Although some types of native speakers have a reputation for being nearly impossible to understand, particularly those with a strong regional accent and / or who mumble, the structure and style of their presentations is generally appreciated.

Things that non-natives like about native speakers' presentations (and Scandinavians' too):

1. attractive slides with minimal text

2. friendly delivery

3. lots of examples

4. not too much detail

5. feeling involved

6. narrative style e.g. *So then you think 'Hey, we could do this instead'*

7. speaker's passion for his / her topic

Although some non-native speakers adopt some of the points above, many don't. This is because their education system tends to be much more formal. Academics are not supposed to be too friendly or fun. They are not supposed to make it easy for their listener. The idea for them is to show off rather than show how.

So use the above seven points to show that you really care about the audience. And if you say everything slowly and clearly, you are guaranteed to get a good reception!

19.10   Be careful of cultural differences

Avoid making references to the cultures of others as you may not be sure that what you are saying is positive or negative. Whilst teaching English in Cairo, my wife posed a hypothetical scenario to her audience: *Imagine that the Nile dried up*. The debate that ensued was extremely heated and many of the students were upset: the topic was to sensitive for them (the Nile, for some, was a life source).

Stick to making references about your own culture, where you should be on safer ground.

19.11   Avoid humor, but have fun

Although the humor of Laurel & Hardy and Mr Bean is fairly universal, much Anglo humor either gets lost – or worse – may offend your audience.

While preparing another book in this series, *English for Writing Research Papers*, I wrote a few spoof abstracts that I considered using as examples. Below is one such abstract from an imaginary paper entitled *Revisiting Gibbon's decadent Rome: parallels in social media and the downfall of the West*.

> In 1789 Edward Gibbon published the last volume of his epic tome *The History of the Decline and Fall of the Roman Empire*, with a clear allusion as to where civilization in the west was heading in the 19th century. He summed up history as being: *little more than the register of the crimes, follies, and misfortunes of mankind*. New research has brought to light a surprising number of parallels between Roman decadence and the social media of

today. This paper reports on manuscripts, recently discovered in the Vatican archives, which were written at the height of Rome's excesses. These manuscripts reveal hitherto unknown services that operated within the empire. These include *tuba tua*, where citizens would bring their wind instruments to the Forum and perform in public (feedback was left in the form of graffiti on the walls near the *cauponiae* - fast-food restaurants), *vox populi* (with its offshoot "Rome's got talent"), *Liber Faciērum,* and *twitterus* (inane blathering amongst slaves). Our findings combined with Gibbon's prognosis would seem to suggest that the west's self obsession and self indulgence will lead to self destruction and possibly a new wave of barbaric invasions.

I was pleased with my abstract. I even sent it to a professor of Latin at the University of Sassari in Sardinia so that she could check the 'Latin'. I then sent it around to various teachers in Europe for them to test it out on their students. My aim was to see whether any students might at best find it amusing or at worst plain stupid or vulgar.

The answers came back: most students (particularly the Germans and Austrians) had no idea that it was a spoof, one teacher wrote to me saying: *They didn't find it offensive, nor funny (but they didn't find it not funny either: they just took it at face value with a barely a reaction).* In fact, it hardly raised a smile amongst teachers either!

So what I had thought was rather clever and amusing got no reaction at all!

In 2015, Nobel prize winner professor Tim Hunt was forced to resign from his position after telling an audience at the World Conference of Science Journalists in South Korea:

> Let me tell you about my trouble with girls. Three things happen when they are in the lab:
> You fall in love with them, they fall in love with you, and when you criticize them they cry.

The reaction he received was generally one of outrage and disgust. Hunt claimed his comments were meant to be ironic and lighthearted but had been "interpreted deadly seriously by my audience."

And that's my point – what you may find amusing may be interpreted very differently by your audience.

Essentially, we cannot ever be sure that people will share our sense of humor, unless, of course, we test it out on many other people. Below is a letter written by Peter White and sent to the editor of the British journal *The Oldie* in 2015. It went viral immediately, and it's not hard to understand why.

Sir: I haven't got a computer, but I was told about Facebook and Twitter and am trying to make friends outside Facebook and Twitter while applying the same principles.

Every day, I walk down the streets and tell passers-by what I have eaten, how I feel, what I have done the night before and what I will do for the rest of the day. I give them pictures of my wife, my daughter, my dog and me gardening and on holiday, spending time by the pool. I also listen to their conversations, tell them I 'like' them and give them my opinion on every subject that interests me…whether it interests them or not.

And it works. I have four people following me; two police officers, a social worker and a psychiatrist.

Basically, if you have something funny that you want to say, check with others first whether (i) it is actually funny, (ii) it is appropriate for your intended audience.

However … if you are doing a presentation late in the conference, and you notice that the audience has consistently reacted well to what you would consider humorous in other people's presentations, then you can cautiously try out your own brand. But test it out on colleagues first.

19.12   Explain key words

It helps your audience if you explain any key words to them.

19.13   Choose appropriate vocabulary

Here is a very potted history of the English language (55 BC to 1301 AD):

Julius Caesar invaded 'Britain' in 55 BC - several military words were introduced into the language. More Latin came with St Augustine who was sent by the pope in 697 AD to convert the Irish (and then mainland 'Britain') to Christianity, hence the predominance of Latin-based religious words (e.g. *spirit, priest, religion, redemption*). In the meantime 'Britain' was invaded by the Angles, Saxons and Jutes, then by Vikings - all these invaders came from Northern Europe and contributed to the 'Anglo Saxon' element in our language (e.g. our 'four-letter' words!). By 1066 English (Old English) was a complex, but fairly regular, language. All this changed with the Battle of Hasting in 1066 when the Normans killed the English King Harold, and French became the 'official' language until 1301.

Latin and French-based words in English thus tend to be considered more erudite and formal: compare a 'hearty welcome' with a 'cordial reception'.

All this has big implications on the words that you should choose for your presentation.

ANGLO-SAXON	LATIN / FRENCH
aim	objective
comprehend	understand
mankind	humanity
unbelievable	incredible
indication	clue
amusing	funny
result	outcome
drawback	disadvantage
irresponsible	reckless
earnings	profits

Try this short test. Simply underline the words that are in the wrong column in the table above. The key is at the end of this subsection.

So which words are non-native speakers likely to understand most?

The answer is that speakers of nearly all languages are more likely to understand more formal English words (i.e. those that derive from Latin, Greek and French). And this is true irrespectively of whether their own language is Latin/French/Greek-based or not. This is because:

- when learning English, many non-natives study quite formal texts

- the longer the word, the more time the non native has to hear it (compare *hard* with *difficult*)

This means that although you may feel that you sound very formal, the audience may not perceive this. In any case, if you do speak in a formal way, they will probably understand more of what you say.

However, one sign of informality is shorter sentences, and this is an aspect that you should certainly adopt. Short sentences clearly spoken are much easier to understand than long formal sentences.

Try getting into the habit of being able to think of synonyms for words. This will enable you to communicate better when your counterpart doesn't understand a particular word. This is true not just for presentations (and socializing at conferences), but also in email correspondence.

The email below (written by a British speaker) might be very hard to understand for a non-native who is not proficient in English – the 'offending' words and expressions are in italics.

Sorry for not getting back to you till now, but *I've had my back up against the wall*. To answer your two questions:

1) Attached are the notes you need to read. Let me know when you're *up to speed*.
2) *Re* the meeting. Looks as if I'm going to be *totally bogged down* for the next *fortnight*, but if you'd like to *give us a buzz* on Fri *aft* that would be *brill*.

Nice one, Phil

Try to write your emails in a more formal way.

KEY Anglo-Saxon: aim, understand, mankind, unbelievable, clue, funny, outcome, drawback, reckless, earnings

19.14   Mind your language!

As already mentioned (19.13), multi-syllable words are better for three reasons:

1. they are longer, so there is a greater chance of the audience knowing them

2. for Latinate speakers (i.e. Italian, Spanish, French, Portuguese and Romanian) these words are likely to be the same as in their own language

3. they tend to be words that non-natives learn at school (so even those whose language does not have its roots in Latin or Greek are more likely to understand them)

More examples: *aim* vs *objective, drawback* vs *disadvantage, clue* vs *indication, reckless* vs *irresponsible* (prefer the second choice in each case).

The choice of words applies not just to what you say, but also to what you write on your slides. Although workshops and seminars tend to be less formal, it is worth remembering that too much informality may be hard for non-natives to understand.

In the Ruby on Rails (see Sect. 19.8) presentations, the Americans used some colloquial expressions that would have been very hard for most of the audience to understand. Here are some examples:

it has a bunch of useful features

you have to do a backflip in your head

people who are newbies like me

it is certainly not all plain sailing

it's just part and parcel of

you might get a kick out of this

19.15   Speak slowly and enunciate very clearly

If you say the following you will depress your audience immediately:

I know I speak fast, so if I go too quickly then raise a hand.

You are basically saying:

Sorry, but I am native speaker. I have never learned a foreign language. I have no idea what it is like not to understand. I know I speak fast, so unfortunately you are not going to understand much. Sorry about that.

In any case, anyone who has the courage to 'raise a hand' would be admitting that they didn't understand (even though the rest of the audience probably didn't understand either) and would likely think that they would lose face in front of colleagues.

As native speakers we also tend to slur our words, and drop our voice at the end of a sentences. Both these factors make us harder to understand.

Finally, remember NOT to apply Boren's first law: *When in doubt, mumble.* The problem is that to a non-native a lot of what native speakers say sounds like mumbling! So never mumble, and when in doubt, say so (clearly!). By the way who was Boren? I have been unable to find out!

19.16   Workshops and seminars: try to reduce anxiety levels of the audience as soon as possible

One of your primary and constant goals should be to reduce your audience's anxiety levels to the absolute minimum. You can do this by:

- putting yourself in your audience's shoes

- speaking slowly and clearly

- ensuring that you never put anyone in a position where they might lose face

- explain that when you ask a question, you will always say it twice and you will try to phrase it in a way that is easy to understand and easy to respond to

19.17 Never equate a person's level of English with their level of intelligence

If someone says to you 'he can hardly speak a word of English', what is your reaction? Most people would consciously or subconsciously think that 'he' was somewhat lacking in intelligence. But probably the only reason 'he' doesn't speak English is that he wasn't born in a country where English is the official language.

Don't forget the enormous advantages you have by being born in a native-English speaking country.

So avoid making assumptions that someone's ability to speak English reflects their level of intelligence.

19.18 Take responsibility for any lack of understanding by your interlocutor

Many non-native researchers, particularly those of the older generation or in countries where the Internet is not freely available, have been mainly exposed to English through standardized textbook recordings of clear-speaking actors and actresses reading simplified scripts, or through their English teacher who was probably not a native speaker. Such learners are thus likely to have great difficulty when encountering regional accents, informal register, colloquial structures/expressions, high-speed 'youth-speak', and the like. You need to modify your normal spoken variety accordingly.

I asked Chandler Davis, Professor of Mathematics at Toronto University, whether there was a need for a chapter in this book on helping native speakers communicate more effectively with non-natives. He wrote to me saying:

Your question reminds me of the reaction of my late friend Moe Schreiber to his first scientific travel in Europe: "There's a common language for Poles, Hungarians, and Italians to communicate with each other. It's English; and I don't speak it." Moe's dilemmas was: *How do I frame my English utterances so they are not only good English but also unbaffling to non-native speakers.*

19.19   Ask your participants questions during workshops

The success of your workshop or seminar depends on how much your audience understand. There are two main ways to check if they have understood:

1. by setting them a practical task to do which is related to what you have just explained. Their level of success in this task will be a clear indicator of whether they have understood or not

2. by asking them pertinent questions

The first solution is unlikely to be suitable at a conference. But the second is entirely feasible ... and fundamental. You need to be absolutely sure they understand. If you don't ask any questions, the risk is that you will be the only person talking and this will be extremely tiring for your participants.

An additional problem is that people of whatever culture:

- are reluctant to admit that they haven't understood, particularly as they erroneously conclude that the rest of the audience will have understood

- do not ask questions because they fear that they may not be relevant for other members of the audience, or because they are embarrassed about their level of English

The result is that only those with good English will ask the questions. And those with the low English will probably not even understand the questions asked by the good-English-speaking colleagues.

19.20   Avoid saying 'OK?' to check understanding during workshops

If you ask participants in a workshop or seminar if they have understood, some will certainly say 'yes' including some people who have understood nothing, simply because they don't want to lose face. So it may be useful to get someone to repeat back in their own words what they think they have understood.

Constantly be on the look out for vacant expressions. It is very easy to fall into the habit of addressing only those people who you know are following you and thus ignoring those who are not.

Note that when checking whether your audience are following, the questions below are rarely effective – they are the equivalent of just saying *OK?*

Is that clear? Does everyone understand? Everybody with me? Does anyone have any questions at this point? Does that all seem to make sense?

As with putting their hand up (see 00 above) participants are likely to be too embarrassed to admit that they don't understand.

One possibility is to get everyone to write down a couple of questions to ask. They can then compare questions with the person sitting next to them. They might be able to answer the questions without your help, if not you can read their questions and choose some to focus on. Either way, it takes the focus off you for a while and they can relax without having to concentrate on listening to you.

19.21   Remind the audience of the big picture

Make sure the audience is always aware of the big picture, by:

- referring back to the agenda to show where you are

- referring back to previous slides either verbally or by reshowing them the same slide

- reminding them why you are telling them something

- giving them mini summaries (remember you are very familiar with what you are talking about, but they may need reminding)

- warning them about what's coming next

19.22 Have recap slides in addition to or as an occasional alternative to questions slides

You can create variety in your workshop if you occasionally insert slides containing a summary (i.e. a recap slide). You can ask your audience to read the summary and ask them which points they would like you to explain again, or which points they found the most difficult to understand. You can then say

Can you explain exactly what it is that you did not understand?

This should then automatically force them to ask you for clarifications.

In any case, always go over key points more than once.

19.23 Reduce your talking time during workshops, seminars and training sessions

Being a participant at a workshop that is held in your own language is very different from being a participant and listening to a foreign language. When listening to your own language the effort is minimal, you can happily listen to the speaker telling jokes and anecdotes, going off at a tangent. You also know when you can tune out and tune back in again when the speaker goes back to the main point.

When the presentation or workshop is in another language, you don't have this control over your own level of participation.

This means that you as a presenter need to heavily adapt any workshops you've done in your native country, when you hold them outside that country.

Whereas in your own country you might speak for about 40-50% of the time, with non-natives you need to cut down your talking time as much as possible by avoiding:

- anecdotes

- digressions

- improvising

In the above three cases we tend to use a lot more words and to speak more quickly, neither of which are going to help our audience.

Finally, when giving any instructions make them short, clear, and phrase them in short sentences spoken very slowly.

19.24   Timing and breaks: using exercises in workshops

Exercises and demos take much longer to set up with a non-native audience, so you are likely to achieve much less in a session than you would with native speakers.

You also need to schedule in breaks. This is because it is quite exhausting listening to someone speaking in another language for long periods of time.

19.25   Handouts

Every audience appreciates a handout with the key points summarized.

19.26   If you are a participant, never dominate the discussion

If you are not actually holding the workshop or seminar, but are instead attending it, make sure you don't ally yourself with the other native speakers and take over the workshop. Remember that you have a distinct advantage over the non-native participants. You can understand and react much more quickly. So always give the others time to collect their thoughts and mentally prepare what they want to say.

The same guidelines apply to when having a conversation on a social occasion – it is very easy for those with the best command of English to take over the discussion.

Chapter 20

Useful Phrases

20.1 PART 1 PRESENTATIONS AND POSTERS

20.1.1 Introductions and outline

Introducing institute/department

Hi. Thanks for coming …
I am a PhD student/researcher/technician at …
I am doing a PhD/a Masters/some research at …
I am part of a team of 20 researchers and most of our funding comes from …
The work that I am going to present to you today was carried out with the collaboration of the University of …

Telling the audience what point your research has reached and in what context it is

What I am going to present is actually still only in its early stages, but I really think that our findings so far are worth telling you.
We are already at a quite advanced stage of the research, but I was hoping to get some feedback from you on certain aspects relating to …
Our research, which we have just finished, is actually part of a wider project involving …

Giving a general outline (formal)

In this presentation I am going to/I would like to/I will

discuss some findings of an international project
examine/analyze/bring to your attention
introduce the notion of/a new model of
review/discuss/describe/argue that

© Springer International Publishing Switzerland 2016
A. Wallwork, *English for Presentations at International Conferences*,
English for Academic Research, DOI 10.1007/978-3-319-26330-4_20

address a particular issue, which in my opinion, ..
give an analysis of/explore the meaning of
cite research by Wallwork and Southern

Giving your agenda (traditional)

I will begin with an introduction to …
I will begin by giving you an overview of …
Then I will move on to …
After that I will deal with …
And I will conclude with …

Giving your agenda (less formal)

First, I'd like to do x/I'm going to do/First, I'll be looking at X.
Then we'll be looking at Y/Then, we'll focus on Y.
And finally we'll have a look at Z/Finally, I'm going to take you through Z.
So, let's begin by looking at X.

Giving your agenda (informal)

So this is what I am going to talk about …
… and the main focus will be on …
… and what I think, well what I hope, you will find interesting is …
I'm NOT going to cover P and Q, I'm just going to …

Giving your agenda (more dynamic)

This is what I'm planning to cover.
I've chosen to focus on X because I think

    it has massive implications for …
    it is an area that has been really neglected …
    I'm hoping to get some ideas from you on how to …
    that what we've found is really interesting

I think we have found a

    radically new solution for …
    truly innovative approach to …
    novel way to ..

We are excited about our results because this is the first time research has shown that …
Why is X is so important? Well, in this presentation I am going to give you three
    good reasons …
What do we know about Y? Well, actually a lot more/less than you might think.
    Today I hope to prove to you that …

Referring to handout

I've prepared a handout on this, which I will give you at the end - so there's no need
to take notes.
Details can also be found on our website. The URL is on the handout.

20.1.2   Transitions

Moving on to the main body of the presentation

Okay, so let me start by looking at …
So first I'd like to give you a bit of background.
So why did we undertake this research? Well, …
So what were our main objectives? Well, …

Introducing a new element or topic

With regard to x …
As far as x is concerned …
Regarding x …

Signaling that the topic is about to change

Before I give you some more detailed statistics and my overall conclusions, I am
just going to show you how our results can be generalized to a wider scenario.
In a few minutes I am going to tell you about X and Y, which I hope should explain
why we did this research in the first place. But first I want to talk to you about …

Showing where you are in the original agenda

Okay so this is where we are ..
This is what we've looked at so far.
So, we're now on page 10 of the handout.

Referring to previous topic to introduce next topic

Before moving on to Z, I'd just like to reiterate what I said about Y.
Okay, so that's all I wanted to say about X and Y. Now let's look at Z.
Having considered X, let's go on and look at Y.
Not only have we experienced success with X, but also with Y.
We've focused on X, equally important is Y.
You remember that I said X was used for Y [go back to relevant slide], well now
we're going to see how it can be used for Z.

Getting the audience interested in the next topic

Did you know that you can do X with Y? You didn't, well in the next section of this presentation I'll be telling you how.

Direct transition

Let me now move onto the question of …
This brings me to my next point …
Next I would like to examine …
Now we're going to look at Z. // Now I'd like to show you Z. // Now I'd like to talk about Z.
Okay, let's move on to Z.
Now we are going to do X. X will help you to do Y.

20.1.3   Emphasizing, qualifying, giving examples

Emphasizing a point

I must emphasize that ..
What I want to highlight is …
At this point I would like to stress that …
What I would really like you to focus on here is …
These are the main points to remember:
The main argument in favor of/against this is ..
The fact is that …
This is a particularly important point.
This is worth remembering because …
You may not be aware of this but …

Communicating value and benefits

So, the key benefit is…
One of the main advantages is…
What this means is that …
We are sure that this will lead to increased …
What I would like you to notice here is …
What I like about this is …
The great thing about this is …

Expressing surprise in order to gain interest

To our surprise, we found that …
We were surprised to find that …
An unexpected result was …
Interestingly, we discovered that …

Qualifying what you are saying

Broadly speaking, we can say that ...
In most cases/In general this is true.
In very general terms ...
With certain exceptions, this can be seen as ...
For the most part, people are inclined to think that ...
Here is a broad outline of ...

Qualifying what you have just said

Having said that ...
Nevertheless, despite this ...
But in reality ...
Actually ...
In fact ...

Giving explanations

As a result of ... Due to the fact that ... Thanks to ...
This problem goes back to ...
The thing is that ...
On the grounds that ...

Giving examples

Let's say I have ... and I just want to ...
Imagine that you ...
You'll see that this is very similar to ...
I've got an example of this here ... show slide
I've brought an example of this with me ... show object
There are many ways to do this, for example/for instance you can ...
There are several examples of this, such as ...

20.1.4 Diagrams

Making initial reference to the diagram

Here you can see ...
I have included this chart because ...
This is a detail from the previous figure ...
This should give you a clearer picture of ...
This diagram illustrates ...

Explaining what you have done to simplify a diagram

For ease of presentation, I have only included essential information.
For the sake of simplicity, I have reduced all the numbers to whole numbers.
This is an extremely simplified view of the situation, but it is enough to illustrate that …
In reality this table should also include other factors, but for the sake of simplicity I have just chosen these two key points.
This is obviously not an exact/accurate picture of the real situation, but it should give you an idea of …
I have left a lot of detail out, but in any case this should help you to …
if you are interested you can find more information on this in my paper.

Indicating what part of the diagram you want them to focus on

Basically what I want to highlight is …
I really just want you to focus on …
You can ignore/Don't worry about this part here.
This diagram is rather complex, but the only thing I want you to notice is …

Explaining the lines, curves, arrows

On the x axis is … On the y axis we have …
I chose these values for the axes because …
In this diagram, double circles mean that … whereas black circles mean … dashed lines mean … continuous lines mean …
Time is represented by a dotted line.
Dashed lines correspond to … whereas zig-zag lines mean …
The thin dashed gray line indicates that …
These dotted curves are supposed to represent …
The solid curve is …
These horizontal arrows indicate …
There is a slight/gradual/sharp decrease in …
The curve rises rapidly, then reaches a peak, and then forms a plateau.
As you can see, this wavy curve has a series of peaks and troughs.

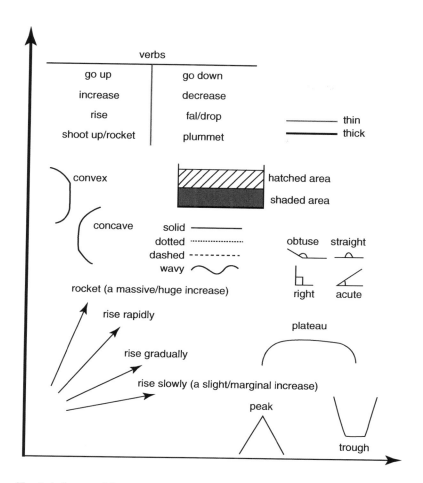

Explaining positions

on the left is … on the left side here …
in the middle …
here, at the top …
down in this section …
over here is a …
the upper/lower section …

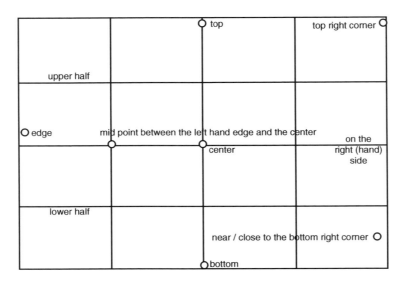

20.1.5   Making reference to parts of the presentation

Referring forward

I'm going to do X, Y, and Z.
I'm not going to cover this aspect now, I'm just going to …
I'll go into a bit of detail for each concept.
I'll explain this in a moment/I'll talk about that later.
As we will see later …

Referring backward

As I said before …
Remember I said that …
The concept I mentioned earlier …
As I mentioned a moment ago …
To return to my earlier point …
If we go back to this slide … (shows an earlier slide)

Referring to current slide

Here you can see …
Notice that it has …
As you can see …

20.1.6 Discussing results, conclusions, future work

Very strong affirmations (but see Section 14.4)

These results definitely prove that ...
We are convinced that our results show that ...
What these results prove is ...

Tentative affirmations

Our results would seem to show that ...
What these findings seem to highlight is ...
I think that these results may indicate that ...
It seems probable from these results that ...
I think it is reasonable to assume that ...
Under the hypothesis that $x = y$, what these results probably mean is ...
We are assuming that the reason for this discrepancy is ...
We are presuming that this nonagreement is due to ...
This may indicate that ...
A possible explanation is ...
I believe this is due to ...

Future work

So, we've still got quite a long way to go. What we need to do now is ...
Given these results, it seems to us that the best thing to do now is ...
A promising area for future research would probably be ...
What we are planning to do next is ...

Eliciting audience help

To be honest, we are not exactly sure what these results may implicate ...
We think our results show that $x = y$, and we were rather hoping to find other people who may be doing similar research to confirm this for us ...
We are not really sure why the results appear to be so contradictory, and we were wondering whether someone here might be able to help us out with this.
We are actually looking for partners in this project, so if anybody is interested, please let us know.

20.1.7 Ending

Warning audience that presentation is near the end

Okay, we're very close to the end now, but there are just a couple of important things that I still want to tell you.

Final summary

Well that brings me to the end of the presentation. So, just to recap …

Telling the audience where they can find further information

I am afraid that I don't have time to go into this in any further detail. But you can find more information about it on this website (which is on the back page of your handout).

If you would like more information on this, then please feel free to email me. My address is on the back page of the handout./My address is in the congress notes.

Thanking the audience

Thanks very much for coming.
Thank you for your attention.

20.1.8 Questions and answers

Beginning a Q&A session

Does anyone have any questions on this?
I'd be really interested in hearing your questions on this.
[If no one asks as a question] One question I am often asked is …

Referring to level of English just before Q&A session

If you ask any questions I would be grateful if you could ask them slowly and clearly, as

– my English is a bit rusty
– many attendees here today are not native speakers of English

Handling the session

Okay, could we start with the question from the gentleman/lady at the back. Yes, you.
[Interrupting someone] Sorry, first could we just hear from this woman/man at the front.
Do you mind just repeating the question because I don't think the people at the back heard you.
I think we have time for just one more question.
Okay, I am afraid our time is up, but if anyone is interested in asking more questions I'll be in the bar and at the social dinner tonight.

What to say when you don't understand a question from the audience

Sorry, could you repeat the question more slowly please?
Sorry, could you speak up please?
Sorry, I didn't hear the first/last part of your question.
Sorry, I still don't understand—would you mind asking me the question again in the break?
Sorry, but to answer that question would take rather too long, however you can find the explanation on my web pages or in my paper.
I'm not exactly clear what your question is.

Going back to the presentation after taking questions mid presentation

Okay, would you mind if I moved on now, because I've still got a couple of things I wanted to say?

Interpreting the questions

If I'm not wrong, I think what you are asking is …
Can I just be sure that I understand? You are asking me if …
So what you are saying is …
So your question is …

Avoiding difficult questions

I'm not familiar with the details regarding that question.
I can't give you an exact answer on that, I am afraid.
That's a very interesting question and my answer is simply I really don't know!
That's a good question and I wish I had a ready answer, but I am afraid I don't.
You know, I've never been asked that question before and to be honest I really wouldn't know how to answer it.
I would not like to comment on that.
I am sorry but I am not in a position to comment on that.
I am not sure there really is a right or wrong answer to that. What I personally believe is …

Asking for time or deferring

I think it would be best if my colleague answered that question for you.
Can I get back to you on that one?
Could we talk about that over a drink?
I need to think about that question. Do you think we could discuss it in the bar?
You've raised a really important point, so important that I think I would rather have a bit of time to think about the best answer. So if you give me your email address at the end, I'll get back to you.
At the moment I don't have all the facts I need to answer that question, but if you email me I can get back to you.
Offhand, I can't answer that question but if you …

Commenting on audience questions

I know exactly what you mean but the thing is …
I take your point but in my experience I have found that …
You're quite right and it is something that I am actually working on now.
I'm glad you raised that point, in fact one of my colleagues will be able to answer that for you.
Yes, the additional experiments you suggest would be very useful. Maybe we could talk about them over lunch.

Suggesting that Q & A session can continue at the bar

Does anyone fancy going for a drink? because it would be very helpful to have your feedback.
Would anyone like to go for a drink? because I'd be really interested to hear your views on this.

20.1.9   Things that can go wrong

Equipment doesn't work

I think the bulb must have gone on the projector. Could someone please bring me a replacement? In the meantime let me write on the whiteboard what I wanted to say about …
The microphone/mike doesn't seem to be working. Can everyone hear me at the back?
I don't know what has happened to my laptop but the program seems to have crashed. Please bear with me while I reboot.
Okay, it looks as if I will have to continue my presentation without the slides. Let me just look at my notes a second.

You realize that a slide contains a mistake

You know what, there's a mistake here, it should be …
Sorry this figure should be 100 not 1,000.

Your mobile phone rings and you have to turn it off

I'm really sorry about that. I thought I had switched it off.

You forget where you are in the presentation

Sorry, what was I saying?
Where were we up to? Can anyone remind me?
Sorry I've lost track of what I was saying.
Sorry, I seem to have forgotten what I was saying.

If you are about to go over your allocated time

It looks as if we are running out of time. Would it be okay if I continued for another 10 minutes?
If any of you have to leave straight away, I quite understand.
I am really sorry about this. But in any case, you can find the conclusions in the handout.
I will put a copy of the presentation on our website.

Getting the person interested

Hi, would you like some more information?
Would you like me to take you through the process?
I have a short demo here if you would like to look at it.
Would you like to hear some more details on the methodology?

Offering further help

Would you like a copy of this handout/brochure/document? It basically says the same as the poster but in a lot more detail.
Here is my paper, if you would like a copy.
You can find more details on my website, which is written on my card here.

Asking questions about the person's research

May I ask what field you are in?
Where are you based?
How long have you been working in this field?

Opening up possibilities for further contact

Would you like to give me your email address?
Are you giving a presentation yourself?
Are you going to be at the dinner tonight?
Might you be interested in setting up a collaboration?

Saying goodbye

Thank you very much.
It was very nice to meet you.
Hope to see you around.
Hope to see you again.
I'll email you the website/my paper/the documentation.
Let's keep in touch.
Goodbye.

20.1.10   What to say during a poster session

Getting the person interested

Hi, would you like some more information?
Would you like me to take you through the process?
I have a short demo here if you would like to look at it.
Would like to hear some more details on the methodology?

Asking questions about the person's research

Can I ask what field you are in?
Where are you based?
How long have you been working in this field?

Opening up possibilities for further contact

Would you like to give me your email address?
Are you giving a presentation yourself?
Are you going to be at the dinner tonight?
Might you be interested in setting up a collaboration?

Offering further help

Would you like a copy of this handout / brochure / document? - it basically says the same as the poster but in a lot more detail.
Here is my paper, if you would like a copy.
You can find more details on my website, which is written on my card here.

Saying goodbye

Thank you very much.
It was very nice to meet you.
Hope to see you around.
Hope to see you again.
I'll email you the website / my paper / the documentation.
Let's keep in touch
Goodbye.

20.2   PART 2: NETWORKING

20.2.1   Introductions

Meeting people for the first time (previous contact via email, phone)

Hello, pleased to meet you finally.
So, finally, we meet.
I'm very glad to have the opportunity to speak to you in person.
I think we have exchanged a few emails, and maybe spoken on the phone.

Meeting people for the first time (no previous contact)

Hello, I don't think we've met. I'm …
Pleased to meet you.
Nice to meet you, too.
May I introduce myself? My name is …
I'm responsible for / I'm in charge of … I'm head of …
Good morning, I'm …
How do you do?
Here is my card.
Do you have a card?

Introducing people

Can I introduce a colleague of mine? This is Irmin Schmidt.
Hello, Pete, this is Ursula.
David, this is Olga. Olga, this is David.
I'm afraid Wolfgang cannot be with us today.

Telling people how to address you

Please call me Holger.
OK, and I'm Damo.
Fine, please call me Damo.

20.2.2   Meeting people who you have met before

Meeting people who you think you may have met before

Excuse me, I think we may have met before, I'm …
Hi, have we met before?
Hi, you must be …

Seeing people you have already met before

Hi, Tom, good to see you again, how are you doing?
Hi, how's it going? I haven't seen you for ages.
How's things?
Great to see you.
I'm (very) pleased to see you again.

Catching up

How did the trip to Africa go?
How's the new job going?
How's your husband? And the children?
How is the new project going?

20.2.3 Small talk

Asking questions

Is it that the first time you have attended this conference?
Where are you staying?
Where are you from?
What did you think of the last presentation?
What presentations are you planning to see this afternoon?
What was the best presentation so far do you think?
Are you going to present something?
Had you ever seen Professor Jones present before? She's great don't you think?
Are you coming to the gala dinner?
So, you said you were doing some research into x. Do have any interesting results yet?
So you were saying your were born in x—what's it like there?

Showing interest

Oh, are you?
Oh, is it?
Oh, really?
Right.
That's interesting.
Oh, I hadn't realized.

Apologizing for something you shouldn't have said

Sorry, I didn't mean to …
Sorry, I thought you meant …
I meant …
I didn't mean to offend.
Sorry I obviously didn't make myself clear.

20.2.4   Arranging meetings

Suggesting a time / day

Would tomorrow morning at 9.00 suit you?
Could you make it in the afternoon?
Shall we say 2.30, then?
Could you manage the day after tomorrow?
What about after the last presentation this afternoon?

Making an alternative suggestion

Tomorrow would be better for me.
If it's OK with you, I think I'd prefer to make it 3.30.
Could we make it a little later?

Responding positively

OK, that sounds like a good idea.
Yes, that's fine.
Yes, that'll be fine.
That's no problem.

Responding negatively

I'm sorry, I really don't think I will have time. I have a presentation tomorrow and I
    am still working on some of the slides.
I don't think I can manage tomorrow morning.
I'm not sure about what I am doing tonight, I need to check with my colleagues and
    then get back to you.
The problem is that I already have a series of informal meetings lined up.

Cancelling a meeting set up by the other person

Something has come up, so I'm afraid I can't come.
Sorry but the other members of my group have arranged for me to …
Sorry but it looks as though I am going to be busy all tomorrow. The thing is I have to …

Postponing a meeting that you set up

I'm really sorry but I can't make our meeting tomorrow morning because my pro-
    fessor needs me to …
I am very sorry about this, and I am sorry I couldn't let you know sooner. I hope this
    has not inconvenienced you.
In any case, I was wondering whether we could rearrange for tomorrow night.

20.2.5 At an informal one-to-one meeting

Initiating a topic

First of all, I wanted to ask you about …
What is your view on … ?

Changing a topic / returning to a topic

I've just thought of something else …
Sorry to interrupt, I just need to tell you about …
Can I interrupt a moment?
But going back to what you said earlier …
I've been thinking about what you said and …

Stalling and deferring by interviewee

Could I just think about that a second?
Just a moment, I really need to think about that.
Could I get back to you on that? I'll email you the answer.

Concluding by interviewer

Well, I don't want to keep you any longer.
Well, I think that's covered everything.
I think the next session is starting in a couple of minutes, so we had better stop.

Asking for a follow up

Would it be OK if I email you with any other questions that I think of?
Would you have time to continue this conversation at lunch today?

Thanking

Thank you so much. It has been really useful.
That's great. You have told me everything I needed to know.
It was really very kind of you to …
Thanks very much for …
Thank you very much indeed for …
I don't know how to thank you for …
You've been really helpful.

Responding to thanks

You're welcome.
Don't mention it.
Not at all.
It's my pleasure.
That's alright.

20.2.6   At the bar, restaurant and social dinners

Formal invitations for dinner

Would you like to have lunch next Friday?
If you are not busy tonight, would you like to … ?
We're organizing a dinner tonight, I was wondering whether you might like to come?
I'd like to invite you to dinner.

Accepting

That's very kind of you. I'd love to come. What time are you meeting?
Thank you, I'd love to.
That sounds great.
What a nice idea.

Responding to an acceptance

Great. OK, well we could meet downstairs in the lobby.
Great. I could pass by your hotel at 7.30 if you like.

Declining

I'm afraid I can't, I'm busy on Friday.
That's very nice of you, but …
Thanks but I have to make the final touches to my presentation.
No, I'm sorry I'm afraid I can't make it.
Unfortunately, I'm already doing something tomorrow night.

Responding to a non-acceptance

Oh that's a shame, but not to worry.
Oh well, maybe another time.

Informal invitation to go to the bar / cafe

Shall we go and have a coffee?
Would you like to go and get a coffee?
What about a coffee?
Do you know if there is a coffee machine somewhere in the building?

Offering drink / food

Can I get you anything?
What can I get you?
Would you like a coffee?
Black or white? How many sugars?
So, what would you like to drink?
Would you like some more wine?
Shall I pour it for you?

Accepting offer

I'll have a coffee please.
I think I'll have an orange juice.
No, nothing for me thanks.

Toasting

Cheers.
To your good health.
To distant friends.

Questions and answers at the bar / cafe

Do you often come to this bar?
Yes, either this one or the one across the road.
Is there a bathroom here?
Well, I think we'd better get back—the next session starts in 10 minutes.
Shall we get back?

Arriving at a restaurant

We've booked a table for 10.
Could we sit outside please?
Could we have a table in the corner / by the window?
Actually we seem to have got here a bit too early.
Are the others on their way?
Would you like something to drink / Shall we sit down at the bar while we're waiting for a table?
OK, I think we can go to our table now.

Menu

Can / May / Could I have the menu please?
Do you have a set menu / a menu with local dishes?
Do you have any vegetarian dishes?

Explaining things on the menu and asking for clarification

Shall I explain some of the things on the menu?
Well, basically these are all fish dishes.
I'd recommend it because it's really tasty and typical of this area of my country.
This is a salad made up of eggs, tuna fish, and onions.
Could you tell me what xxx is?

Making suggestions

Can I get you another drink?
Would you like anything else?
Shall I order some wine?
Would you like anything to drink? A glass of wine?
Would you like a little more wine?
Would you prefer sparkling or still water?
What are you going to have?
Are you going to have a starter?
Why don't you try some of this?
Can I tempt you to … ?
Would you like to try some of this? It's called xxx and is typical of this area.
What would you like for you main course?
Would you like anything for dessert? The sweets are homemade and are very good.

Saying what you are planning to order

I think I'll just have the starter and then move on to the main course.
I think I'll have fish.
I'd like a small portion of the chocolate cake.
I don't think I'll have any dessert thank you.

Requesting

Could you pass me the water please?
Could I have some butter please?
Do you think I could have some more wine?

Declining

Nothing else thanks.
Actually, I am on a diet.
Actually, I am allergic to nuts.
I've had enough thanks. It was delicious.

Being a host and encouraging guests to start

Do start.
Enjoy your meal.
Enjoy.
Tuck in.
Help yourself to the wine / salad.

Being a guest and commenting on food before beginning to eat

It smells delicious.
It looks really good.

Asking about and making comments on the food

Are you enjoying the fish?
Yes, it's very tasty.
This dish is delicious.
This wine is really good.

Ending the meal

Would you like a coffee, or something stronger?
Would anyone like anything else to eat or drink?

Paying

Could I have the bill please.
I'll get this.
That's very kind of you, but this is on me.
No, I insist on paying. You paid last time.
That's very kind of you.
Do you know if service is included?
Do people generally leave a tip?

Thanking

Thank you so much—it was a delicious meal and a great choice of restaurant.
Thanks very much. If you ever come to Berlin, let me know, there's an excellent restaurant where I would like to take you.
Thank you again, it was a lovely evening.

Replying to thanks

Not at all. It was my pleasure.
Don't mention it.
You're welcome.

20.2.7   Saying goodbye

Excuses for leaving

I am sorry—do you know where the bathroom is?
It was nice meeting you but sorry I just need to go to the bathroom (GB) / restroom (US).
Sorry but I just need to answer this call.
I have just remembered I need to make an urgent call.
It has been great talking to you, but I just need to make a phone call.
Sorry, I've just seen someone I know.
Sorry, but someone is waiting for me.
Listen, it has been very interesting talking to you but unfortunately I have to go … may be we could catch up with each other tomorrow.

Using the time as an excuse for leaving

Does anyone have the correct time because I think I need to be going?
Oh, is that the time? I'm sorry but I have to go now.
Sorry, I've got to go now.
I think it's time I made a move.

Wishing well and saying goodbye (neutral)

It's been very nice talking to you.
I hope to see you again soon.
I really must be getting back.
I do hope you have a good trip.
It was a pleasure to meet you.
Please send my regards to Dr Hallamabas.

Wishing well and saying goodbye (informal)

Be seeing you.
Bye for now.
Keep in touch.
Look after yourself.
Say "hello" to Kate for me.
See you soon.
See you later.
Take care.
See you in March at the conference then.
Hope to see you before too long.
Have a safe trip home.
OK, my taxi's here.

Acknowledgements

My biggest thanks go, as always, to Anna Southern, for editing and improving the manuscript.

Thanks to the following authors for personally giving me permission to quote from their books, presentations, and interviews:

Thomas Gilovich, Ben Goldacre, Trevor Hassall and Jon Joyce, Jeffrey Jacobi, Bjørn Lomborg, Andrew Mallett, Shay McConnon, and Maria Skyllas-Kazacos.

The following researchers and professors shared their thoughts with me on the art of giving presentations and also helped in getting this book published:

Robert Adams, Francesca Bretzel, Martin Chalfie, Chandler Davis, Wojciech Florkowski, David Hine, Marcello Lippmann, William Mackaness, Osmo Pekonen, Pierdomenico Perata, Beatrice Pezzarossa, Roberto Pini, Magdi Selim, Enzo Sparvoli, Eliana Tassi, Robert Shewfelt (thanks for your encouragement), and Donald Sparks.

The following people did research for me about their countries (for Chapter 3), or gave me advice - thank you!

Tatiana Alenkina, Alessandra Chaves, Ajla Cosic, Eriko Gargiulo, Jaeseok Kim, Ilze Koke, Sofia Luzgina, Maral Mahad, Irune Ruiz Martinez, Randy Olson, Sue Osada, Valentina Prosperi, and Shanshan Zhou.

I would like to thank all my PhD students from the last 15 years without whom this book would have been impossible. In particular, the following PhD students allowed me to use extracts from their presentations

Sergiy Ancherbak, Cristiane Rocha Andrade, Jayonta Bhattacharjee, Michele Budinich, Nicholas Caporusso, Cynthia Emilia Villalba Cardozo, Lamia Chkaiban, Begum Cimen, Angela Cossu, Emanuel Ionut Crudu, Annalisa De Donatis, Chiara Ferrarini, Karolina Gajda, Francesco Gresta, Sven Bjarke Gudnason, Ali Hedayat, Lei Lan, Dmitri Lee, Ana Ljubojevic, Arianna Lugani, Leanid Krautsevich, Nirupa Kudahettige, Leonardo Magneschi, Stefania Manetti, Ahmed Said Nagy, Nadezda Negovelova, Mercy Njima, Rossella Mattera, Peng Peng, Chandra Ramasamy, Pandey Sushil, Md. Minhaz-Ul Haque, Michael Rochlitz, Irfan Sadiq, Tek B Sapkota, Igor Spinelli, Giovanni Tani, and Yudan Whulanza.

A final thanks to Mike Seymour for being a never ending source of interesting information.

© Springer International Publishing Switzerland 2016
A. Wallwork, *English for Presentations at International Conferences*,
English for Academic Research, DOI 10.1007/978-3-319-26330-4

Sources

If no source is given the information is in the public domain or I have been unable to find the original source. While I have attempted to ensure that the factoids only contain accurate information, I can give no guarantee that the information is 100% accurate. The numbers in brackets indicate the number of the factoid, e.g. (2) = the second factoid or quotation.

Chapter 1

1.1 Quote by Osmo Pekonen from personal communication.

Chapter 2

All presentations taken from ted.com. They can be found by typing in the name of the presentation or the presenter into TED's search engine.

2.13 The TED response to my email requesting permission to quote from TED talks began as follows:

Thanks for writing in! In the spirit of ideas worth spreading, TED Talks are free to share – as long you follow the terms of the Creative Commons license "Attribution – NonCommercial – NonDerivative." This means that when sharing TED Talks, the content must be

+ attributed to TED as the original source

+ non-commercial – talks cannot be used for commercial purposes

+ non-derivative – talks cannot be altered in any way

© Springer International Publishing Switzerland 2016
A. Wallwork, *English for Presentations at International Conferences*,
English for Academic Research, DOI 10.1007/978-3-319-26330-4

Chapter 3

Nobel prizes: http://www.nobelprize.org/nobel_prizes/lists/women.html; China http://sklpre.zju.edu.cn/english/redir.php?catalog_id=12375&object_id=60602; http://www.moe.edu.cn/public-files/business/htmlfiles/moe/s8493/201412/181720.html; Iran: http://www.presstv.com/Detail/2014/08/26/376635/Iran-womens-share-in-education-rising; UK: https://www.hesa.ac.uk/stats; Japan: http://nenji-toukei.com/n/kiji/10064/大学進学率; Korea: personal communication from Jaeseok Kim; Latvia:http://www.csb.gov.lv/en/notikumi/women-science-42350.html; Spain: personal communication from Irune Ruiz Martinez; USA: courtesy of Randy Olson

3.1 Women in parliament: http://www.ipu.org/wmn-e/classif.htm

3.3 Facts about Russian women in science: personal communication from Tatiana Alenkina.

Chapter 4

(3, 4) *Yes! 50 secrets from the science of persuasion*, Goldstein, Martin & Cialdini, Profile Books, 2007

Chapter 5

(1,2) quoted in *Business Options*, Adrian Wallwork, OUP; (3) personal observation; (4) http://blog.jazzfactory.in/2009/05/what-is-ideal-font-size-for.html; (5) various experts; (6) *Yes! 50 secrets from the science of persuasion*, Goldstein, Martin & Cialdini, Profile Books, 2007; (7,8) *The McGraw-Hill 36-Hour Course: Business Presentations*, Lani Arredondo, 1994

Chapter 6

(1) probable cause: pollution builds up over the week from exhaust fumes, this seeds rain clouds and alters the weather on a global scale. [Daily Mail 20 Mar 2000]; (2) Britney Gallivan wrote up her achievement for the Historical Society of Pomona in her 40 page pamphlet, "*How to Fold Paper in Half Twelve Times: An "Impossible Challenge" Solved and Explained*". http://www.abc.net.au/science/articles/2005/12/21/1523497.htm

1.1 Point 3 Martin Fewell, deputy editor of Channel 4 news, (Business Life Aug 2007)

Chapter 7

(1-9) *Quirkology*, Richard Wiseman, Macmillan 2007: (10) *David and Goliath: Underdogs, Misfits, and the Art of Battling Giants*, Malcolm Gladwell, Penguin 2015

Chapter 8

(1-10) *Life-Spans* Frank Kendig and Richard Hutton, publ. Holt, Rinehart and Winston, 1979. The statistic for radioactive waste varies massively depending on what source you read. Orange peel (1-24 weeks).

Chapter 9

(1,2) *The Ultimate Lists Book*, Carlton Books Ltd; (3,4) *The Dictionary of Misinformation*, Tom Burnham, Futura Publications, 1975; (5-8) *Freakanomics*, Levitt & Dubner, Penguin 2006; *More sex is safe sex*, Steven E Landsburg, Pocket Books, 2007.

9.8 *Bad Science*, Ben Goldacre, HarperCollinsPublishers, 2008

Chapter 10

The original book of laws, called *Murphy's Law - And Other Reasons Why Things Go Wrong* was written by Arthur Bloch and published by Price/Stern/Sloan Publishers in 1977. But all these laws are now available on many websites. The last law was invented by me based on 30 years of reading tediously long papers with minimal added value.

Chapter 11

(1-10) *The Dictionary of Misinformation*, Tom Burnham, Futura Publications, 1975

Chapter 12

(1) *More sex is safe sex*, Steven E Landsburg, Pocket Books, 2007; (2) http://boards.theforce.net/threads/; (3) *The Lists Book* Mitchell Symons (4-10) *The Lore of Averages: Facts, Figures and Stories That Make Everyday Life Extraordinary*, Karen Farrington, Sanctuary Publishing Ltd, 2004

12.1 Shay McConnon, Presenting with power, How To Books, 20; *The McGraw-Hill 36-Hour Course: Business Presentations*, Lani Arredondo, 1994

12.13 *Outliers*, Malcolm Gladwell, Penguin 2011

12.14 Martin Chalfie personal communication; *How we know what isn't so: The Fallibility of Human Reason in Everyday Life*, Thomas Gilovich, The Free Press 1991

Chapter 13

13.1 *The McGraw-Hill 36-Hour Course: Business Presentations*, Lani Arredondo, 1994

Chapter 14

(1,3): quoted in *Discussions AZ*, Adrian Wallwork, CUP; (2) *The New Believe It or Not*, Robert L Ripley, Simon Schuster, 1931; (4) *Successful selling with NLP*, Joseph O'Connor and Robin Prior, Thorsons 1995; (5) http://www.independent.co.uk/news/world/asia/seoul-tries-to-shock-parents-out-of-linguistic-surgery-573153.html

14.1 *Second Language Learning and Language Teaching*, Vivian Cook, Routledge, 2008

Chapter 15

(1) http://psych.colorado.edu/~vanboven/teaching/p7536_heurbias/p7536_readings/kruger_dunning.pdf; (2-4) *Unusually Stupid Americans*, Ross Petras and Kathryn Petras, Villard Books, 2003.

Chapter 16

(1) *Quirkology*, Richard Wiseman, Macmillan 2007; (2,3,5,6,7) quoted in *Business Vision*, Adrian Wallwork, OUP; quoted in *Discussions AZ*, Adrian Wallwork, CUP

Chapter 17

(2) *How to prepare, stage, and deliver winning presentations*, Thomas Leech, AMACOM, 1982; (3) http://www.blocksclass.com/TOK/LISTENING.pdf; (4,5) quoted in *Business Vision*, Adrian Wallwork, OUP.

Chapter 18

(1) http://www.asco.org/about-asco/asco-annual-meeting; **(3-6)** https://en.wikipedia.org/wiki/Poster; (7) busyteacher.org; (8) http://smbcinsight.tv/web/worlds-biggest-film-poster-unveiled-in-south-india/

Good sites for tips on creating posters:

http://betterposters.blogspot.it/

http://www.asp.org/education/howto_onPosters.html

https://www.asp.org/education/EffectivePresentations.pdf

http://www.lib.ncsu.edu/documents/vetmed/research/Poster_Layout.doc

http://www.the-scientist.com/?articles.view/articleNo/31071/title/Poster-Perfect/

http://colinpurrington.com/tips/poster-design

Chapter 19

(1,7) *The Future of English*, The British Council, first published in 1997, http://englishagenda. britishcouncil.org/publications/future-english; (2) http://www.cambridge.org.br/authors-articles/ interviews?id=2446; (3) personal observation based on how much researchers spend in Pisa, Italy; (4) the book in question is *English Grammar in Use*, CUP; (5) *Business Communications*, Claudia Rawlins, HarperCollins Publishers, Inc; (6) Daily Telegraph 14.2.97; http://soovle.com/top/ 21.7.2015; (8) 1994: The Times 23.12.1994 https://www.gov.uk/government/uploads/system/ uploads/attachment_data/file/340601/bis-13-1082-international-education-accompanying- analytical-narrative-revised.pdf

19.1 *How to prepare, stage, and deliver winning presentations*, Thomas Leech, AMACOM, 1982

19.11: http://www.nytimes.com/2015/06/12/world/europe/tim-hunt-nobel-laureate-resigns-sexist- women-female-scientists.html?_r=0

19.18 Chandler Davis personal communication

Index

Numbers in **bold** refer to complete chapters (e.g. **5** = Chapter 5), numbers not in bold refer to subsections (e.g. 5.7 = Section 7 in Chapter 5).

© Springer International Publishing Switzerland 2016
A. Wallwork, *English for Presentations at International Conferences*,
English for Academic Research, DOI 10.1007/978-3-319-26330-4

Printed in Great
Britain
by Amazon